ISBN 978-1-330-41279-4
PIBN 10056618

For support please visit www.forgottenbooks.com

English
Français
Deutsche
Italiano
Español
Português

www.forgottenbooks.com

Mythology Photography **Fiction**
Fishing Christianity **Art** Cooking
Essays Buddhism Freemasonry
Medicine **Biology** Music **Ancient
Egypt** Evolution Carpentry Physics
Dance Geology **Mathematics** Fitness
Shakespeare **Folklore** Yoga Marketing
Confidence Immortality Biographies
Poetry **Psychology** Witchcraft
Electronics Chemistry History **Law**
Accounting **Philosophy** Anthropology
Alchemy Drama Quantum Mechanics
Atheism Sexual Health **Ancient History**
Entrepreneurship Languages Sport
Paleontology Needlework Islam
Metaphysics Investment Archaeology
Parenting Statistics Criminology
Motivational

ISAIAH·

HIS LIFE AND TIMES

AND THE WRITINGS WHICH BEAR HIS NAME.

BY

REV. S. R. DRIVER, D.D.

REGIUS PROFESSOR OF HEBREW, AND CANON OF CHRISTCHURCH, OXFORD.

SEVENTH THOUSAND.

London.

JAMES NISBET AND CO.,

$$\frac{33}{1927} \varepsilon$$

PREFACE.

—◆—

THE present volume almost speaks for itself. It is an endeavour to exhibit the character and position of the greatest of the prophets, and to exemplify. by means of the brilliant illustrations which the Book of Isaiah supplies, the historical significance of prophecy. Prophecy is intimately connected with history ; and recent discoveries have added greatly to our knowledge of the position and political relations of both Israel and Judah in Isaiah's day. The writer has endeavoured to utilize this knowledge as far as possible. He has sought to interpret the writings which bear Isaiah's name in the light of history, to show how they are correlated throughout with the needs and circumstances of the times which gave them birth, while at the same time they embody elements of permanent validity, and speak to all future generations. The writings of the prophets—as indeed the Biblical writings generally—when studied attentively, are seen to possess definite and distinctive features, reflecting the individuality of their authors, which are apt to escape the notice of ordinary readers : these the writer has made

Isaiah, and as those who have earned most emphatically the gratitude of subsequent labourers in the same field. Two other writers also deserve mention in the same connection, on account, especially, of the attention bestowed by them on the historical side of Isaiah's work, viz., Sir Edward Strachey, in his "Jewish History and Politics in the times of Sargon and Sennacherib" (ed. 2, 1874), and Dr. W. Robertson Smith, in his "Prophets of Israel" (1882). The scope of the present volume was obviously such as to forbid a constant citation of authorities, or discussion of competing views ; but references have usually been added in all important cases.

The Inscriptions, wherever possible, have been quoted from the standard work of Eberhard Schrader, "The Cuneiform Inscriptions and the Old Testament" (ed. 2, Giessen, 1883 [1]), in which the passages illustrative of the Old Testament are excerpted, translated, and annotated with a thoroughness and sobriety of judgment, which leave nothing to be desired. Reference has also been made to the series of Inscriptions translated under the title, "Records of the Past" (Bagsters), where the passages quoted can be read in their original connection. The translations are not mere reproductions of Schrader's German versions : with the view of exhibiting as closely as possible the sense and rhythm of the original, they have usually been compared throughout with his transliterations of the Assyrian text. The Authorized Version of the Book of Isaiah often, unfortunately, misses the sense of the Hebrew ; in quotations, therefore, the writer has generally availed himself of either the Revised Version, or the translation of Prof. Cheyne. Except in a few extreme cases he has accommodated his renderings to the traditional Hebrew text,[2] without, however, desiring thereby to be understood to pronounce an opinion on its integrity in individual passages. The notes occasionally appended will, it is hoped, be found useful in the elucidation and illustration of the text.

S. R. D.

∴ In citations the letters *a* and *b* denote respectively the first and second halves of the verse cited.

---

[1] The citations are according to the German pagination, which is repeated on the *margin* of the English translation (vol. i., 1885). In 1883 Schrader wrote (p. 331), "Respecting the assassination of Sennacherib (2 Kings xix. 37), the Assyrian Inscriptions are silent ;" but since Chapter VII. Part I. of the present work was in type, Mr. Pinches has published the text of an Inscription acquired by the British Museum in 1884, and containing the following notice of it :—"On the 20th day of Tebet Sennacherib, king of Assyria, | his son in a revolt killed him. For . . . years Sennacherib | had ruled the kingdom of Assyria. From the 20th day of Tebet to | the 2nd day of Adar the revolt in Assyria continued. | On the 18th day of Adar, Esarhaddon, his son, sat on the throne in Assyria, | &c." ("Journal of the Royal Asiatic Society," Oct., 1887, p. 678). The Inscription is a Babylonian Chronicle, and throws no additional light on the relations existing between Judah and Assyria in Isaiah's lifetime.

[2] On the nature of this text the reader will find much information in an article in "The Church Quarterly Review" for April, 1887.

CONTENTS.

———•+•———

PART I.

ISAIAH AND HIS OWN AGE.

CHAPTER I.

CHAPTER II.

figure of " Jehovah's Servant"—The author's literary style—The character of his poetry.

CHAPTER V.

ERRATA.

Page 91, line 21, *for* 75, *read* 38.
189, last line, *for* own, *read* coming.

CHRONOLOGICAL TABLE.

B.C.

745 TIGLATH-PILESER II.

740 Arpad taken. *Uzziah* named (probably : see p. 8).

739 Hamath taken.

738 *Menahem* tributary (pp. 7, 13).

734 *Pekah* deposed, and slain ; succeeded by *Hoshea*. Deportation of inhabitants of N. and N.E. districts of Israel (pp. 8, 13).

732 Damascus taken.

727 SHALMANESER IV.

722 SARGON. Fall of Samaria, and end of the Northern Kingdom.

720 Defeat of Egyptians under Sabako at Raphia.

711 Siege and capture of Ashdod. Philistia, Judah, Edom, and Moab, " speaking treason " with Egypt (p. 45).

710 Defeat of Merodach-Baladan, after " sending ambassadors during twelve years " (pp. 45, 96). Babylon entered by Sargon.

705 SENNACHERIB.

703 Defeat of Merodach-Baladan. Palace in Babylon entered and spoiled by Sennacherib.

701 Campaign against Phœnicia, Philistia, and Judah.

696 Babylon entered, and in part demolished, by Sennacherib.

681 ESARHADDON.

672 Esarhaddon conquers Egypt (comp. the allusion, Nah. iii. 8-10).

668 ASSHURBANIPAL (to 626).

633 CYAXARES founds the Median Empire.

625 NABOPOLASSAR increases the power of Babylon.

607 Nineveh destroyed by Medes and Babylonians.

---

604 Nebuchadnezzar defeats Pharaoh Necho at Carchemish. NEBUCHADNEZZAR succeeds Nabopolassar.

599 *First* deportation of Jewish exiles, with Jehoiachin.

593 ASTYAGES succeeds Cyaxares in Media.

588 Destruction of Jerusalem by Chaldæans, and *second* deportation of exiles, with Zedekiah.

561 EVIL-MERODACH.

559 NERIGLISSAR.

555 NABO-NAHID.

549 CYRUS overthrows the Median empire of Astyages.

549-538 Period of Cyrus' successes in Western and Central Asia.

538 Cyrus captures Babylon. Main body of exiles return under Zerubbabel.

458 Second return of exiles under Ezra.

PART I.

ISAIAH AND HIS OWN AGE.

CHAPTER I.

PERSONAL LIFE OF ISAIAH.

Particulars of Isaiah s private life—Relation of the prophets to the history
of their age.

OF the personal life of Isaiah little is known. From notices in his
own book we learn that he received the prophetic call in the last
year of the reign of King Uzziah (vi. 1), from which it may be
inferred that he was at that time not less than 20 or 21 years of
age, possibly rather older. He was married (viii. 3) ; and two
sons are alluded to ; one, Shear-jashub, sufficiently old in 736–5
to accompany his father on the occasion of his interview with
King Ahaz during the Syro-Ephraimitish war (vii. 3) ; the other,
Maher-shalal-hash-baz, born about a year afterwards (viii. 1–4).
The scene of his labours appears to have been chiefly, if not
exclusively, Jerusalem ; and from the position which was evidently accorded to him at Court, under both Ahaz and Hezekiah,
it has been supposed that he was of noble blood. The Rabbi-
nical tradition, however, which made the prophet's father Amoz
to be a brother of King Amaziah, and Isaiah consequently to be
cousin to King Uzziah, rests probably upon nothing better than
a fanciful etymological combination ; and, as the great mediæval
commentator, David Kimchi, of Narbonne, remarks, nothing is
in fact known respecting the prophet's genealogy and connections.

2

From notices either in his own book or in the Book of Kings, it cannot with certainty be inferred by how many years he survived the great crisis of Hezekiah's reign in 701 ; but according to a tradition current among the Jews in the second century A.D., and alluded to by many ancient writers, both Jewish and Christian, he suffered martydom in the heathen reaction under Hezekiah's successor, Manasseh. In one of the treatises of the Mishnah (collected about A.D. 200) mention is made of a " roll of genealogies " in Jerusalem, in which it was stated that " Manasseh slew Isaiah ; " and other authors specify the manner in which he was reputed to have suffered. Thus Justin Martyr, writing about A.D. 150, in his controversial Dialogue with the Jew Trypho (ch. 120) reproaching the Jews with the deed, writes—" Whom ye *sawed asunder* with a wooden saw ; " and the same account of his martyrdom, together with details as to the circumstances which led to it, is given in the apocryphal work called " The Ascension of Isaiah," which is assigned by critics to the beginning of the second century. Whether the tradition be a true one we do not know ; but there is a definiteness and (in its earliest form as here cited) a simplicity attaching to it which is in its favour. The martyrdom of Isaiah has been supposed to be alluded to in the Epistle to the Hebrews (xi. 37 : " were sawn asunder "), and this is possible : the passage cannot, however, be quoted in *proof* of the tradition, for, of course, the reference in it *may* be to other martyrs. The chronology of the reigns of Jewish kings contemporary with Isaiah is in some particulars uncertain, but upon the shortest possible scheme, that, viz., which places Uzziah's death in 740, Isaiah's prophetical ministry will have embraced a period of at least forty years (740–701) ; and if he survived the accession of Manasseh, he will hardly at the time of his death have been less than seventy years of age. In addition to the prophecies embodied in the book which bears his name, he was, according to the Chronicler (2 Chron. xxvi. 22 ; xxxii. 32), the author of a history of the reign of Uzziah, and also of a work (called a " vision ") containing an account of the reign of Hezekiah ; the latter was incorporated in the (lost) " Book of the Kings of Judah and Israel," which is one of the authorities often referred to by the Chronicler in the course of his work.

But though little can be told concerning the incidents of Isaiah's private life, his personality and character stand before us in his writings with all the certainty and clearness that could be desired. True, a considerable part of the contents of the book which bears his name cannot (as will be seen) be attributed to him ; but in the parts which are indubitably his we can watch him, and, as it were, walk by his side, through all the varied and eventful phases of his forty years' ministry. We can observe him as a reformer, denouncing social abuses, sparing neither high nor low in his fearless and incisive censure. We can follow him as a statesman, devoted patriotically to his country's interests, and advising her political leaders in times of difficulty and danger. We can see him as a theologian, emphasizing old truths, developing new ones, bringing fresh ideas to light which were destined to exercise an important influence in the generations which followed. Throughout the reigns of Ahaz and Hezekiah he is the central figure in Jerusalem, and the position which he there took—his motives, principles, policy, the character of his teaching, the nature and extent of his influence—are all reflected in the collection of his prophecies which we possess. It will be the object of the following pages to present a picture of Isaiah's character and work, under the three aspects mentioned, such as may both justify this estimate of his position, and assist the reader who may desire to understand the volume of his prophecies better.

It may be desirable at the outset to call attention to a characteristic of the prophets, which must be steadily kept in view if their position and significance is to be rightly apprehended. The prophets, one and all, stand in an intimate relation to the history of their times. Whatever be the truth which they announce, it is never presented by them in an abstract form ; it is always brought into some relation with the age in which they live, and adapted to the special circumstances of the persons whom they address. Of course, the principles which the prophets assert are frequently capable of a much wider range of application ; their significance is not exhausted when they have done their work in the prophet's own generation ; but still his primary interest is in the needs of his own age. The vices which Amos or Hosea denounces are those of the kingdom of Israel, in the middle of the eighth century B.C., and though they would have raised their voice not less loudly had they lived at some other period of Israelitish history, in which the same faults were prevalent, the form which their denunciations assume, the characteristic features of society which they attack, are those of the age in which they themselves lived. Similarly in their theology, while there are naturally a series of fundamental principles common to the prophets generally, each prophet in particular possesses a special individual element, partly conditioned by his own genius and temperament, partly determined by the course of general events in the world in which he moves. As men expressing habitually their judgment on the conduct of public affairs, and holding decided political views, it will be still more evident that the principles advocated by them must stand in a definite relation to the circumstances of particular junctures, and to the attitude assumed on such occasions by the nation generally. The position taken by Amos, for instance, in view of the Assyrians, is very different from that taken by Jeremiah at a subsequent period with reference to the Babylonians. As we shall see, many of Isaiah's most important prophecies are dependent, in their most characteristic features, upon the relation which Judah, through the action of its responsible rulers, occupied alternately towards one or other of the two great empires of Assyria and Egypt. It is thus essential, if the work of any prophet is to be properly understood, to study it in the light of contemporary history. In the case of Isaiah we are peculiarly fortunate in being able to do this; for the decipherment of the Cuneiform Inscriptions of Assyria—one of the most brilliant scientific achievements of the present century—has enabled us to watch the movements of the Assyrian kings, almost year by year, through the whole period of his ministry, and the result has been to exhibit this great prophet's character and position with a distinctness and completeness which, antecedently, would assuredly not have been anticipated. Before proceeding, however, to the details of Isaiah's work it will be necessary, for the reasons stated, to give some account of the condition and prospects, at home and abroad, of the kingdom of Judah, at the time when Isaiah first stepped into public life, in the last year of Uzziah's reign.

NOTE.—The " Ascension of Isaiah," alluded to above, exists only in an Ethiopic Version, which has been edited, with a Latin translation and Introduction, by the veteran Ethiopic scholar, Aug. Dillmann (Lipsiae, 1877). The book appears to consist of a ground-work of Jewish origin, into which passages have been inserted, bearing a decidedly Christian impress.

CHAPTER II.

ASSYRIA AND JUDAH IN THE EIGHTH CENTURY B.C.

Influence of Assyria upon Israel and Judah in the eighth century B.C.—
Reign of the Assyrian king, Tiglath-Pileser II. (745–727)—Reigns of
Uzziah (Azariah) and Jotham in Judah (790–736).

TILL the eighth century B.C., the kingdoms of Israel and Judah,
with the solitary exception of Shishak's invasion in the reign of
Rehoboam, had escaped serious attack from any really formidable power.   There had been indeed no lack of hostilities from
time to time between themselves, and each in its turn was liable
to incursions on the part of one or other of the neighbouring
nationalities which, when the empire of Solomon was divided,
had cast off the yoke of Israelitish rule ; but the best organized
of these, the Syrian kingdom of Damascus, was scarcely more
than an equal match even for the northern kingdom alone.   In
the course, however, of the eighth century, the political relations
of all these kingdoms underwent an entire change.   A new power
was making itself felt in the regions of Western Asia, destined,
as the great prophets of both Israel and Judah quickly discerned,
to determine for many years to come the history of both
countries.   The monuments have revealed to us the character of
that vast civilization which had its seat at Nineveh : the prodigious
activity of the Assyrians, in letters, in science, in architecture,
in sculpture, in the industrial arts, in military enterprise, as-
tonishes us : we are familiar with the single expedition sent by
Sennacherib against Jerusalem, but to form an adequate idea of
their ceaseless movement, as disclosed in the annals of one
king after another for centuries, we must multiply that expedition
indefinitely, and conceive it to be but the type of what took

place almost yearly against one or other of the tribes of Media,
or Armenia, or Syria, or whatever other district it might be of
the regions bordering on the great plain watered by the Tigris
and the Euphrates. The Assyrians have been termed the
Romans of Asia, and though the parallel is not intended to be complete (for, to notice but one difference, the Assyrians possessed
no genius for civilizing or consolidating a conquered province),
it nevertheless suggests a true idea of their skill in military organization, and of their mastery of the principles and methods
of war. To be sure, it must not be imagined that the Assyrians
were now about to interfere in Western Asia for the first time.
Between Assyria and Damascus there had been already many
a rough encounter. In the previous century Shalmaneser II.
had been victorious against Benhadad, the contemporary, and
for a while the ally (1 Kings xx. 34), of Ahab, as well as against
his successor Hazael. He had also (as the Black Obelisk in the
British Museum informs us) received tribute of Jehu (842 B.C.),
as Rammannirar received it from his son Jehoahaz (or possibly
his grandson Jehoash) in 803. But these interferences left no
lasting impression on the history of Israel, and did not affect
Judah at all ; nor was either nation involved by them in any
grave political complication.

It was probably towards the end of the long and prosperous
reign of Jeroboam II. (790–749) that Amos, amid his presages
of disaster for the northern kingdom, first alludes darkly to a
nation soon to be brought actively upon the scene of history
for the purpose of humbling the proud and too confident people
(vi. 14) : " Behold, I raise up against you a nation, O house of
Israel, saith Jehovah, the God of hosts ; and they shall afflict
you from the entering in of Hamath, unto the torrent of the
Arábah," i.e., from the far north to one of the torrent-valleys
constituting a boundary on the east or south-east of the Dead
Sea. As it happened, both in Israel and Judah, the first intervention of the Assyrian was at the invitation of the ruling king.
With a power of unlimited capabilities so near at hand, the
temptation was as irresistible as it was a century and a half
afterwards in Jerusalem, as it was three centuries afterwards in
the great struggle for supremacy between Sparta and Athens,
for either party in a political contest to aim at securing its
support against their antagonists ; and thus though Hosea
(viii. 9f. ; x. 4–6) foresaw the consequences, Menahem, to retain

name of the same king who is called elsewhere Tiglath-Pileser. In accordance with the position of dependence which Menahem hereby assumed, we find him included in an inscription relating to the year 738, among many other princes of Syria and Phœnicia, as paying tribute to the Assyrian king.

The reign of Tiglath-Pileser has an intimate bearing on the state of political feeling in Judah during the early years of Isaiah's ministry. Let us take a rapid survey of the principal events belonging to it. The dates are fixed in most cases by the Assyrian monuments, and, as is still more the case in the subsequent reigns, afford an invaluable clue amid the uncertain, and sometimes conflicting, chronology of the Hebrew historical hooks.[3] Tiglath-Pileser's reign extended from B.C. 745 to 728, its termination thus nearly synchronizing with the accession of Hezekiah in Judah. Almost in his first year he was engaged in a successful campaign in Babylonia, which was quickly followed by other expeditions in the direction of Media and Armenia. In 742 he marched against Arpad, in Syria ; and after a siege of three years succeeded in reducing it (B.C. 740). To the same period, probably to 740, belongs his reduction of the little kingdom of Hamath, a place not far distant from Arpad, and named beside it more than once in the Old Testament. Tiglath-Pileser's notice of this success is interesting on account of its containing a name which can hardly be any other than that of Uzziah (or, as he is called in 2 Kings, *Azariah*) of Judah : " Nineteen districts of the city of Hamath, together with the towns round about them, which are by the sea of the setting of the sun, which in their faithlessness had made revolt to Azriyahu, to the territory of Assyria I annexed; my officers,

[1] From the allusions in Hosea it is plain that at this time there were opposite factions in the northern kingdom, which placed reliance upon Assyria and Egypt respectively. (*See* v. 13 ; vii. 11 ; xii. 1.)

[2] Schrader, "Cuneiform Inscriptions and the Old Testament," on 2 Kings xv. 19.

[3] See note at the end of this chapter.

my deputies, I appointed over them."[1] It would seem from
this notice as though Uzziah shortly before his death had concluded an alliance with Hamath, probably in conjunction with
other states as well, for the purpose of resisting Assyrian aggres
sion—a step which, as we proceed, we shall see exemplified in
other instances.   Shortly afterwards, in 738, Tiglath-Pileser
mentions his receiving tribute from numerous princes of Syria
and Asia Minor—amongst others, from Rezin of Damascus,
Menahem of Samaria (p. 7), and Hiram of Tyre.

From 737 to 735 Tiglath-Pileser was occupied in the East,
but his twelfth year, 734 B.C., was one of critical importance for
both Israel and Judah.   In an inscription relating to this year
the Assyrian king narrates how he advanced further to the
south than he had previously done, as far, in fact, as the Philistine
city of Gaza, with an eye, not improbably, to the possibility at
some future time of penetrating into Egypt.   " . . . . the city
of Gal-[ed?] . . . . [A]-bel   . which was above the land of
the House of Omri, . . . in its whole extent to the territory of
Assyria I annexed ; my [officers], the deputies, I appointed
[over them].   Hanno of Gaza, who fled before my troops, to the
land of Egypt escaped.   Gaza [I captured] ; his possessions,
his gods [I carried away], and my royal effigy [I erected]."
" The land of the House of Omri, the distant . . . . the whole
of its inhabitants, together with their possessions, to Assyria I
deported.   *Pekah, their king, I slew.   Hoshea* [to rule] *over
them I appointed*.   Ten [talents of gold, one thousand talents
of silver, together with . . . .] I received from them."[2]   Though
there must be some exaggeration in the statement that " the
whole " of the inhabitants of the " land of the House of Omri "
were deported to Assyria, the rest of the notice is in evident
accordance with 2 Kings xv. 29, 30 : " In the days of Pekah
king of Israel, came Tiglath-Pileser king of Assyria, and took
Ijon, and Abel-beth-maacah, and Janoah, and Kedesh, and
Hazor, and Gilead, and Galilee, all the land of Naphtali "—all

---

[1] See the argument of Schrader (pp. 217-223).   It is from this notice of
Uzziah, taken in combination with another which, though fragmentary,
describes Tiglath-Pileser as receiving tribute from " . . . . riyahu of the
land of Judah," that we seem compelled to bring down the date of Uzziah's
death to 740.

[2] Schrader, p. 255 f., the " land of the House of Omri " is the name by
which the kingdom of Israel is designated in the Inscriptions.

districts in the north-east and north of Israel—"and carried them captive to Assyria. And Hoshea, the son of Elah, made a conspiracy against Pekah the son of Remaliah, and slew him, and reigned in his stead." The new point not mentioned in the Old Testament, but made clear by the Inscription, is that the conspiracy in Samaria, which cost Pekah his throne and life, was carried through with the aid of the Assyrians, and that Hoshea's elevation to the throne was due to his recognition of Assyrian supremacy. How this action on the part of the Assyrian king affected Judah will appear subsequently. Pekah, as we learn from Isaiah, had been in close alliance with Rezin, king of Damascus, against which city Tiglath-Pileser proceeded next to turn his arms. The Inscriptions assign the siege of Damascus to the years 733 and 732. It ended with the capture of the city, the flight or deportation of the inhabitants, and the devastation of its territory. With this agrees substantially the account in 2 Kings xvi. 9 : "The king of Assyria went up against Damascus, and took it, and carried (the people of) it captive to Kir, and slew Rezin." The occasion on which (2 Kings xvi. 10-16) Ahaz went to meet Tiglath-Pileser in Damascus was doubtless a levy of tributary princes held in the conquered city : an inscription of the same king's last year mentions, with many other princes of the neighbouring districts, " Joahaz (*i.e.* Ahaz) of Judah " as paying him tribute. The concluding years of Tiglath-Pileser's reign, 731-728, were not marked by any special enterprise.

The preceding outline will be sufficient to convey some idea of the power which the Assyrians at this time wielded in Western Asia, and of the uses to which they were apt to apply it. The problem which a statesman, whether in Israel or in Judah, had to face, was by no means a simple one, even when it was not complicated, as was frequently the case, by the intrigues of opposing factions. Both states, in fact, were passing through a critical period in which nothing short of the greatest wisdom

Elated by his successes against Edom, Uzziah's father, Amaziah, had sent a foolhardy challenge to Jehoash, king of Israel. The parable of the thistle and the cedar, by which Jehoash sought to divert him from his purpose, fell upon unheeding ears. Amaziah persisted, and in the battle which ensued suffered a humiliating defeat. Nor was this all. Jehoash, following up his success, marched upon Jerusalem; resistance was impossible: it was treated as a captured city; a considerable length of wall was broken down; treasure was carried off, both from the temple and the royal palace; and hostages were led back by the conqueror to Samaria (2 Kings xiv. 8–14). It is not improbable that the passage of Amos which speaks of the "breaches" of the "booth of David that is fallen" (ix. 11) may contain a reminiscence of this disaster. Uzziah, however, who followed Amaziah upon the throne, proved himself a vigorous and able ruler. Under his administration the kingdom rapidly recovered itself; its resources were replenished; its military defences reorganized; commerce and the arts of peace again flourished undisturbed. Thus one of his first acts (2 Kings xiv. 22) appears to have been to push forward to the Gulf of Akabah and rebuild the port of Elath, probably with the object of utilizing the Red Sea for commercial enterprise after the example of Solomon (1 Kings ix. 26), and hoping for better success than had rewarded Jehoshaphat (1 Kings xxii. 48). The fortification of Elath and its recovery for Judah implies that Uzziah's hands were too strong for resistance to be effectually opposed by Edom, which indeed must have been still sorely crippled by the sanguinary defeat inflicted upon it by Amaziah (2 Kings xiv. 7). This is almost the only event of importance related in the somewhat meagre account of this reign contained in the Book of Kings; further particulars, derived apparently from a credible source, are supplied by the Second Book of Chronicles (chap. xxvi.). From this we learn that Uzziah obtained various military successes upon his south and southwest frontiers—a quarter in which Judah was always exposed and liable to invasion, whether from its old and restless enemy, the Philistines, or from nomad Arab tribes. Gath, Jabneh, and Ashdod were dismantled; and garrisons were established in the surrounding parts to keep the district under proper control. Edom, as we have seen, was not at present in a position to resume hostilities, so that the whole southern frontier of Judah was thus secure. Even the Ammonites, on the east of the Dead Sea, were again (2 Sam. viii. 2) reduced to the condition of tributaries. Further, Uzziah improved the defences of the capital, and greatly strengthened the army. He built new towers for the walls of Jerusalem—amongst others, one at the same "corner-gate" (probably at the north-west corner of the city) which marked one limit of the four hundred cubits destroyed by Jehoash (2 Kings xiv. 13), of course repairing the breach itself (if it had not been repaired already) at the same time. The walls were also provided by him with elaborate "engines" of defence "to shoot arrows and great stones withal;" and the army was newly equipped with "shields, and spears, and helmets, and coats of mail, and bows, and stones for slinging." By these and other precautionary measures he secured peace for himself and his subjects, and was able to encourage commerce and agriculture, to the latter of which he was himself personally devoted. Thus "he built," we are told, "towers in the wilderness" for the protection of flocks, "and hewed out many cisterns, for he had much cattle; in the lowland[1] also, and in the plain:[2] and he had husbandmen and vinedressers in the mountains and in the fruitful fields; for he loved husbandry." Clearly the material prosperity of Judah was ably cared for under this firm and wise administration. In religion Uzziah appears to have been a sincere worshipper of the true God. Towards the end of his reign he was smitten with leprosy —according to the Chronicles[3] on account of his presumption in attempting to exercise the office of priest, and to sacrifice incense—and passed the closing years of his life in a "several house," his son Jotham acting, in his stead, as regent.

How long Jotham filled this position the Biblical narrative does not state. Sixteen years are, however, assigned as the length of his reign; but it is now generally supposed (upon chronological grounds) that the greater part of these years

[1] *I.e.*, in the "Shephélah," or low country, in the direction of the Mediterranean. See Dean Stanley's "Sinai and Palestine," App. § 8.

[2] *I.e.*, the downs, or high "table-land" (Revised Version *marg.*), on the east of Jordan (Deut. iii. 10).

[3] For 2 Chron. xxvi. 5-20 is an addition made by the Chronicler to the narrative of Kings. This passage, though it may be *based* upon the work of Isaiah, alluded to in *v.* 22, cannot, however, be an extract from it; for it abounds with marks of the peculiar style and diction of the Chronicler, of a late type which Isaiah could not have used.

belongs to the period of his regency, and that, in fact, he did not
survive his father Uzziah by more than a very few years.
Whether as regent or as monarch, he adhered to the same
administrative principles as his father. The narrative in Kings
is again meagre, but may be supplemented, as in the case of
Uzziah, by the Chronicles (2 Chron. xxvii.). Jotham continued
the public works commenced by Uzziah ; he built a new gate in
the temple court, and increased the fortifications of Jerusalem
at a spot called Ophel, or "the Mound," immediately below the
royal palace on the south-east of the city. Cities were also
built by him in the hill-country of Judah, and castles and towers
in the exposed forest districts. The Ammonites, who sought
to regain their independence, were speedily reduced and obliged
to pay a large annual tribute. Other warlike enterprises are
alluded to by the Chronicler, and the terms in which he speaks
authorize us in the inference that Jotham was a brave and successful ruler, and maintained his country in the same honourable
position to which it had been raised by his father.

Not, probably, until shortly before his death does a change
begin to be perceptible. In 2 Kings xv. 37 we read : " In those
days Jehovah began to send against Judah Rezin the king of
Syria and Pekah the son of Remaliah." This is the first
instance at this period of an outbreak of hostile feeling upon
the part of Syria and Israel—an outbreak destined shortly to
assume grave proportions and to involve Judah in serious trouble.
But the further course of the Syro-Ephraimitish war must be
reserved for a subsequent chapter.

Note on the Chronology of Isaiah's Time.

The Biblical chronology of the Kings of Judah and Israel is in perplexing
disagreement with that fixed by the contemporary Assyrian Inscriptions. It
is allowed by modern commentators and historians that in cases of diver-
gence the latter is to be preferred (for the system of the Book of Kings, at
least in some items, was only arrived at through computation by the compiler), the only question being how the figures of the Book of Kings are to
be rectified so as to be brought into agreement with it. The following
table exhibits a synopsis of dates, from 1 Jehu=1 Athaliah, in accordance both with the chronology of Ussher (affixed to the margin of reference
Bibles), and with the principal modern systems :—

JUDAH.	1. Ussher.	2. Welh.	3. Kamp.	4. Dunck.	5. Ch. Qu.	ISRAEL.	1. Ussher.	2. Wellh.	3. Kamp.	4. Dunck.	5. Ch. Qu.
Athaliah (6)	884	84?	843	843	844	Jehu (28)	884	84?	843	843	844
Joash (40)	878	83?	837	837	838	Jehoahaz (17)	856	81?	815	815	817
Amaziah (29)	839	801	797	797	800	Jehoash (16)	839	802	798	798	801
Uzziah (52)	810	792	778	792	772	Jeroboam II. (41)	825	786	782	790	786
						Zechariah (½)	773	746	741	749	746
						Shallum (1-12th)	772	745	741	749	746
						Menahem (10)	772	745	741	748	746
Jotham (16), regent		(750)	(751)		(749)	Pekahiah (2)	761	737	738	738	737
„ sole ruler	758	740	736	740	735	Pekah (20)	759	735	736	736	736
Ahaz (16)	742	735	735	734	734	Hoshea (9)	730	733	730	734	730
Hezekiah (29)	726	715	715	728	727	Fall of Samaria	722	722	722	722	722
Manasseh (55)	698	686	686	697							
Amon (2)	643	641	641								
Josiah (31)	641	639	639								

In columns 2 and 3 the figures will sometimes be observed to be higher by a unit than those in the author's own tables. The dates given here are those of the years of *accession ;* in the original tables they are those of the *first year of reign, i.e.,* the first whole year following the accession. The figures immediately after the name indicate the regnal years as stated in the Bible. On the authorities cited, see the end of this note.

Upon the Assyrian Inscriptions—[1]

Ahab is named ...	854 B.C.
Jehu	842 ,,
Uzziah (probably [2])	740 ,
Menahem	738 ,
Pekah (dethroned by Tiglath-Pileser and succeeded by Hoshea)	734 ,,
Ahaz	734[3] ,,
Fall of Samaria ...	722 ,,
Campaign against Hezekiah ...	701 ,,

It is evident at once that Ussher's chronology is irreconcilable with these *aata ;* the aim of all the other schemes is so to adjust the figures that the dates mentioned may fall within the reigns of the respective kings. It is impossible here to discuss each scheme at length. The most important difference between them relates to the date assigned to Hezekiah's accession. According to the Inscriptions there was an interval of twenty-one years between the fall of Samaria and Sennacherib's invasion of Judah : according to 2 Kings xviii. 10, 13 the former occurred in Hezekiah's 6th year, the latter in his 14th year—in other words, the interval between them was not more than eight years. The dates in *both* these verses cannot be correct. (2) and (3) now abandon the date in *v.* 10, adhering to the "14th year" in *v.* 13 ; (4) and (5), on the contrary, abandon the date in *v.* 13, adhering to

---

[1] Schrader, pp. 463-466.　　[2] Ibid., pp. 217-223.　　[3] Ibid., p. 257 f.

the " 6th year" in *v.* 10. (2) or (3), if adopted, necessitates a shortening
of the subsequent long reign of Manasseh by 10 years ; (4) or (5) necessitates an alteration in the ages of Ahaz and Hezekiah at their succession [1]
(to avoid the absurdity of Ahaz dying at the age of [20 + 6 or 7=] 26
or 27 years, and leaving a son aged 25 l) ; the age of Ahaz at his accession
must be increased—say, to 25 years (as 2 Chron. xxviii. 1 in the Sept. and
Pesh.), and that of Hezekiah reduced (probably to 15 years). It follows
from (4), (5), that Hezekiah's sickness (Isa. xxxviii., see *v.* 5, " fifteen years "),
and probably also Merodach-Baladan's embassy (chap. xxxix.), must *precede*, chronologically, the events narrated in chaps. xxxvi., xxxvii. (Sennacherib's invasion) by some 12 years. Upon the system of (2), (3),
Hezekiah's sickness, at any rate, will nearly synchronize with the Assyrian
invasion. Merodach-Baladan's embassy may be placed, consistently with
what we know of him from the Inscriptions, somewhat prior to either 710
or 703.

The system (2), or (3), has much to recommend it, and has been accepted
by recent writers in Germany ; [2] but the system (4), from which (5) does not
differ in principle, has been generally followed in this country, and for
that reason it is adopted in the present volume. Fortunately, the difficulties
in question form no impediment to the study of Isaiah's life. It is certain,
in any case, that Ahaz and Pekah were reigning in 735-4, and that Hezekiah was on the throne in 702-1. In the prophecies belonging to the interme-
diate period no king's name is mentioned ; and the attitude assumed by
the prophet is determined, not by the personal views or character of the
reigning king of Judah for the time being, but by the movements of the
Assyrians, and by political feeling in Judah as influenced by them.

The chronological question is treated at length by Wellhausen, in a
luminous essay in the " Jahrbücher für Deutsche Theologie," 1875, pp.
607-40 ; also by W. R. Smith, " Prophets of Israel," pp. 416-19 ; by
Kamphausen, " Die Chronologie der Hebr. Könige " (Bonn, 1883);
Duncker, " History of Antiquity" (Eng. Tr.), vol. iii. pp. 16-18, &c. ;
and in *The Church Quarterly Review*, Jan., 1886, pp. 257-271.

---

[1] A point which the reviewer in *The Church Quarterly* has overlooked.
[2] *E.g.* by Guthe, " Das Zukunftsbild des Iesaia " (1885), p. 37.

CHAPTER III.

THE BEGINNINGS OF ISAIAH'S MINISTRY.

¶Isaiah's "call" (chap. vi.)—Prophecies belonging to the end of Jotham's reign (chap. i. ?), or the beginning of the reign of Ahaz (chaps. ii.–iv., and v.).

THE prophecies of Isaiah have the misfortune not to be arranged in chronological order. The effort to view the events of the prophet's life in their proper perspective is, in consequence, attended with some difficulty. Thus Isaiah's "call," though not described till chap. vi., must evidently precede, in order of time, the delivery of the prophecies which stand now as chaps. i. and ii.–v. This presumption derived from the nature of the prophetic call is confirmed by internal evidence ; for while the call is expressly stated to have taken place in the last year of King Uzziah's reign, chaps. i.–v. contain indications that they were written at a later date. Why the narrative of the prophet's call was not, as in the cases of Jeremiah and Ezekiel, allowed to occupy the first place in the book, is a question which cannot be certainly answered. One conjecture is that chaps. i.–v. were placed first for the purpose of preparing the reader of the book for the severity of tone which marks the end of

What, however, is the "call" which Isaiah here describes?
The prophets uniformly speak of themselves as actuated in
their work by a power not their own.   It is the God of Israel in
whose service they stand, whose purposes they declare, whether
of judgment or salvation, whose message they deliver to His
people.   Their declarations are continually prefaced or attested
by the words, *Thus saith Jehovah*, or *Oracle of Jehovah*. Such
expressions as these are not, indeed, to be taken as implying
that the words which they utter were placed mechanically upon
their lips—the varying style and phraseology of different prophets, to say nothing of other grounds, forbids this supposition ;
but they must be understood to imply the conviction that the
substance and purport of what they utter is not their own,
only the form in which it is cast bearing the stamp of their own
genius and literary art.   Not only is this conviction a characteristic of the whole activity of a prophet, it is especially prominent in all the accounts which we possess of the occasion on
which a prophet was first made aware of the vocation which he
was destined to pursue in life.   The prophets do not speak of
a resolution or purpose, framed by themselves, to devote themselves to their vocation ; but they describe a moment in which
they received a *call*—*i.e.*, to speak from a human point of view,
were conscious of a sudden intuition, impressing itself upon
them with irresistible clearness and force, and, in certain
instances, communicated to them in the form of a vision.
Thus Amos refers to this moment of his life in the following
words (vii. 14-15) : "I was no prophet, neither was I a prophet's son (*i.e.*, no professed member of a prophetic guild) ; but
I was an herdman, and a dresser of sycomore trees : and
Jehovah took me from following the flock, and Jehovah said
unto me, Go feed my people Israel." Amos was thus diverted
from secular employment by an inward prompting, the guidance
of which he could not resist.   He does not, however, state that
the call came to him in a vision.   But Ezekiel, and apparently
Jeremiah as well, like Isaiah, both experienced a vision at the
time of their call (Ezek. i. 1, ii. 1-3 ; Jer. i. 4-10). The necessity
of obeying the prophetic summons is finely expressed by Amos
(iii. 8) : "The lion hath roared, who will not fear? the Lord
Jehovah hath spoken, who can but prophesy?"

The vision in which Isaiah's future vocation was thus made
known to him bears the impress of that grandeur of imagination,

which is the distinctive mark of his genius. " In the year that king Uzziah died, I saw the Lord sitting upon a throne high and lifted up, and his train filled the palace." The scene is the heavenly palace of Jehovah's sovereignty, modelled upon, though not a copy of, the earthly temple at Jerusalem. The comparatively small chamber of the Temple on Zion is indefinitely expanded, the lofty throne takes the place of the mercy-seat, the skirts of the royal mantle, falling in ample folds, fill the space about and below the throne, and conceal from the prophet, as he seems to himself to be standing beneath, the Form seated upon it. The two colossal cherubim, whose extended wings overshadowed the ark in the Holy of holies, are absent, their place being taken by a choir of living creatures encircling the throne. The seraphim are not mentioned elsewhere in Scripture ; and the origin and meaning of the name can only be supplied by conjecture. Here their presence seems intended to symbolize the adoration unceasingly due from the highest of created beings to the Creator. Possessed apparently of human form, and in an erect posture, they stand in a double choir about the throne, each with two of his wings seeming to support himself upon the air, with two covering his face in reverence, that he might not gaze directly upon the Divine glory, and with two his own person in humility, not deigning to meet directly the Divine glance. Isaiah, standing, as it were, by the doorway, hears the seraphs' hymn of adoration ; and as the sound of their united voices peals through the expanse the pillars of the door shake to their foundation, and smoke, indicating probably an approaching manifestation of God (Exod. xix. 18), fills the space around. The prophet, overpowered for the time by the vision, as he recovers self-possession, is conscious only of his unworthiness to be where he is. Unlike the seraphs, he is a man of unclean lips ; the nation of which he is a mem-

teacher of his people ; but with the result of making them only
less ready to listen, less fit to recover moral and intellectual [1]
soundess.   The very earnestness of his preaching will but confirm them in their unwillingness to obey.   Whatever it may
accomplish secretly, his work is to be in appearance fruitless.
Is this to continue always? he wonders.   He asks anxiously,
How long? and, in reply, another prospect as discouraging,
though in a different way, as the first, is opened before him ; it
must continue until the desolating tide of invasion has swept
over the land, and purged to the utmost the sin-stricken nation ;
so severe should the judgment be that even though a fraction
(" a tenth ") should escape, or recover, from the first assault, a
second and a third should follow till the purgation was complete (*v.* 13*a*).   But the dark prospect is not left without a
gleam of hope ; a new figure abruptly shapes itself in the prophet's imagination : as a terebinth or an oak, which, when
it is felled and left apparently without chance of recovery,
will yet germinate afresh, for its *stock* remains unimpaired, so
the *core* of the Jewish nation will survive the judgment, and
burst out afterwards into new life ; it is a " holy seed," and, as
such, is indestructible (*v.* 13*b*).   In the words just explained we
have the first germs of an idea which will frequently meet us
in Isaiah, and which we shall find to be one of his most characteristic doctrines.

Such was the moment in which Isaiah beheld, as through a
veil, the glory of his God, and was given to understand his own
mission in life.   The truths thus vividly presented before him
left upon his mind an indelible impression.   · *t* and
the *holiness* of Israel's God are the two aspects of the Di
nature pre-eminently conspicuous in his writings ; of the former
an illustration will recur before long in the grand picture of
Jehovah's " Day " (ii. 10 ff.) ; the latter is perpetually brought
before us in the prophet's favourite phrase, " the Holy One of
Israel "—the Holy One, that is, who is peculiarly Israel's own,
and who reigns in Israel as its Monarch and King.   And the
conviction that the chosen seed, however severe the trials
through which it must pass, is indestructible, and that " a remnant will return," was embodied almost immediately [2] in the

[1] " Heart "=understanding, as Hos. vii. 11 (see R. V.), Jer. v. 21, &c.
[2] For in 736–5 the child is old enough to accompany his father to meet
Ahaz (vii. 3).

name given to his son _Shear-jashub_, and is the principle which is ever afterwards his support and hope when disappointment vexes or dangers threaten.

Whether in chap. I. we have Isaiah's first public utterance is a question difficult to determine.

Undoubtedly this chapter is fitted, both by its contents generally, and by its fine exordium in particular, to have been the first address publicly delivered by Isaiah : but it is not less fitted, upon the same grounds, to open the volume of his prophecies ; and though written subsequently it may have been placed here—whether by Isaiah himself, or by a collector of his prophecies—as an introduction to the following discourses. The evidence of internal criteria is not decisive. The passage which speaks apparently most definitely is _v._ 7–9, especially _v._ 7 : " Your country is a desolation ; your cities are burned with fire ; your land, _strangers are devouring it_ in your presence, and it is a desolation, as the overthrow of strangers :" but these words are capable of being referred not only to the Syro-Ephraimitish invasion, which (as has been already stated) began at the end of Jotham's reign, but to an Assyrian invasion many years later (cf. xxxiii. 8). It is urged in favour of the latter date, that the expressions correspond more closely with the Assyrian than with the Syro-Ephraimitish invasion ; and, in particular, that the picture of isolation and disaster which the verses set before us is darker than the facts at the earlier date would justify. Still, an army of which Syrians formed a large—perhaps the larger—part might not inaptly be described as " strangers ;" and, from allusions elsewhere, the ravages perpetrated by the allied troops appear to have been considerable. It is possible, too, that the description itself may be somewhat idealized : the prophets seldom use the language of mere prose ; and Isaiah discerning beforehand what the ultimate issue would be, may have heightened the colours of his description in "fusing the actual present with the expected future."[1] At the same time, it cannot be denied that the passage is exactly appropriate to the period of Sennacherib's invasion in 701, when, as the Assyrian monarch tells us himself, he had shut up Hezekiah in Jerusalem " like a bird in a cage," had captured forty-six Judæan cities, and had bestowed the territory around them upon his Philistine vassals. The very fact, however,

[1] Sir Edward Strachey, "Jewish History and Politics," p. 24.

that the historical allusions are thus ambiguous makes the
question of its date one of minor importance. On the whole,
though without any confidence that his view is correct, the
present writer prefers to suppose, upon the *prima facie* ground
of its position, that it is the first of Isaiah's spoken discourses, and to assign it accordingly to the end of the reign
of Jotham.

The chapter is so suggestive and significant that it is impossible to do more here than point to a few of its more salient
features, for in several cases even a single expression would
demand some pages for its proper elucidation. The chapter
has been styled by Ewald " The Great Arraignment ;" and a
more appropriate title could not be proposed. The long period
of prosperity under Uzziah and Jotham has blinded the nation
to its real condition ; the prophet pulls the veil aside, and
exhibits to it its own image without concealment or disguise.
The nation evinced an unworthy neglect in the discharge of the
claims due from it ; like unnatural children, its members have
disowned their father ; they have frustrated the purpose
(Exod. xix. 6), which their national existence was designed to
realize. Hence the peril in which they at present find themselves ; the " body politic " is unsound, morally and materially ;
it is diseased alike in intellect ("heart") and will ; it succumbs
in consequence the more quickly to an attack from without which
it might otherwise have effectually resisted (*v.* 2-9). The
defence which the nation is supposed to offer, that the Temple
services are maintained with splendour and regularity, and that
thus all religious obligations are completely discharged, is in-
dignantly disallowed by the prophet ; no ritual, however costly
and elaborate, can supply the place of sincerity of heart and integrity of purpose : God indeed accepts such service from His
worshippers, but only as the token and expression of a right
mind (*v.* 10-17). Still the day of grace is not yet past, and
upon condition of the nation's amendment, an offer of re-
conciliation is made. But the prophet foresees too truly that
the offer will not be listened to, or at least that it will be
listened to only by a minority ; the nation as a whole will
not be reformed (*v.* 18-23), and judgment is accordingly
passed   " Ha ! I will appease me through mine adversaries"
—so God now calls those who were formerly his "sons"—" and
avenge me of mine enemies ; and I will bring back my hand

upon thee, smelting out as with lye thy dross, and I will take
away all thy lead-alloy ; and I will bring back thy judges
as aforetime, and thy counsellors as at the beginning : afterwards thou shalt be called Citadel of righteousness, Faithful
city." Nothing but a severe discipline will restore the nation to its
former and ideal character—a discipline that will result in the
destruction of evildoers, and the survival of a worthy residue
alone (*v.* 24–31).

Such (if the view here taken of the chronology be correct) is
Isaiah's first endeavour to awaken in his nation its slumbering
spiritual susceptibilities, to arouse it by the offer of pardon, and
to bring it back to singleness and sincerity of life. His aim is
to produce what would now be described as a great social and
moral reform—a reform, however, consisting, not merely in the
removal of palpable anomalies and injustice, but having its
root in a complete change of heart—μετάνοια, as it is termed in
the New Testament (Matt. iii. 2, &c.)—in the individual. In
the picture which Isaiah draws, it will be noticed that the upper
and ruling classes form a prominent feature. Corrupt rulers,
unjust officials, are, and always have been, a crying evil in the
East : legislators in vain denounced them (*e.g.* Exod. xxii.
21–24 ; xxiii. 6–9) ; they flourished in Judah during the prosperous days of Uzziah as they flourished in the neighbouring
kingdom during the prosperity which similarly marked the
long reign of Jeroboam II. (Amos ii. 6 ; v. 10–11). Their
misgovernment is largely the cause of the calamities under
which the nation is suffering, and their bad example is a permanent obstacle to reform : thus their downfall is the essential
condition of national improvement. But all other unworthy
members of the nation must perish with them. And these, as
the prophet perceives, are so numerous that when the judgment
comes only a *remnant* will survive it. This principle of the
survival of a worthy remnant, which, as we saw, was fore-
shadowed on the occasion of Isaiah's call, is here enunciated
more distinctly. The idea was not a new one : it had been
already dropped by the prophet Amos (chap. v. 15 ; cf. ix. 19).
But in Isaiah's hands it acquires a new significance. It is the
principle by which he reconciles God's faithfulness with His

cast off and perish. But it has been untrue to its high vocation;
it has abandoned itself to sin; and justice demands that it
should reap the penalty. It will be purged therefore, but not
destroyed. Judah will pass through the furnace of trial and
come out refined, freed from the admixture of evil—her rulers
no longer corrupt, but displaying ideal perfection; her capital
the home of justice and faithfulness. Isaiah pictures to himself
a catastrophe which will remodel the national life, and in-
augurate a new epoch. The inhabitants of Judah, in so far as
they either remain faithful, or are led by the judgment to reform,
will be rescued: those who thus "turn" to Jehovah ("her
converts") and are saved, form the nucleus of a new community
which will then be established, and which will exhibit the true,
or, as we may term them, the *ideal*, characteristics of the "Israel
of God." This thought of an ideal society, to succeed and take
the place of the existing corrupt one, will often meet us in
Isaiah. No other prophet dwells upon it so frequently, or
paints it with the same distinctness and force. To be sure, it
was never actually realized in the form in which he himself
anticipated it, but his visions of it are not on that account deprived of their value; for he conceives and gives expression in
them to an ideal of life and conduct, which was an example
and a model both to his contemporaries and to succeeding
ages; while to us they remain as a foreshadowing of what may
one day be accomplished by the Gospel.

Chapters ii.–v.—divided by a natural break at the end of
chap. iv.—belong either to the end of the reign of Jotham or the
beginning of that of Ahaz. The language of chap. iii. 12,
"My people—his governor is a wilful child, and women rule
over him," points to a time when the vigorous administration
of Uzziah and Jotham had been succeeded by the weak and
inefficient government of Ahaz; and, on the other hand, the
general impression derived from the chapters is that they were
written at a time when the disasters of the Syro-Ephraimitish
war had not yet commenced, but were only imminent. It is
possible that prophecies belonging to the two periods mentioned
have been fused together. Whether this be so or not the
chapters present a vivid picture of the condition of Judah and
of its prophets, as they were viewed by the prophet at the
time indicated, while the tide of prosperity which (p. 10 f.) had
continued to flow throughout the age of Uzziah and Jotham

showed still no signs of intermittence. The reader will recall the sketch which has been given of the material progress which the kingdom of Judah had made during the reign of these two kings. The particulars derived from the historical books may be supplemented by Isaiah, whose allusions in the chapters before us make it evident that Jerusalem had become, in a word, a fashionable capital, where wealth increased daily, and where luxury and dress, with their accessories, were a first object in everybody's thoughts. Foreign relations were, moreover, amicable : trade was flourishing ; military defences were in a high state of efficiency ; was it possible for a nation to be more prosperous or to feel more secure?

All those who thought thus were speedily disillusioned by Isaiah. The scene at the beginning of his discourse is effectively conceived by Ewald. The verses ii. 2–4, it should be premised, recur with slight variations in the fourth chapter of Micah, and are supposed by many to have been borrowed by both writers from some older source. The prophet appears before an assembly of the people, perhaps on a Sabbath, and recites this passage, depicting in beautiful and effective imagery the spiritual pre-eminence to be accorded in the future to the religion of Zion. He would dwell upon the subject further : but scarcely has he begun to speak when the disheartening spectacle meets his eye of a crowd of soothsayers, of gold and silver ornaments and finery, of horses and idols; his tone immediately changes, and he bursts into a diatribe against the foreign and idolatrous fashions, the devotion to wealth and glitter, which he sees about him, and which extorts from him in the end the terrible wish *Therefore forgive them not* (*v.* 5–9). And then in one of his stateliest periods, Isaiah declares the judgment about to fall upon all that is "tall and lofty," upon Uzziah's towers and fortified walls, upon the great merchant ships at Elath, upon every object of human satisfaction and pride, when wealth and rank will be impotent to save, when idols will be cast despairingly aside, and when all classes alike will be glad to find a hiding-place, as in the old days of

of water : hero and warrior, judge and prophet, and soothsayer and elder ; the captain of fifty and the man of repute, and the counsellor, and the skilful artificer, and the expert enchanter. And I will make youths to be their princes, and with wilfulness (*or* capriciousness) shall they rule over them." Society is to be dissolved ; and the prophet names as typical examples the different professional classes which usually constitute an element of stability in a state, but which will all be involved in the impending ruin. The army, which had been newly organized and equipped by Uzziah, the "elders" and others responsible for justice and order, the prophets, who formed a recognized order in the state (Jer. xviii. 18), the artizan class, who no doubt were numerous in Jerusalem, especially at a time when luxury and wealth would ensure them employment, and who are expressly named among those carried away to Babylon (Jer. xxiv. 1), will all be broken up ; and a similar fate will befal the "soothsayers" and "enchanters," a class which clearly, in Isaiah's day (cf. ii. 6 ; viii. 19), enjoyed no small reputation among the people. The king, it has been remarked, is not named : Ahaz has no independence of character ; he is under the guidance of companions, young and thoughtless, like the advisers of Rehoboam ; ere long the state will be abandoned to the rule of mere caprice, and then, government being at an end, every one will be free to pursue his own interests and assert his imagined rights, regardless of those of his neighbour. So desperate will be the condition of society, that even should the office of *kadi*—judge, or, as we might say, dictator (cf. Jud. xi. 6)—be tendered to a man, with power to use his authority in the restoration of order, he will decline the proffered honour ; the task he will at once see to be beyond his powers (*v.* 6, 7). And why is it that the state is drifting to this deplorable condition? As in chap. i., it is the rulers at whose doors the guilt lies : "O my people, they which lead thee cause thee to err, and destroy the way of thy paths." The king and his advisers, the men of authority and influence, have forgotten their responsibilities, have had no thought for the moral and social well being of the nation, have "eaten up" the vineyard instead of tending it, have sought only to amass the means of enjoyment for themselves, heedless of the cruelty or injustice which may in the process have been inflicted upon others. Isaiah here (chap. iii. 13) imagines a judgment scene : the

the "elders" and "princes," runs in these terms : "It is ye that have eaten up the vineyard : the spoil of the poor is in your houses ; what mean ye that ye crush my people and grind the face of the poor? saith the Lord, Jehovah of hosts."

The prophet next attacks a fresh feature in the society of the capital—the dress and luxury of the women. The ladies of Jerusalem hardly impress Isaiah more favourably than those of the capital of Samaria, a generation earlier, had impressed the prophet Amos (iv. 1). The ground, however, upon which the attack here rests is not selfishness or devotion to the pleasures of the table, but vanity and ostentatious display. Isaiah's indignation, it may be, was suddenly aroused, as he watched their demeanour whilst they were escorted in state through the public places of Jerusalem, or caught sight of the costly and curious attire which was the chief object of their thought ; and he enumerates, with bewildering minuteness, the various articles of dress and adornment which thus constituted their pride ; declaring emphatically that the day will come when they will be forcibly stripped of it all, and obliged to assume the coarse and humiliating attire of captives. The image which the prophet has in his mind is that of a disaster in the field : the warriors of Judah defeated and slain ; their wives and daughters defenceless in the hands of the conquerors ; the gates which had seen them march forth in the full assurance of victory, mourning over their fall ; the city itself desolate and empty. "And seven women shall take hold of one man in that day, saying, Our own bread will we eat, and our own clothing will we wear ; only let us be called by thy name ; take away our reproach " (iv. 1). The women that remain crowd round the few survivors : they do not claim the support which it was the natural duty of a husband to confer ; they will provide

growth[1] of Jehovah be for beauty and for glory ; and the fruit of
the land for majesty and adornment, unto the escaped of Israel.
And it shall come to pass that he that is left in Zion and that
remaineth in Jerusalem, shall be called holy, even every one
who is written down for life in Jerusalem." The thought is the
same as that which we found in chap. i., but it is developed
with richer and more magnificent imagery. A remnant will
survive the judgment, and under changed and brighter auspices
will found an ideal community in the future. A new social state,
established without man's intervention, is what the prophet
pictures as about to commence. A new glory and ornament
will appear, and take the place of that which has perished.
The very growth of the land, for *those that escape*, fostered by
Jehovah's care, will be clad with preternatural splendour. The
inhabitants of Zion will realize the ideal character of the nation :
every one of the survivors, *written down for life in Jerusalem*,
i.e., inscribed in the register of its living citizens, shall be called
holy (Exod. xix. 6). By "life" Isaiah means not life hereafter,
but life on earth, though under new conditions ; a glorified life,
freed from sin and trouble. The purification of the nation
being thus completed, provision is next made for its continued
safety. It is defended by the protecting presence of Jehovah,
described, in imagery drawn from the story of the Exodus
(Exod. xiii. 21 f.), as "a cloud and smoke by day, and the shining
of a flaming fire by night." Nor are more material comforts neglected : a pavilion, or canopy, extended over the whole site of
Zion, will be a shelter against those violent extremes of weather
to which an Eastern climate is always exposed.

Such is Isaiah's second picture of the ideal Zion of the
future—the vision which, when he looks out beyond the dark
and disheartening present, his eye of faith enables him to
descry.

Chap. v., in its general scope, is parallel to chap. iii., and
demonstrates afresh the grounds upon which sentence has
been already passed upon the nation. In the parable of the

---

[1] See Gen. xix. 25 ; Psa. lxv. 10 ("the *springing* thereof"). Not the word
rendered rightly *Branch* in ch. xi. 1. Jeremiah (xxiii. 5) applies the term
to the Messiah ; but it is doubtful if it is so used here. In Jeremiah the
sense of the figure is limited by the context (" I will raise up *unto David* a
righteous growth *or* sprout ") ; but here the parallel clause ("fruit of the
land") is in favour of the view that it is to be understood literally.

vineyard, with which it opens, Isaiah shows how, in spite of the advantages profusely lavished upon it, Israel has not borne the expected fruits—" He hoped for justice, but behold bloodshed ; for righteousness, but behold a cry."[1] And then one by one the national sins are summed up (v. 8-23). The inordinate desire for the possession of large estates which now asserted itself, and was accompanied, doubtless, not by an increased sense of the duties of landed proprietors, but by the unfair or violent ejectment of less fortunate possessors ; the immoderate indulgence in enjoyments of the table, which, in the minds of many, left no room for more serious thought (v. 12) ; the devotion to sin for sin's sake, attended by a scoffing and defiant unbelief; the confusion of moral distinctions, blinding men to the true nature and issue of the course which they were pursuing ; the self-satisfied astuteness of the leading politicians,[2] who conceived that their management of affairs was above criticism (v. 21); the systematized corruption of the authorized administrators of justice—these are the sins against which Isaiah hurls his denouncing 'Woe,' showing (v. 24) how in truth they are already working their natural effects in the disintegration of the national life, and the slow but steady deterioration of the national vigour. And he ends his discourse with a picture, imitated by Jeremiah, but not surpassed, of the rapid advance, the compact array, the unerring aim, the iron grasp, of an unnamed but terrible invader, whose shock none can resist, and at whose presence clouds of impenetrable darkness will shroud the political horizon.

These, then, were the thoughts which presented themselves to Isaiah, as his eye penetrated beneath the surface of society in Judah, and showed him how deceptive its plausible exterior was. Not only did Isaiah perceive clearly the unsound elements which underlay it—he saw also, what the popular leaders of opinion did not see, how ill-fitted Judah was to sustain the attack of a really formidable foe, and how delusive the imagined security of the country was. The approaching future is represented in chap. ii. (v. 12 ff.), under the form of a "Day of Jehovah," a figure used frequently by the prophets, and implying a signal and triumphant manifestation of Jehovah in vindication of His laws and rights.[1] Though this vindication may be effected by means of human agents, the conception puts their instrumentality out of sight, and regards the decisive movements of history as an exclusive manifestation of Jehovah's purpose and power. The prophets elaborate the figure under varying imagery, suggested partly by the occasion, partly by their own imagination. n Joel ii. 1 ff., for instance, the imagery is evidently suggested by the recent visitation of locusts, described by the prophet in chap. i.[2] Isaiah effectively represents the " Day " as directed against the various objects of pride and strength which the nation had accumulated in the days of Uzziah. Here, then, the judgment is depicted on its *Divine* side ; and the case is similar in v. 16, where it is treated also as an exhibition or assertion of Jehovah's holiness.[3] Viewed on its *human* side, it takes the form of a defeat and desolation of Judah (iii. 25–iv. 1 ; v. 9 f., 13, 17), effected through the instrumentality of the Assyrians (v. 25–30), whom the demoralized people are powerless to resist (v. 24). The event did not actually prove as serious as Isaiah had an-ticipated ; but his object is to reform his nation, to brace up its energies, to quicken its perceptions ; and with this purpose in view he holds up before it the true principles which its respon-sible leaders are disregarding, and paints vividly the con-sequences to which their continued neglect may be expected to lead. In the next chapter we shall, see the false and short-sighted principles which he here exposes operating disastrously at a grave political juncture.

[1] Based, probably, upon the Hebrew use of *day* as = victory (Ezek. xiii. 5 ; comp. Isa. ix. 4). See W. R. Smith, " The Prophets of Israel," p. 131 f. 396 f.

[2] For other examples, see Amos v. 18, 20 ; Zeph. i. 7, 14-16 ; Isa. xiii. 6-10.

[3] " Is sanctified," R.V. : rather, " shows himself holy " (Cheyne) comp. Ezek. xxxvi. 23 ; xxxviii. 16 (holiness vindicated in an act of judgment).

CHAPTER IV

THE SYRO-EPHRAIMITISH WAR.

Isaiah and the Syro-Ephraimitish war (chaps. vii. 1–ix. 7 ; ix. 8–x. 4 ,
xvii. 1–11)—The prophecy of Immanuel.

WE arrive now at the first great political crisis through which
Judah passed during Isaiah's lifetime. The prophet assumed
in it a conspicuous part, and it proved the occasion of two of
his greatest and most famous prophecies. In order to understand how it arose, we must go back a few years. Menahem, it
will be remembered, owed his throne to Assyrian help, and had
naturally in consequence acknowledged the suzerainty of Assyria ; but Pekah, who overthrew Menahem's successor and established himself in his place, was in his sympathies anti-Assyrian.
It was, probably, a willingness to co-operate against a common
foe that now drew together the two kingdoms of Israel and
Syria, which in the past had usually viewed one another with
feelings of inveterate hostility. Hence the league between
Pekah and Rezin, the object of which, in so far as it was
directed against Judah, appears to have been to force it to join
a coalition formed for the purpose of opposing more effectual
resistance to the Assyrians. The beginning of hostilities is
referred (2 Kings xv. 37) to the end of the reign of Jotham. At
first, to judge from the description there given, the incursions
were probably of a desultory kind ; but after the accession of
Ahaz they took the form of an organized campaign. It is
difficult to follow the stages precisely, and especially to feel any

The tradition of a particular incident in the war appears to
have reached the Chronicler, which he has amplified in accordance with his usual plan, without giving any clue as to the place
occupied by it in the struggle as a whole.   The numbers in
verse 6, it is clear, have been largely exaggerated ; but the fact
that a grave disaster befel the troops of Ahaz in the progress of
the war may be fairly held to underlie the Chronicler's narrative.
From the language of Isaiah vii. 2, which appears to describe
danger anticipated rather than danger already experienced, it may
perhaps be inferred that the disaster in question did not take
place till subsequently.   But, however that may be, it is plain
that the territory of Judah must have suffered severely from the
continued incursions, and that the people, unable to repel them,
became gradually demoralized.   There are other indications
that the position of Judah was now no longer what it had been
under the two previous reigns.   Uzziah (p. 10) had fortified the
port of Elath, and many Judæans had settled in it, probably for
commercial purposes.   But in the account of Ahaz's reign we
read (2 Kings xvi. 6) that Rezin ended all this : his forces
swept past Judah unimpeded, obtained possession of Elath, expelled from it the Jewish settlers, and restored it to Edom.[1]
Nor was this all.   According to the Chronicler (2 Chron. xxviii.
17 f.) the Edomites and Philistines, both old enemies of Judah,
took advantage of the exposed and defenceless state of the
country to make marauding expeditions, and the latter—retalia-
ting what Uzziah had done—even captured some of the towns
and villages, carrying away their inhabitants. · So little was the
army, in spite of all that had been done for it by Uzziah (p. 11),
able now to protect its country.

But to return to the occasion of which Isaiah tells us.   The
object of the attack on the part of the allied forces was, as has
been stated, to force Judah to join them in offering resistance to
Assyria.   It was against the " House of David " that the combination was specially directed ; and the intention was to substitute a more subservient ruler in place of Ahaz, the son of
Tabeel, to judge from the form of his name, a Syrian.   Ahaz, it
would seem, had been antecedently favourable to Assyria ;
deficient himself in independence, he was probably disposed to

[1] So we must doubtless read, for "Syria," and the "Syrians :" the
words for Syria ("Aram"), and Edom, written in the old Hebrew characters, would be scarcely distinguishable.

throw himself upon the support of a strong external power. Hence his resistance to the solicitations of Rezin and Pekah and their consequent appeal to arms. The narrative of Isaiah opens with what would seem to have been the beginning of the danger; or possibly with the approach of a more numerous and better organized body of forces. How great the alarm in Jerusalem was appears from the comparison which the prophet uses, "And the king's heart shook, and the heart of his people, as the trees of the forest shake before the wind." The people, in a word, were paralysed at the approach of danger: nor was Ahaz the man to come forward at a crisis and allay the general alarm, or to adopt with decision a prompt and well-considered line of action. On the contrary, he was already meditating the expedient which he ultimately adopted, and which, though perilous, when viewed in relation to the consequences which it might involve, was one which, nevertheless, promised immediate relief. He meditated following the precedent set by Menahem a few years before, and inviting the assistance of Tiglath-Pileser to rid him of his troublesome invaders. The step cost him his independence: it cost him also now and subsequently a heavy expenditure of treasure—so terribly was he impoverished by the Assyrian demands that he had even to strip the Temple of its ancient ornaments: but in its immediate result it was successful (2 Kings xvi. 7-9). Tiglath-Pileser accepted the terms offered by Ahaz; he invaded the territory of Damascus and Israel in the rear, thereby at once necessitating the withdrawal of the allied forces from Judah. It was on the occasion of this invasion (fixed by the Inscriptions to B.C. 734) that the districts in the north-east of Israel, including Gilead, Galilee, and Naphtali, were lost to Israel, and their inhabitants deported to Assyria (p. 8 f.).

We have, however, somewhat anticipated the course of events. At the date of Isaiah's interview with Ahaz (chap. vii.), the application to Assyria was meditated, but not actually carried into effect. To understand this interview two things must be borne in mind. Firstly, Isaiah is aware of the king's intention to solicit aid from Assyria, but it is not openly admitted between them. Secondly, the power and resources of the allied kings, especially of Rezin, so impressed the popular imagination that they were held to be practically invincible: Isaiah views both differently; describes them as "smoked out firebrands," and

intimates that he considers the terror of the people to be unreasonable. Hence, the words in verses 8, 9, in Isaiah's mouth,
have a contemptuous import : it is as though he said : " For the
head of Syria is Damascus, and the head of Damascus is *a mere*
Rezin ; .. and the head of Ephraim is Samaria, and the head
of Samaria is *only* Remaliah's son." Rezin and Pekah constitute
in his eyes no ground of real alarm.

It was close outside the walls, " at the end of the conduit of
the upper pool, in the highway of the fuller's field "—whither,
we may conjecture, Ahaz had gone to make provision for a supply of water within the city, in the event of a siege—that Isaiah,
accompanied by Shear-Jashub his son, met Ahaz, upon the
memorable occasion described in the seventh chapter of his
book. The contrast of character and bearing between the king
and the prophet is marked. Ahaz is timid and helpless, takes
no position, and displays no promptitude or courage. Isaiah,
on the contrary, steps forward with assurance : he is collected
and calm : and his complete control of the political situation
impresses us forcibly. With prophetic intuition he has discerned already that the power and splendour of the allied kingdoms is doomed to extinction—" Take heed, and be quiet : fear
not, neither be faint-hearted, for these two tails of smoking
fire-brands, for the fierce anger of Rezin with Syria, and of the
son of Remaliah ;" and declares with emphasis that their plan
for the ruin of Judah is not to succeed : " It shall not stand,
and it shall not be ;" the head of Syria is only Rezin, the head
of Ephraim is but Pekah : and " within threescore and five
years, Ephraim will be broken that it be not a people." " If
ye do not believe," he adds (*v.* 9), " surely ye shall not be
established." The prophet in these words assumes the part of
a practical statesman, and warns the nation that their safety
lies not in the help to be derived from some external alliance,
but in reliance upon their own resources strengthened and sustained by faith in Jehovah. He pauses, waiting to observe the
impression made by his words upon Ahaz. The king hesi-
tates to reply : the prospect opened by Isaiah is too distant
for his faith : his hopes rest in reality upon the Assyrians, to
whom he may even already have made overtures : and his
consciousness that Isaiah disapproves makes him silent and
reserved. Isaiah, endeavouring to win his confidence, and interpreting his hesitation in the most favourable sense, is ready

to reassure him. " Ask thee a sign of Jehovah thy God ; ask it
either in the depth, or in the height above." " I will not ask,
neither will I put Jehovah to the test." His answer, though
couched in the language of resignation and piety, is not sincere :
he declines the sign because he has a secret dread of the truth ;
and sees too well, that if given it would be the condemnation of
his distrust, the ruin of his fondly cherished scheme. The
reply, addressed not to the king only, but to the princes of the
royal house, who approved, perhaps guided, his policy, follows :
" Is it not enough for you to weary men" (*i.e.*, the prophet himself, in his human capacity), " that ye will also weary my God,"
by refusing *His* gracious offer to renew and confirm your faith ?
"Therefore," as you have declined the proffered choice, "Jehovah"
withdraws the offer, and "will Himself give you a sign :" and
there rises before the mental eye of the prophet the vision of the
maiden, ere long to give birth to the child who, in spite of the
destitution through which his country must first pass,[1] is still the
mysterious pledge and symbol[2] of its deliverance (*v.* 13–16).
And now, at last, what has been in the background all along is
no longer concealed : abruptly (*v.* 17) the prophet confronts
Ahaz with the naked truth. " The power on which you rely for
safety, and which will indeed for the moment save you, will
afterwards bring upon you a retribution which you have not
foreseen : it will make your land the arena of a conflict with
Egypt (*v.* 18 f.) ; your country will be swept bare, and the
simplest pastoral produce — curdled milk and honey—will be
the sole means of subsistence for the survivors" (*v.* 20–25).[3] The
sequel will show how true Isaiah's forecast, expressed in these
verses, was, and how accurately they indicate the natural results
of Ahaz's policy. A generation hence, Judah passed through
perils greater than any which had befallen it since the division
of the kingdom ; and though Isaiah's worst anticipations were
happily not realized to the letter, the conflict between Assyria

---

[1] His only fare, in infancy (*v.* 15), being of the simplest kind, viz.,
curdled milk and honey, such as implies privation (cf. *v.* 22).

and Egypt took place on the very borders of Judah, and the land itself was terribly devastated by the wild Assyrian soldiery.

The danger which Ahaz dreaded was not, however, removed at once ; and if it be true that the scene just described occurred at the beginning of the campaign, it must even have grown more grave as the allied forces proceeded to ravage and plunder the territory of Judah. But Isaiah continued to assert his unabated confidence in the issue (viii. 1–4) : in some conspicuous spot, perhaps the court of the Temple, he inscribed in large characters the motto, which every one could understand, " Swift spoil, speedy prey ; " and after an interval approaching a year, he recorded his conviction in a still more permanent form by naming his son, *Maher-shalal-hash-baz*—" For before the boy shall know how to cry, My father, and My mother, the riches of Damascus and the spoil of Samaria shall be carried away before the king of Assyria." And now follow words of consolation addressed to those who could see below the surface, and had realized the truth of Isaiah's contention a year before, viz., that the fall of Damascus and Samaria was fraught with peril for Judah as well : " Forasmuch as this people—the entire nation, North and South alike—hath rejected the waters of Shiloah which flow softly, and rejoice with Rezin and the son of Remaliah : therefore, behold, Jehovah bringeth upon them the waters of the river, mighty and great," which first inundating Israel will afterwards sweep on with impetuous violence into Judah, " and the stretching out of its wings shall fill the breadth of thy land, O Immanuel ! " There is little consolation as yet : but no sooner has the magic word escaped the prophet's lips than his tone at once changes, and with bold defiance he challenges the combined nations (whether near, as the Syrians and Israelites, or distant as the Assyrians), and announces triumphantly their overthrow (*v.* 9, 10). Nothing shows more forcibly than this sublime apostrophe how vividly Isaiah must have conceived the reality of the unborn child of his imagination, Immanuel, and with what lofty attributes he must have invested him. But he reverts to the nearer present : he has grounds for his assurance ; for an hour of sacred ecstasy [1] had made it clear to him. The cry in Judah had been, " There is a conspiracy against us, a formidable combination, which can

---

[1] " With strength of hand " (*v.* 11), *i.e.*, seizing him, and casting him into the prophetic trance : see 2 Kings iii. 15 ; Ezek. i. 3, iii. 14, viii. 1.

only be met by a counter-alliance with Assyria"[1] : Isaiah and his
little circle of adherents had been warned not to join in it, not
to judge of the enterprise, or probable success, of Rezin and
Pekah, by the worldly and superficial estimate of the masses.
A truer guide for action had been revealed to them. "Do not,"
such is the lesson which he has been taught, "do not follow the
common people in their unreasonable alarm" (v. 12) : "Jehovah
of hosts, Him shall ye count holy ; and let Him be your fear,
and Him your dread," i.e., in modern phraseology, "Do not be
guilty of a practical abandonment of Jehovah ; do not sacrifice
principle to expediency. If you do not lose faith, 'He will be
for a sanctuary' " (v. 14), i.e. (apparently), He will be as a sanctuary protecting the territory in which it is situated, and securing
for those who honour it safety and peace ; "but" (it is ominously added) "a cause of stumbling and ruin to both the houses
of Israel," to you of Judah not less than to those of Ephraim, to
whom alone you might think that the warning can apply. Translated into modern language, the prophet's lesson is this—that
those who in a time of difficulty and temptation, sacrifice principle to expediency, and abandon the clear path of duty for a
course which may seem to lead to some greater immediate
advantage, must not be surprised if the penalty which they
ultimately have to pay be a severe one.

"Bind thou up the admonition, seal the teaching among
my disciples." So important a formula of action is not to be
entrusted to the memory alone ; it is to be written down, and
deposited, carefully bound and sealed, in the custody of the
prophet's disciples. The time will come, when though mis-
understood and neglected now, the lesson may be divulged,
and its value will be recognized. Meanwhile Isaiah, though
the time is dark, and God's favour withdrawn, will wait and
hope. He, and his children, he recollects, are the living omens
of a happier future[2] (v. 17 f.). But darker days are destined
to come first—days in which those who once refused to listen
to the prophet's voice, and who in their despair and anxiety to
learn the future had recourse, like Saul, to the aid of necro-
mancers and wizards, will be only too eager to know what

Isaiah said, and to submit to his direction—" To the teaching
and to the admonition ! "—this will be their cry, when it is too
late, and the darkness closes finally around them.[1]   In the two
verses following, the gloom thus alluded to, with the blank and
utter despair accompanying it, is inimitably represented.   But
a sudden change ensues.   Deep as is the humiliation now
falling upon the land of Zebulun and Naphtali (which, with the
region " beyond Jordan," was just the district depopulated by
Tiglath-Pileser in 734) ; dark and hopeless as their prospect
seems to be, the prophet transports himself into the " latter
time," and sees the clouds lifted, and a brilliant day shining ;
the very region which suffered most should then rejoice most
unrestrainedly.   The nation is restored and triumphant ; the
rod of the taskmaster is broken ; the garments of war become
fuel for a bonfire.   " For a child is born unto us, a son is given
unto us "[2] who will restore the empire of David upon an imperishable basis ; and in a few brief but pregnant sentences
Isaiah describes his wonderful and glorious rule (ix. 1-7).

We reach here the climax of the series of prophecies which
begins with vii. 1.   As regards the announcement made to
Ahaz in vii. 14 it is to be observed that it is not one wholly of
encouragement ; nor, after the insincerity which Ahaz had
displayed, could it be expected that it would be such.   Not
only is the promised deliverance itself only to be obtained
through privation and suffering (v. 15) ; but, whether Ahaz had
the capacity to see it or not, the terms of the promise imply a
repulse.   Not Ahaz, not some high-born son of Ahaz's house, is
to have the honour of rescuing his country from its peril : a
"nameless maiden of lowly rank" (Delitzsch) is to be the
mother of the future deliverer.   Ahaz and the royal house are

---

[1] So Revised Version, *margin*. " This word " means the saying just
quoted, " To the teaching and to the testimony."   The text of the Revised
Version expresses nearly the same sense, stated hypothetically : " If they
speak not according to this word," &c., *i.e.* if they do not agree in making
their appeal to the prophet's teaching, " they will have no morning," *i.e.*,
no brighter days will ever dawn for them.   *Testimony* = solemn admonition : comp. the cognate verb, Exod. xix. 21 (" charge ") ; 2 Kings xvii. 15
("testify ") ; Jer. xi. 17 ("protest ").

[2] Authorized Version and Revised Version, " For unto us a child is born,
unto us a son is given "—the rhythm of which is immortalized by Handel's
" Messiah."   But it is undeniable that this rendering gives to the words a
false emphasis : *child* and *son*, not *unto us*, are the emphatic words in the
sentence.

thus put aside : it is not till chap. ix. 7—spoken at least a year subsequently—that we are able to gather that the Deliverer is to be a descendant of David's line.

Before considering in what manner Isaiah's predictions were fulfilled, it will be desirable to notice two other prophecies which, from internal evidence, must be assigned to the same period, viz., chap. ix. 8-x. 4 and chap. xvii. 1-11. These two prophecies differ from the one which has just been reviewed, in that while this deals primarily with the future of Judah, the subj˒ ct of chap ix. 8-x. 4 is the condition and prospects of *Ephr˓ im*, and that of chap. xvii. 1-11 is the issue of the conflict in its effects upon Syria and Ephraim together. The prophecy, chap. ix. 8-x. 4, forms a well-articulated whole, divided into four strophes, each marked by a closing refrain. In its general purport, it may be described as a development of the thought expressed more concisely in chap. vii. 16 or viii. 4. In the first strophe Isaiah depicts the Ephraimites' proud superiority to danger, and their placid assurance after defeat : "The bricks," they say, "are fallen, but we will build with hewn stone ; the sycomores¹ are cut down, but we will put cedars in their place" : no sooner, in other words, has one scheme miscarried than they are prepared with a more magnificent one to take its place ; no sooner is one dynasty overthrown than another rises in its stead. The proverb gives apt expression to the temper habitually displayed by the northern kingdom, and may be compared to the one used by the prophet Amos about thirty years before for a similar purpose (vi. 13) : "Which say, Have we not taken to us horns by our own strength ?" In the present instance, the result which Isaiah foresees for Israel is that the country will be beset on all sides (*v.* 11, 12) by its foes. But the temper of the nation remains unimproved ; and so the prophet adds the refrain : "For all this His anger is not turned away, but His hand is stretched out still." In the next strophe a second stroke is described as descending upon it ; a great and sudden disaster befalls it, by which the plans of its statesmen are in a moment wrecked : "therefore Jehovah cutteth off from Israel head and tail, palm-

reform ensues ; and a third stroke accordingly follows. Internal lawlessness results in general anarchy, and the strife of
rival factions (v. 0). The nation is given up to internecine
conflict : the two sons of Joseph engage with each other in
mortal fray, yet do not forget their old animosity against Judah.
The figures in v. 18 are applied effectively by the prophet. Un-
righteousness, like burning fire, when once it has attacked the
nation, spreads with destructive fury and rapidity ; its flames encircle first the humbler plants, then the forest itself (symbolizing
the nation), till the whole mass seems to roll upwards in a proud
column of smoke. That factions such as those to which Isaiah
alludes were the bane and ruin of the northern kingdom is well
known. 1 Kings xvi. 21 f. may exemplify the fact for the earlier
period of the history ; the rapid succession of short-lived
dynasties, which followed after the assassination of Zechariah
(2 Kings xv. 10, 13 f., 25, 30), will illustrate it for the period
within Isaiah's own lifetime. Pekah himself, who now occupied
the throne, had obtained it by a successful conspiracy, in which
he was aided by a band of Gileadite adventurers ; by another
conspiracy, of which Hoshea was the head, he was destined
soon to lose it. Possibly, as Isaiah wrote, during the absence
of Pekah with his forces in Judah, the conspiracy was already
being planned. But again, as Isaiah contemplates the nation,
he can discern no sign of improvement ; so in a fourth and last
strophe, the final sentence upon it is declared. Injustice and
oppression are rampant amongst its rulers, self-interest is the
dominant passion ; strength and independence of character is
undermined ; how can a nation thus demoralized expect to
cope with misfortune? It will succumb at the first shock ; and
its magnates will then discover that their only place of safety
will be beneath the corpses on a battle-field ! And, as though
this prospect were not dark enough, "For all this," the
prophet ominously adds, "his anger is not turned away, but
his hand is stretched out still !" (x. 1-4).

In chap. xvii. 1-11, the prophet begins by declaring the
impending fall of Damascus, and afterwards passes on to show
how the ruin of Syria will be followed rapidly by that of Ephraim
as well. It is probably owing to the prominence given in this
prophecy to Damascus that it has been placed by the collector
among the " foreign prophecies " of Isaiah (see Chap. VIII.).
After describing how the storm which breaks upon Damascus

(*v.* 1), will afterwards (*v.* 2) sweep over the region east of Jordan, and finally (*v.* 3) cross over into Israel itself, until both nations share a common doom, Isaiah dwells next (*v.* 4, 5) upon the scene of desolation which the Northern kingdom will then present. The few who survive the judgment—not more numerous than the berries which escape after the last strokes have been given by the beaters (Deut. xxiv. 20) to an olive-garden—will indeed be spiritually transformed, and recognize Him who is the true source of their strength ; but, as a whole, the cultivated plains and fortified cities of Ephraim will again be deserted by their inhabitants, as they were deserted by the Canaanites of old in presence of the invading Israelites (*v.* 7–9). For Israel had abandoned the service of its Maker ; it had offered a home upon its soil to foreign cults ; the plantations (such is the metaphor by which the prophet describes the foreign worships imported into Israel [1]) had been carefully enclosed and otherwise tended ; the seed had even blossomed, and there was promise of an abundant crop ; but the day of harvest would be a sad one (*v.* 10–11). The people of Israel had "transplanted heathen gods into their worship, and they must reap God's abandonment of their nation as the fruit." [2]

How Isaiah's predictions, so far as Syria and Ephraim were concerned, received their fulfilment, is disclosed by the annals of Tiglath-Pileser (above, p. 8, 9). Ephraim was crippled by a serious loss of territory and population in 734 ; Damascus capitulated in 732 : Samaria itself did not fall until it was captured by Sargon in 722. Tiglath-Pileser's advance upon the north-east provinces of Israel obliged the allied forces to withdraw from Judah, and brought the Syro-Ephraimitish invasion to an end. Pekah, returning to Samaria, is slain by the conspirators, who, it may reasonably be conjectured, had taken advantage of his absence in Judah to organize their plan of rebellion : Tiglath-Pileser marches forward to Samaria, gives his support to Hoshea, and banishes to Assyria the nobles who had favoured or defended Pekah. For the present Syria escaped, but in the following year, 733, the Assyrian king laid siege to Damascus, which, after a stubborn resistance, was

[1] "Gardens" were a common site for the practice of idolatrous rites (i. 29) ; there may even, in the word rendered "pleasant," be a specific allusion to the worship of Adonis (comp. R.V. *marg.*)

[2] Sir Edward Strachey, "Hebrew History and Politics," &c., p. 209.

reduced in 732, just at the time anticipated by Isaiah (viii. 4).
Its inhabitants were punished with deportation, and henceforward we read no more of a Syrian kingdom of Damascus in
the Old Testament.   No fresh peril, however, threatened Judah.
The Assyrian king was occupied with affairs at home ; he made
no attempt to invade Egypt, nor did his troops molest Judah.
For the present the danger which Isaiah had feared (vii. 17 ff. ;
viii. 8) passed by.

But who is the child Immanuel, the subject of the famous
verse, vii. 14?   Many readers, more familiar perhaps with the
quotation in St. Matthew's Gospel (i. 23) than with the place
which the prophecy holds in Isaiah, see in it *merely* a prediction
of the birth of Christ of a Virgin.   This view of the meaning of
the prophecy is, however, insufficient ; it offers no explanation
of its *historical setting*.   It is the prophet's plain intention to
intimate to the men of Judah that a temporal deliverance is imminent ; and his words would be singularly unreal had it been
implied in them that many centuries must elapse before the limit
of time which he was fixing could arrive.   To do better justice,
therefore, to the historical setting of the prophecy, different
suggestions have been made.   It has been thought that the
allusion may be to a child shortly to be born to Ahaz himself,
and this either as exhausting the significance of the prophecy,
or as a first fulfilment, typical of a further fulfilment in the more
distant future ; or, again, it has been held that a child about to
be born to the prophet is intended ; or, thirdly, the words have
been supposed, like the not dissimilar ones in viii. 3 f., to be
meant as a simple note of time, as though the prophet said,
" Before the time when a maiden, now of marriageable age, shall
have brought forth her firstborn (whom, in token of the coming
deliverance, she will name *Immanuel*), and before that child
shall be old enough to distinguish good and evil, the power
which you dread will be no more."   None of these suggestions,
however, supplies a satisfactory solution of the difficulty.   It is
decisive against the first that, whatever scheme of chronology
be adopted, Hezekiah was already born at the time of the interview of Isaiah with Ahaz.[1]   Against the second view it is to be

---

[1] Being 25 years old (2 Kings xviii. 2) at his accession, if this be placed
in 715, his birth will have been in 740 ; if his accession be placed in 728,
and his age at that time have to be reduced for the reason stated (p. 14), it
would still be most arbitrary to suppose him not yet born in 735-4.

observed that, though viii. 3 f. is referred to in support of it, the parallel is a very imperfect one ; not only is Isaiah's wife there called the "prophetess"; but, while the language used with reference to Maher-shalal-hash-baz does not imply that Isaiah saw in him anything remarkable beyond the symbolism of his name, the announcement of Immanuel's birth is made with peculiar solemnity, and the mention of his name afterwards (viii. 8) stirs the prophet's soul with profound emotion. The same objection, *viz.*, that it does not account for the hope and wonder with which Isaiah evidently regards the child, holds against the third suggestion that his words are intended solely to mark pointedly a limit of time. And an objection which is of force against each view equally is the fact that in viii. 8, Immanuel is conceived as *owner of the land:* is it credible that Hezekiah should be passed by, and a younger son of Ahaz be so designated? or that the prophet's own child, or even the child of no one in particular, could be invested by him with such a dignity?' The manner in which Isaiah reverts to him in chaps. viii.–ix. should also be noticed. Even after the interval of a year (viii. 1–4) the child is still none visibly present before him ; he is located by the prophet in a period *yet future,* when Zebulun and Naphtali have been restored, the dwindled nation replenished, and the glorified realm of David inaugurated (ix. 6 f). The language of Isaiah forces upon us the conviction that the

---

¹ The word rendered "virgin," Heb. *'almah,* cannot be urged against the suggestions proposed. For it is not the term ordinarily employed in Hebrew for *virgin,* and cannot be shown to be exclusively applicable to one who was unmarried. It occurs besides in Gen. xxiv. 43 ; Exod. ii. 8 ; 1 Chron. xv. 20 ; Psa. xlvi. *title;* lxviii. 25 ; Prov. xxx. 19 ; Cant. i. 3 ; vi. 8 : the corresponding masculine occurs 1 Sam. xvii. 56 ; xx. 22. From the sense borne by the root in Arabic, it appears to denote properly *one of marriageable age.* The corresponding term in Aramaic (strictly a diminutive) unquestionably does not connote virginity (see *e.g.* Deut. xxii. 28, 29 [for *damsel*], Targ. and Pesh.). Probably the English word *damsel* would be the fairest rendering. From the prophecy as a whole, it may indeed be inferred that Isaiah saw something remarkable in the birth of the child Immanuel ; and it may even be plausibly contended that his use of the

figure of Immanuel is an *ideal one*, projected by him upon the shifting future—upon the nearer future in chap. vii., upon the remoter future in chap. ix., but grasped by the prophet as a living and real personality, the guardian of his country now, its deliverer and governor hereafter. The circumstances under which the announcement is made to Ahaz are such as apparently exclude deliberation in the formation of the idea; it is the unpremeditated creation of his inspired imagination. This view satisfies all the requirements of the narrative. The birth of the child being conceived as *immediate* affords a substantial ground for the assurance conveyed to Ahaz; and the royal attributes with which the child speedily appears to be endued, and which forbid his identification with any actual contemporary of the prophet's, become at once intelligible. It is the Messianic king, whose portrait is here for the first time in the Old Testament sketched distinctly. Earlier prophets or psalmists had told of the promises bestowed upon David, and had spoken of the permanence thus assured to David's line,[1] but by Isaiah these comparatively vague hopes are more closely defined, being centred upon a concrete personality, to whose character we shall find fresh traits added, more than thirty years afterwards, in chap. xi.[2]

[1] See 2 Sam. vii. 12-16, xxiii. 5 ; Psa. xviii. 43-5 ; 1 Kings xi. 34-6 ; Hosea iii. 5. See further below, Chap. IX.

[2] This view of the prophecy of Immanuel is supported by Micah v. 3, written not many years later, and with apparent reference to Isa. vii. 14. Judah, it is there said, will be given up " until the time when *she that beareth hath brought forth* ;" and there similarly the advent of the deliverer is placed *within Assyrian times*, though he is not, as in Isaiah (ix. 4), to break the power of the Assyrians, but only to ensure his country's safety by repelling their attacks (*v.* 6: "And he shall deliver us from the Assyrian, *when he cometh into our land, and when he treadeth within our border*").

CHAPTER V.

THE REIGNS OF SHALMANESER IV. AND SARGON.

Influence of Egypt upon the politics of Palestine—End of the Northern Kingdom (B.C. 722)—Sketch of the reign of Sargon (B.C. 722-705)—Ahaz succeeded by Hezekiah—Rise of a party in Judah whose watchword was alliance with Egypt—Prophecies of Isaiah belonging to this period (chaps. xxviii., xx.).

TIGLATH-PILESER died in 727, being succeeded by Shalmaneser IV., who reigned till 722. The period of Shalmaneser's reign marks the first beginning of an altered attitude on the part of both Israel and Judah towards Assyria, due, at least in a measure, to the encouragement which it received from the valley of the Nile. The glorious period in the history of Egypt had indeed passed by—the period of the Thothmes and the Ramses, when the Egyptian arms penetrated far and wide, and when Egyptian monarchs could command terms, not only with the powerful kingdom of the Hittites, on the Orontes, but even with the empire of Assyria itself. Nevertheless, although no longer the brilliant power which she had once been, Egypt had suffered no direct humiliation ; she had tendered no submission to Assyria. The Assyrian kings, though they had carried their arms into the country of the Philistines, had been content hitherto to rest there. Thus the reputation of Egypt was unimpaired ; a new dynasty, the twenty-fifth, founded by

their efforts to stem successfully the tide of Assyrian aggression, would instinctively turn thither for support. The fact that the Assyrian kings had not yet essayed the invasion of Egypt was far from being a guarantee that they would not do so in the future ; and Sabako would be aware that it was to his interest to anticipate attack by uniting the elements of resistance existing in Syria. Hoshea, weary after a while of paying tribute, entered into negotiations with Sabako, and ultimately revolted (2 Kings xvii. 4). No Assyrian annals of the short reign of Shalmaneser have come down to us ; but we read in the Book of Kings that he immediately took steps to reduce his rebellious vassal to subjection : no effectual aid was rendered by the Egyptians, and, after holding out for three years, Samaria fell (B.C. 722). Shalmaneser himself, however, died before this success was achieved : and it is assigned by the Assyrian annals to the first year of Sargon. The terms in which Sargon speaks of it is in complete agreement with what we read in the Book of Kings : " The city of Samaria I besieged, I took ; 27,280 of its inhabitants I carried into captivity ; fifty of their chariots I seized ; the rest of their possessions I let (my dependents) have ; my officers I appointed over them ; the tribute of the former king I laid upon them." The Biblical statement that people from Babylonia and other parts of the Assyrian Empire were subsequently settled in the conquered country is confirmed by a parallel Inscription, which contains the words, " In their place I settled the men of countries conquered [by my hand]."[1]

Sargon's reign was of sixteen years' duration (722-705). The principal events may be briefly told as follows. Ilubid (or Jaubid), an aspirant to the throne of Hamath, induced some of his neighbours to unite with him in rebellion against Assyria ; but this was speedily suppressed in 720, and the land of Hamath made " a heap of ruins." Sargon now directed his arms towards the south, where Hanno, king of Gaza, had contracted an alliance with Sabako. The joint forces gave battle at Raphia, a spot about half-way between Gaza and the " torrent of Egypt." Sabako saved himself by an ignominious flight ; Hanno fell into the hands of Sargon. At Raphia the old antagonism between the rival powers was revived ; and the issue of the encounter was an omen of the future. Sargon did not, however, pursue the advantage which he had gained ; he was satisfied with the impo-

[1] Schrader, p. 272, 274; " Records of the Past," vii. p. 28.

sition of tribute ; and the actual invasion and conquest of Egypt
was reserved for Esarhaddon (681–668) and Asshurbanipal, many
years after. During the following years Sargon was principally
occupied with expeditions against Armenia, Media, and other
countries on the north of Mesopotamia. But the spirit of the
Philistines was not yet broken, and Egypt was soon ready again
with promises of support. This time Ashdod was the centre of
disaffection. Azuri, its king, refused his accustomed tribute,
and incited some of the neighbouring princes to join him in
open revolt. Sargon arrives upon the scene, deposes Azuri, and
places on the throne his brother Ahimit. But the anti-Assyrian
party in Ashdod were in the ascendant, and came to an understanding with some of their neighbours, who were nominally
Assyrian tributaries. " The people of Philistia, Judah, Edom,
and Moab, dwelling beside the sea, bringing tribute and presents
to Asshur my lord, were speaking treason. The people and
their evil chiefs, to fight against me, unto Pharaoh, king of Egypt,
a prince who could not save them, their presents carried, and
besought his alliance." [1] Ahimit was deposed, and one Yaman
chosen in his place. The consequence was the siege of Ashdod
by the " Tartan," or Assyrian general-in-chief, alluded to in
Isa. xx. The hopes of effectual assistance from Egypt resulted,
as the prophet foresaw, in disappointment, the Philistine city
capitulated, and its inhabitants were carried into captivity.
This happened in 711. Meanwhile, an important movement
had been advancing in the East. Babylon, mindful of her
ancient greatness, had for long been a recalcitrant and unwilling subject of Nineveh ; and now Merodach-Baladan, the
" Babylonian patriot," whose romantic career forms the subject
of one of M. Lenormant's interesting studies,[2] having "against the
will of the gods of Babylon, for twelve years sent ambassadors,"
presumably for the purpose of securing allies to support him in
his venturesome undertaking, openly threw off his allegiance.
Sargon collects his forces, compels Merodach-Baladan to
evacuate his capital, enters Babylon with triumph, and " estab-
lishes his power in the midst of Merodach-Baladan's palace." [3]
The following year, 709, was occupied by Sargon in com-

pleting his successes, in capturing the city of Dur-Yakin (to
which Merodach-Baladan had retreated), in receiving formally
his submission, and in re-establishing the Assyrian dominion
to the shores of the Persian Gulf.[1]

Such, in outline, were the chief events of Sargon's reign. In
Judah, meanwhile, Ahaz had been succeeded by Hezekiah,
a prince of very different character and temperament from
his father. In his public life, Hezekiah may be said to have
reverted to the ideas of his great-grandfather Uzziah. Thus
he improved the water supply of Jerusalem (2 Kings xx. 20;
2 Chron. xxxii. 30), thereby enabling the city more effectually to
withstand a siege; and the Hebrew Inscription found in 1880
upon the wall of the Pool of Siloam, near the lower exit of a
tunnel pierced through the rock from the Gihon-spring above,
and describing how the excavators, starting from the two ends,
met in the middle, has been not unreasonably supposed to preserve a record of his work.[2]   It appears further that Hezekiah
had a care for the military efficiency and financial resources
of the kingdom : at least, at the time of Merodach-Baladan's
embassy (probably about 712), his armouries and treasuries
were well filled (2 Kings xx. 13 ; also 2 Chron. xxxii. 27). The
only warlike enterprise, however, related of him is the subjugation of the Philistines (2 Kings xviii. 8), who had harassed
Judah during the reign of Ahaz, but who were smitten by
Hezekiah as far as Gaza, in the extreme south-west limit of
their territory. Like Uzziah also, he encouraged the cultivation
of the soil, and made provision for the storage of its produce,
and for the protection of flocks (2 Chron. xxxii. 28–29). At his
court, moreover, literature flourished : a poem attributed to him
is preserved in the Book of Isaiah (xxxviii. 9–20) ; and in Prov.
xxv. i. allusion is made to the patronage bestowed by him upon
literary undertakings. The " men of Hezekiah," who " copied
out " proverbs, were evidently employed in the collection and
preservation of the literary remains of former ages ; and we
would gladly know whether their activity extended to other
departments of literature besides " proverbs."

Lastly, Hezekiah was devoted to the worship of Jehovah ;
and in 2 Kings xviii. 4 (cf. 22 end), a religious reformation is

---

[1] " Records," vii. p. 47 f.

[2] Others, however, hold that the tunnel is really of earlier date : *e.g.*,
Stade, "Geschichte des Volkes Israel," i. p. 593 f.

ascribed to him, which, though not so efficacious as the subsequent one under King Josiah, was at least a movement in the same direction. The temple, which had been treated with violence (2 Kings xvi. 17 f.) and neglect by his father, was purified and restored, the occasion being celebrated with solemn sacrifices (2 Chron. xxix.-xxxi.) ; and measures were taken for the abolition of images and other idolatrous symbols. From the allusions in Isa. xxx. 22, xxxi. 7 (belonging to 702 or 701 B.C.), it would seem either that this reform was not carried out till after the triumph over Assyria had secured Isaiah's position and influence ; or, if it belongs really (2 Chron. xxix. 3 ; xxxi. 1) to the beginning of Hezekiah's reign, that it was limited to a withdrawal of the State recognition hitherto accorded to idolatrous practices, and did not penetrate the life of the people. Hezekiah attempted, further, a centralization of the public worship of Jehovah at Jerusalem, by a removal of the " high places " which lent themselves readily to abuse, and to contamination by heathen cults. That these and similar efforts, in spite of the support which they would receive from Isaiah and the prophetical party, were only partially successful, and that the unspiritual tendencies prevalent in the nation were far from extirpated, appears from the prolonged and violent reaction in favour of heathenism which ensued shortly afterwards under Manasseh. A more radical reform was indeed undertaken a century after Hezekiah's time by Josiah ; but the tendencies in question were not finally overcome until after the return from the Babylonian captivity.

It remains to describe the change which gradually passed over the political feeling of the nation during the period which has been just surveyed. Ahaz, it will be recollected, renouncing his independence, had owned the suzerainty of Assyria ; his immediate aim had been secured ; and, for the time, the nation was doubtless content. But after his death a reaction set in, the beginnings of which may be traced in the prophecies of Isaiah even before the fall of Samaria in 722. The Assyrian protectorate involved naturally an annual payment of tribute, the vexatiousness and humiliation of which began gradually to be

been already alluded to (p. 43). In the case of Judah, the project of an alliance would be the more attractive, for Egypt it was thought, would supply a want of which the Jews were always conscious, and which was a primary requisite in a struggle with such antagonists as the Assyrians—a powerful and active cavalry. The horse does not appear on the oldest monuments of Egypt; but it was introduced into the country from Asia either by the Hyksos (xv.-xvii. dynasties), or by the great conquerors of the xviii. dynasty; and henceforth the renown of the Egyptian cavalry was established.[1] Matters, however, were not ripe for a rupture with Assyria at once. What Hezekiah's personal views at this time may have been we do not know; but even if they verged in that direction, prudential motives would for a while restrain him. Severe losses must have been sustained by the country during the wars under Ahaz, from which it could hardly have recovered at the time of Hezekiah's accession, only six years after the evacuation of Judah by the troops of Rezin and Pekah; an empty treasury (2 Kings xvi. 8), a ruined peasantry, an unprotected frontier, a shattered army, must have warned him that he was not yet in a position to risk the retribution which a refusal of tribute to Assyria would inevitably involve. And Isaiah was opposed to a rupture. He had, it is true, been averse to the original application to Assyria; but when the decisive step had been taken by Ahaz, and a position of dependence accepted by the country, his advice was, " Be content : above all things place no reliance upon Egyptian promises : they will but deceive you." Isaiah, in fact, saw that it was of primary importance to Judah to avoid all political complications with the powers around her; and hence his opposition to the policy of Ahaz: but when, in spite of his remonstrances, the application to Assyria had been made and responded to, he acquiesced, and sought to avert any step which might lead to a rupture. Chap. xxviii., written before the fall of Samaria in 722, shows that the friends of Egypt possessed already influence in Jerusalem, though they were as yet in a minority. The reduction of the strong fortress of Samaria, and deportation of its population to Assyria, must have produced a profound impression in Judah : the fall of Hamath in 720, and the defeat of Egypt at Raphia in the same

[1] Compare Exod. xv. 4; Deut. xvii. 16; 1 Kings x. 26, 28; Cant. i. 9; Ezek. xvii. 15; also Homer, *Il.* ix. 383 f.

year, must have satisfied a majority among Hezekiah's advisers
that the Assyrians were practically irresistible, and that no
scheme of revolt could for the present succeed. But in the
course of the six or seven following years, during which (as the
annals of Sargon show) the Assyrian forces did not show themselves in Western Asia, the dread which they once inspired
would be gradually forgotten, and the influence of the Egyptian
party would proportionately increase : the embassy of Merodach-
Baladan in 713–12 (which, though its ostensible object was a
congratulatory message to Hezekiah, was prompted, doubtless, by a political motive as well) probably encouraged the
Jewish king to hope that a successful diversion might be made
upon the empire of Assyria in the East ; and Judah was
certainly implicated (in conjunction with Edom and Moab) in
treasonable negotiations with Egypt shortly afterwards, in 711
(p. 45). No actual breach, however, appears to have taken
place at this time ; Sargon's troops, whilst engaged before Ashdod
(p. 45) may have intimidated Judah : the Assyrian king may
even have demanded fresh proof of Hezekiah's allegiance ; and
it is at least possible that something may have occurred (though
hardly, as has been thought, an invasion of Judah almost on
the scale of the subsequent one by Sennacherib) to justify
Sargon in styling himself, as he once does, "subjector of the
land of Judah." [1] The renewed appearance of an Assyrian army
in a country immediately contiguous to Judah would itself considerably strengthen Isaiah's hands against the advocates of an
Egyptian alliance. And thus, though the Egyptian party never
ceased to exert itself, and continued to number its representatives
among the politicians of Judah, it was not powerful enough to
carry the king with it, until after the death of Sargon in 705
(see Chap. VI.).

The prophecies, with a distinct bearing upon Judah, which
may be assigned with certainty to the two reigns of Shalmaneser
IV. and Sargon, are chap. xxviii. and chap. xx. Chap. xxviii.

evidence of the first six verses, must have been written prior to
the fall of Samaria in 722, and therefore during the reign of
Shalmaneser IV. The prophet begins with a glance at the
approaching ruin of the strong fortress of Samaria, proudly
seated though it was upon the eminence which the military
genius of Omri had chosen for his capital ; but he soon turns
aside (v. 7, "But these also," i.e., the people of Jerusalem) to
expose the faults, not less grave, of those nearer home. The
haughty spirit of the Ephraimites has been alluded to before
(p. 37) : the immoderate self-indulgence of the magnates of
Samaria is a feature in the picture drawn by Amos of society in
the northern capital (vi. 3–6 ; cf. iii. 12). But Isaiah's aim is
to produce an effect, not so much on Samaria as on Jerusalem.
There also, he exclaims, the same habits are only too conspicuous. – Discreditable levity attends the discharge of the
most solemn offices, even those of priest and judge (v. 7 end).
Impatient of censure, his hearers mock his words : "Whom
will he teach knowledge? and whom will he make to understand the message? them that are weaned from the milk, and
drawn from the hearts?" i.e., Will he teach us, who are no longer
infants, but adults, educated, and able to judge for ourselves?
" For," they continue, "it is precept upon precept, precept upon
precept ; line upon line, line upon line ; here a little, there a
little :" he is always at us : he treats us like children, interfering
perpetually with his petty recommendations and advice. But
Isaiah rises to the occasion; he retorts his opponents' sarcasm,
charged with a new and terrible significance, upon themselves :
"Nay, but with men of strange lips, and with another tongue, will
he speak to this people. . . . Therefore shall the word of Jehovah
be unto them precept upon precept, precept upon precept ; line
upon line, line upon line; here a little, there a little ; that they
may go and fall backward, and be broken and snared and
taken." That is, "Nay, you are mistaken. This childish
monotone (for such, in the Hebrew, are the words in which they
censure the prophet) shall indeed sound in your ears : you shall
listen to the harsh and uncouth tones of a foreign invader. The
word which you have rejected as a series of vexatious com-
mands shall become to you a series of vexatious demands,
culminating in a disaster for which your calculations have
omitted to allow." The prophet is conscious that, whether the
counsel which he offers be palatable or not, if it is not listened

to, retribution will follow, as certain as it will be severe. His meaning becomes plainer as he proceeds. He turns with passion to the "men of scorn, who rule this people that is in Jerusalem," *i.e.*, the politicians who rested all their hopes upon the alliance with Egypt, and imagined that they had found a scheme which would enable Judah to challenge danger with impunity (*v.* 15),[1] but who in reality, as Isaiah saw, were regardless of all ulterior issues, and pursued merely what appeared to offer an immediate advantage; the storm, he declares, will burst soon ; the refuge in which the politicians trusted will be instantly swept away : not once or twice only, but repeatedly, day after day, will the "scourge," which they had hoped to elude, pass over them ; life will be spent amid suspense and anxiety unspeakable. "Will you mock me?" he exclaims ; " will you tell me I am the victim of an illusion? will you persist in your scheme for the recovery of independence? Then you will but fix your bonds; nay, you will do more than this, you will invoke upon yourselves certain destruction" (*v.* 22).

The vehemence of Isaiah's tone makes it evident what a power the politicians now guiding opinion in Jerusalem must have been ; and his utmost efforts were needed in order to counteract their influence. The charge which he brings against them is that of having entirely miscalculated the relative resources of Egypt and Assyria ; in the event of a revolt the help of Egypt will fail them, and the result will be that, instead of securing for Judah the coveted freedom, the bands of servitude will simply be drawn more tightly about her (*v.* 22). As regards the value of Egyptian aid Isaiah's judgment was brilliantly confirmed by the future : in 720, in 721, and (as we shall see) in 701, her troops were powerless in presence of the Assyrians. The picture drawn by him of the consequences of revolt is meant obviously as a dissuasive—an occurrence which as yet it was not given to him to foresee intervened to prevent its being realized to the letter.

The positive side of Isaiah's teaching must not, however, pass unnoticed. In contrast to the illusory hopes cherished by the friends of Egypt, he points with confidence to the secure

Jehovah, Behold I found in Zion a stone, a tried stone, a precious corner-stone of solid foundation : he that hath faith shall not make haste." The prophet borrows his figure from the huge and costly foundation stones upon which the Temple rested (1 Kings v. 17) ; and the thought which he desires to enforce is that in Zion there is an element of *permanency*, a constitutional fabric capable of resisting all shocks ; and that whoso fixes his faith upon this, need not hasten hither and thither in search of some better security, for his refuge is close at hand and certain. The counsel of the prophet may be compared with that offered by him on a previous occasion (viii. 13) : Do not, for the sake of some apparent but unreal advantage, abandon the fundamental principle of your constitution. The element of permanency to which Isaiah here looks is, of course, the theocracy centred at Zion, and represented by the Davidic dynasty, the continuance of which had been promised long since by Nathan to David (2 Sam. vii. 13 ; cf. xxiii. 5 ; 1 Kings xi. 36). As the people of Israel, in Isaiah's view (p. 18), is indestructible, so is the dynasty, which, since it was established, became the centre and pivot of the national life. The prophecy is not in its primary import a Messianic one ; for the element of security to which the prophet appeals is *opposed* to the plan of an Egyptian alliance, and hence must be something not pointing entirely to a distant future, but having some reference to present needs. But it is true that a Messianic reference is *included* in the terms of the prophecy, as it was included similarly in the promise of permanency to David's dynasty. The mistake to be guarded against is that of so limiting the prophet's words as to unfit them for their obvious and primary application.[1]

The discourse closes in a different strain (v. 23-29) with a parable of comfort, addressed by the prophet to his own circle of friends and adherents. The parable is drawn from the opera-

---

[1] The refuge of the politicians (v. 15) is swept away (v. 17) : the stone laid in Zion is secure (v. 16). In order for the "stone" to form an effectual substitute for the unreal refuge to which it is opposed, it must represent some *existent* reality ; that is, it must symbolize something which, however far it may reach into the future, must have its *basis* in the prophet's own present. Undoubtedly the permanency which the figure expresses resolved itself ultimately into the kingdom of the Messiah ; but to the prophet's contemporaries this lay still in the future ; and to them his words could only, in the first instance, have been significant as the assertion of a *present* element of security, upon which he would lead them to rest their faith.

tions of agriculture. The sole aim of the husbandman's labours
is to mature his crops and to produce food. For this end, variety
of treatment (*v*. 24, 25) and sometimes rough and violent
measures (*v*. 27, 28) are needful : nevertheless, arbitrary as
some of these operations may appear to be to a superficial
observer, all are directed to a single object, and each is accommodated to the particular nature of the seed subjected to it.
The wisdom guiding the husbandman in these operations proceeds from God, and is a reflection of His wisdom (*v*. 26, 29).
The lesson, for those who will learn it, is : Has not God similarly
an object in the varied and severe discipline to which he may
subject His people? Is it not His purpose that out of it Israel
may issue forth, a fruit perfected and matured, cleansed from
every admixture of husk or chaff?

The second prophecy which may be assigned with certainty
to the same period is the short one embodied in chap. xx. The
title of this chapter, with which the internal evidence entirely
agrees, fixes its date to the siege of Ashdod, which ended in 711.
The forces of Sargon were in the immediate neighbourhood of
Judah ; but yet so strong was the Egyptian party in Jerusalem that
extraordinary means were adopted by Isaiah for the purpose of
impressing visibly upon the people of the capital the folly of
reliance upon Egypt. The prophets frequently accompanied
their words by symbolical acts, such as would set vividly before
an Eastern audience the truths which they desired to bring
home to them. Such acts, for instance, are recorded of Samuel

humiliated and disgraced, what will be the feelings of those who had bestowed upon her their unsuspecting confidence? Will not "the inhabitants of this coast-land," *i.e.*, the dwellers on the sea-coast belonging to Judah and Philistia, who, as Isaiah spoke, were intent upon forming a league with Egypt—will they not then, when it is too late, begin to tremble anxiously for their own safety? "Behold, such is our expectation, whither we fled for help to be delivered from the king of Assyria : and we, how shall we escape?"

It is not improbable that others of the foreign, or occasional, prophecies of Isaiah (chaps. xiii.–xxiii.) belong also to the reign of Sargon. As, however, these rarely illustrate the state of feeling in Judah, or add substantially to the picture which we have already formed of the position taken during this period by Isaiah, it will be preferable to reserve them for separate consideration (see Chap. VIII.).

CHAPTER VI.

THE EARLY YEARS OF THE REIGN OF SENNACHERIB.

Sargon succceeded by Sennacherib (705-681)—Preparations for rebellion in Palestine—Negotiations with Egypt—Line taken by Isaiah in 702 (chaps. xxix.-xxxii.).

AFTER a reign of seventeen years Sargon died—in point of fact, as it appears, was assassinated [1]—in 705, and was immediately succeeded by his son, Sennacherib. Upon news of the decease of Sargon Babylon again declared its independence, and Merodach-Baladan reappeared from the retreat to which he had withdrawn since his submission five years previously (p. 45). The first task imposed upon the new king was thus the restoration of his authority in Babylonia. This he achieved in 703, in which year (to cite his own words [2]) " Merodach-Baladan, King of Kardunias, together with the troops of Elam, in front of the city of Kish, I defeated. In the midst of the battle he abandoned his baggage ; he fled alone ; into the land of Guzumman he escaped ; he entered in among the marshes and reeds ; his life he saved. The chariots, . . . horses, mules, asses, camels, and dromedaries, which he left on the field of battle, my hands captured. His palace in Babylon I entered with rejoicing , I opened his treasuries ; gold and silver, vessels of gold and silver, precious stones of every kind, his goods and possessions, abundant treasure, his wife, the women of his palace, his nobles, his . . . ? all the officers of his palace, I brought forth, I counted them as spoil, I took possession of them. My soldiers I despatched after him, into the land of Guzumman, into the

[1] Schrader, p. 407, 489.
[2] Bellino Cylinder, " Records," i. p. 25 f. ; Schr., p. 346 f.

midst of the marshes and reeds. Five days passed; but not a trace of him was seen. In the might of Asshur,[1] my lord, 89 strong cities and fortresses of Chaldæa, as well as 820 smaller towns round about them, I besieged, I took, I carried away their spoil. The Arabians, Aramæans, and Chaldæans who were in Erech, Nipur, Kish, Charsakkalama, Kutha, with the inhabitants of the rebellious city, I brought forth, I counted them as spoil." Upon his return from this campaign Sennacherib receives the submission of numerous neighbouring tribes, and returns to Assyria with a fabulous quantity of booty. The rest of 703 and 702 were occupied in other undertakings in the East, amongst other things with improvements in the city of Nineveh itself. Meanwhile, as on previous similar occasions (pp. 44, 45), the cities of Phœnicia and Palestine showed no disposition to neglect an opportune moment for reasserting their freedom. After nearly ten years' intermission, it seemed as if the tide of Assyrian aggression had permanently receded from Western Asia. In the north the centre of revolt was Sidon; in the south, the Philistine cities of Ashkelon and Ekron. Egypt, of course, was intriguing in the background, and encouraging the movement with liberal promises of aid. And now at length the Egyptian party in Judah overcame the remonstrances of Isaiah, and succeeded in carrying the king with them. An understanding had probably been already arrived at with Sidon and the Philistine cities; implicit reliance was naturally placed in the Egyptian promises; Sennacherib was engrossed with imperial interests in the far East; the people of Jerusalem, persuaded by their favourite leaders, deemed themselves in a position to take the critical step with impunity. Chapters xxix.-xxxii. of Isaiah's book remain as monuments of the action which the prophet took at this juncture, while (as it would seem) the plan of revolt was being concerted, but before the decisive step had been actually taken. If the expressions in xxix. 1 are interpreted correctly,[2] the date of the discourse will be fixed to 702 B.C. Within a year, Ariel[3]—such is the mystic name by

---

[1] The tutelary deity of Assyria, to whom the Assyrian kings, in their inscriptions, regularly ascribe their successes.

[2] "Add ye a year to (the current) year; let the feasts run their round," i.e., in a year's time.

[3] I.e., either "God's lion" or "God's hearth"—in either case, applied in v. 3 as a symbol of hope; "but she shall be unto me as an Ariel," i.e., in the extremity of her need I will enable her to verify her name (Cheyne).

which the prophet designates Jerusalem—will be reduced to extremities ; Zion, figured as a woman, will then be seen sitting on the ground in dejection and despair, scarcely able to make her voice heard ; but suddenly the hostile throng pressing around her will be scattered, and vanish away like an unsubstantial dream (*v.* 1-8). But the residents of the capital viewed the situation very differently ; these evil forebodings had no meaning for them. It is not surprising, therefore, that when the prophet pauses, endeavouring to read the effect of his parable upon the countenances of his hearers, he sees them unmoved ; they gaze at him in blank astonishment ; the prophecy seems to them to be out of all relation to the facts.[1] Isaiah proceeds to indicate the cause of this want of discernment. A spirit of infatuation has seized upon the nation, and has blinded in particular its leading representatives : thus to the educated and intelligent classes, who might read the vision if they would, it is a sealed book ; the less intelligent classes, on the other hand, are debarred from reading it by defects of education or training ; the one will not, the others cannot, discern the application of the parable (*v.* 11-12). By the strict observance of external ceremonial the nation imagined that they had secured Jehovah's favour, and could count upon His approval, whatever the project upon which they might embark. The prophet retorts that this is not so ; the very fact that they have sought to conceal their purpose now from Isaiah[2] is evidence that they secretly think otherwise : the wisdom of their self-confident but short-sighted counsellors will stand abashed when the issue of their policy declares itself, and the army of the Assyrians claims vengeance at their gates ! Then it will seem as if Jehovah had dealt " wonderfully " with His people, abandoning them to the natural consequences of their self-delusion, and treating them as if they had renounced all claim upon His protection (*v.* 14, cf. xxviii. 21).

---

[1] The exact sense of *v.* 9 is uncertain. If the rendering of the R.V. be correct, the meaning will be—" Hesitate and wonder at my words, if you will ; take your pleasure whilst you can, and be blind : your amazement and blindness with regard to the prospect which I lay before you is no evidence against its truth."

[2] This is the meaning of *v.* 15. The verse shows incidentally how influential politically the great prophets of the capital were ; a project has to be concealed from Isaiah, lest his opposition should defeat it.

But the prophet does not close here. The vision of a brighter future dawns before him. Ere long, He whom they thus ignore will assert His presence: " Is it not yet a very little while, and Lebanon shall be turned into a garden-land, and the garden-land shall be accounted a forest ? " The aspect of nature will be changed. The mountain region, now unvisited in its native wildness, will become a cultivated tract of orchards and vine yards : so complete will be the transformation that what is now reckoned a garden-land will then be esteemed no better than a forest. But this is but an external transformation : it is significant only as the accompaniment—or perhaps as the symbol—of a more radical and vital change effected in the nation itself. The people now deaf and blind, will then have their ears and eyes unstopped, ready to receive the word which at present they refuse ; and the first to profit by the change will be the poor and humble servants of Jehovah, who, free at last from oppression and contempt, will be able to rejoice thankfully in their God. For the foe without, the scorner within, those who are vigilant (v. 20), not for justice, but for injustice, will have disappeared : the purged and regenerated nation will no more have to endure humiliation or shame ; for the mis-applied shrewdness, which once beguiled its rulers (v. 14), will then have given place to true wisdom, and those who murmured discontentedly at the prophet's warnings will be ready to accept instruction. It is another vision of the ideal future of his nation, which in spite of present appearances will, he is sure, be realized, and to which, in the dark hour which seems to be drawing ever nearer, he turns as to a source of consolation and strength.

In chap. xxx. the negotiations with Egypt are represented as having reached a further stage : an embassy, despatched for the purpose of concluding a treaty, is already on its way to the court of the Pharaohs. Isaiah takes the opportunity of re-iterating his sense of the fruitlessness of the mission, and derides the folly of those who expect from it any substantial result. The plan, he complains, has never received Jehovah's sanction ; those who take part in it are as "rebellious " or "unruly sons," acting in direct opposition to their father's wishes : the prophet, who had a claim to be consulted on such an important occasion (cf. xxix. 15), has been deliberately ignored. An undertaking commenced under such auspices is doomed to failure : " Therefore shall the

strength of Pharaoh be your shame, and the trust in the shadow
of Egypt your confusion." The prophet sees in imagination the
ambassadors arrived in Egypt, and watches them as they meet
there with a disgraceful disappointment (v. 4 f.). Then his
thoughts revert to the period of the journey : he expatiates on
the foolhardiness which they show in undertaking it: they
venture to traverse a perilous region haunted by wild animals,
with costly presents for the acceptance of a people, who, after
all, will render them no aid ! And to crown this exposure of folly,
he sums up, in a brief and pithy sentence, the character of
Egyptian promises and Egyptian aid :—

> " Egypt helpeth in vain and to no purpose ;
> Therefore have I called her *Rahab, that sitteth still !* '

The terseness and force of the original phrase cannot be re-
produced in our language'; but its meaning is evident : Isaiah
describes Egypt as a worthless, procrastinating power, loud
enough with the offer of promises, but sitting inactive when
promptitude is demanded in the performance of them. The
short and pointed form in which the thought is expressed would
adapt it for retention in the memory of his hearers ; it was
further, like " Maher-shalal-hash-baz " on a previous occasion
(viii. 1), to be inscribed in some prominent public spot, as a
permanent record of the prophet's conviction (v. 8).

The people of Judah, he continues, are so blinded that they
will not submit to hear the straightforward truth : they will
only listen to the prophets on condition that they promise what
is agreeable to their wishes ; nay, such is their impiety that they
will have no more of the " Holy One of Israel," they are weary
of the monotony with which a prophet like Isaiah appeals

have striven to maintain; a restless, dissatisfied search for
external alliances will result only in disappointment. The
cavalry of Egypt will ignominiously fail you: on the day of
battle, your few survivors will be found deserted and defenceless.

But again, as in chap. xxix., the strain abruptly changes ; and
in *v.* 18 a gleam of light appears amid the clouds, which expands
before long into a brilliant day. *Because* the prospect is thus
dark, *because* the battle would be thus disastrous, *therefore*
Jehovah, in His longsuffering, will intervene before the crisis
has arrived ; He will *wait* expectantly in order to give you time
to repent, He will even *lift Himself up*—be in readiness—to
show mercy upon you, if you will but respond ! The respite is
accepted ; the nation's cry of penitence has been heard (*v.* 19);
the siege is over; the moral perceptions of the people are
restored ; prophets are as honoured and welcome amongst
them as they are at present the reverse. It is the first stroke
in a fine description of the ideal future which now follows. The
people's altered mind will recognize the uselessness of idols ;
even the costliest will be flung contemptuously aside. The
external aspect of the country will be correspondingly transformed ; in contrast with the scarcity and distress which the
prophet (*v.* 20) saw imminent in the nearer future, means of
livelihood will be abundant, there will be rich and ample
pastures—even cattle employed upon farms (*v.* 24) will not
lack their artificially flavoured provender ; the land itself will
be copiously irrigated. The light, which at present suffices for
an entire week, will then be concentrated in a single day ; night
and day alike will be preternaturally bright (cf. iv. 2, 5, 6).
Isaiah, as iv. 2, 5, 6, imagines a transformation and glorification
of external nature as accompanying the advent of the ideal
future, when the Assyrian will have been discomfited, and the
mistakes of the present will all be at an end.

But the scene of judgment which must precede this happier
future has yet to be described (*v.* 27–33) ; and Isaiah employs
some of his grandest imagery for the purpose. Firstly, the
approach of Jehovah is described ; the effect of His advent is
to " sift the nations in the sieve of vanity (or, destruction); and
a bridle that causeth to err shall be in the jaws of the peoples,"
i.e., they will be scattered and disappear, the path along which
they move only leading them to their ruin. But in the midst
of the confusion in which the " nations " are thus involved, the

Jews are pictured as exulting at the discomfiture of their foes; they rejoice as in the night when a feast (most probably the Passover) is celebrated, or as those who journey up to Jerusalem at one of the annual pilgrimages, and whose way was brightened by music and song: "Ye shall have a song, as in the night when a feast is hallowed, and gladness of heart, as when one goeth with a pipe to come into the mountain of Jehovah, to the Rock of Israel." The judgment itself is next figured under the form of a theophany: "And Jehovah shall cause the peal of His voice to be heard, and the lighting down of His arm to be seen, in fury of anger, and the flame of devouring fire, the bursting of clouds, and a storm of rain and hail-stones. For at the voice of Jehovah shall Asshur be panic-stricken, when He shall strike with the rod." And as blow after blow falls upon their proud foe a fresh shout of triumph rises from the Jews, who watch the scene as spectators: "And every stroke of the appointed (or, destined) staff which Jehovah shall lay upon him shall be with timbrels and with lutes, and with battles of swinging will He fight against them." The close of the drama follows. Already the funeral pile stands prepared, it is waiting only to be kindled; it has been made deep and wide that it may be able to receive the corpses of many dead, for king and army alike are destined for it; and even as the prophet speaks, he sees in imagination a stream of burning sulphur pouring down upon it and setting it ablaze (*v.* 33.) The description is of course figurative: and the details, as is often the case in prophecy, are not to be understood literally; they merely constitute the drapery in which the prophet clothes his idea. No such scene as is here described was ever actually enacted; Sennacherib, in point of fact, perished twenty years after his invasion of Judah in his own land, being assassinated by his own sons (chap. xxxvii. 38).

A third discourse, chap. xxxi.–xxxii., belonging to the same period (see xxxi. 1), reiterates under fresh imagery substantially the same thoughts. Again Isaiah raises his warning voice against reliance upon the help of Egypt, and again there follows a representation of the ideal future. In *v.* 2 he dwells particu-

chief," *i.e.*, defeats it, and " doth not call back his words " (such as those in xxix. 14, xxx. 12–17, condemning the alliance) ; but " will arise against the house of evildoers and against the helpers of those that work iniquity "—in other words, will ruin alike the politicians (whose motives Isaiah discredits) and the Egyptians whose assistance they invoke ; both (*v.* 3) will fall together. For Jerusalem is Jehovah's possession, which Jews and Egyptians combined will be powerless to rob Him of ; like a lion descending from the mountains (Ps. lxxvi. 4) to seize its prey, whom the shepherds are impotent to dismay, so Jehovah, at the head of the Assyrian battalions, will advance against Jerusalem ; the city is already within His grasp—when suddenly the image changes, and the impetuous lion is transformed into a bird protecting and shielding its threatened nest. Jerusalem will escape indeed, but in spite of the Egyptian alliance, rather than because of it, and only after a moment of extreme peril. "And the Assyrian shall fall with the sword, not of man ; and the sword, not of men, shall devour him ; and he shall flee from the sword, and his young men shall become tributary."

Such will be the ignominious end of the proud battalions of Assyria. For Judah a happier future immediately begins. There should be no break between the two chapters. The representation which follows (xxxii. 1–9) is the positive complement to xxxi. 6 f., and is parallel to xxx. 23–26, completing under its ethical and spiritual aspects the picture of which the external material features were there delineated. Society, when the crisis is past, will be regenerated. King and nobles will be the devoted guardians of justice, and great men will be what their position demands that they should be—the willing and powerful protectors of the poor.[1] All classes, in other words, will be pervaded by an increased sense of public duty. The spiritual and intellectual blindness (xxix. 10) will have passed away (*v.* 3) ; superficial and precipitate judgments will be replaced by discrimination (*v.* 4a) ; hesitancy and vacillation will give way before the prompt and clear assertion of principle (*v.* 4b). The present confusion of moral distinctions will cease ; men and actions will be called by their right names. The

---

[1] " A man," *v.* 2, *i.e.*, any particular citizen, but the term, as here used, denotes one individually conspicuous, rather than one taken at random out of the masses. The passage does not allude to the Messiah.

characters of the "fool" and the knave are manifest in their
acts ;[1] and these, it is implied (though at present they are
viewed with indifference), will then be recognized at their true
worth. It is not improbable that Isaiah here alludes to types
of character which were in some way conspicuous among his
contemporaries.

But he turns aside abruptly from his main theme. His eye,
we may suppose, was arrested by the spectacle of some women,
sitting down perhaps at a little distance from where he stood,
and testifying their indifference to his words. In chap. iii.
(p. 25), it was their vanity-and love of display which called forth
the prophet's censure ; here it is their complacency and unconcern.
They have never known want ; they have lived always
in luxury and ease ;—they are light-hearted, and feel perfectly secure. They will soon, he tells them, be disillusioned ;
their comfort and security will be at an end. _Next year's
harvest will never come._ He has not before spoken so unam-
biguously : it is the first distinct intimation of the coming invasion ; and not only does he already see, as it were (v. 12),
the people mourning[2] over their ravaged fields and crops, but
so far has the calamity advanced that the capital itself is desolate,
"the hum of the city is deserted," even the strong hill,[3]
crowned at its summit by the Temple and royal palace, is become the haunt of wild asses[4] and a pasture for flocks. It is
the prophet's darkest utterance ; the desolation anticipated in his
inaugural vision (vi. 11 f.) does not (apparently) touch the
capital ; in his more recent prophecies (xxix. 5 ; xxx. 20) the
picture is one of distress, but not of ruin ; the nearest approach
to it is the scene of disaster and bereavement pourtrayed in iii.
25 f., likewise (as commentators have observed) elicited by the

---

[1] Ver. 6 unfolds in his acts the character of the "fool," *i.e.*, the illiberal,
obstinate churl, who has no regard for God or man [Heb. *nabal* ; see Ps.
xiv. 1 ; 1 Sam. xxv. 10, 11, 14*b*, 17*b*, 25], as *v.* 7–8 unfold the characters
of the knave (R.V. *marg.* "crafty") and the liberal man respectively.
Will in *v.* 6 means *is disposed to, is in the habit of*, as Prov. xix. 6, 24 ;
xx. 6, &c.

[2] In *v.* 12 the scene is represented vividly by the participle ; lit. *men are
smiting.* In *v.* 14 the tenses in the original are all *past ;* the scene appears
to the prophet as though already completed.

[3] "Ophel"—the steep, southern side of the Temple hill, which had been
strengthened recently by Jotham (2 Chron. xxvii. 3).

[4] Implying that it is actually *desert ;* see Job xxxix. 5–8.

spectacle of the women. And the state of ruin is to continue
for an indefinite time, until a vivifying spirit be poured upon it
from on high, which will transform external nature and re-
generate the inhabitants. Then human justice, now so rare,
will dwell throughout the land (cf. i. 26), and its fruits will be
palpable—tranquillity, peace, confidence, a true security in
place of the false security on which at present (v. 9) the women
feed their hopes. Yet the prophet reverts for a moment, before
concluding, to the crisis which must be passed through before
this more blissful future can arrive. "It shall hail in the downfall
of the forest; and the city shall be utterly laid low." There is
the storm in which Assyria (typified by the "forest," as x. 34)
will be brought down; and there is the humiliation through
which Jerusalem itself must simultaneously pass. This double
aspect of the crisis is expressed more distinctly, as we shall
shortly see, in the great prophecy, x. 5–xii. 6. For the present,
the aspect which is chiefly prominent is the thought that Zion
will indeed escape, but not without suffering, and not entirely
unscathed. The same thought has met us before in xxix. 2–4;
xxx. 17, 20; xxxi. 4; and it is evidently one which, at the period
when these discourses were delivered, was dominant in Isaiah's
mind. How well justified it was will before long appear. The
prophet closes, however, with a glance at the brighter, if remoter,
future. The land which (v. 13 f.) is so shortly to be desolated
will eventually be restored to its possessors. Happy they who
survive the catastrophe, and can then avail themselves freely
of its ample pastures and well-watered plains (xxx. 23) l

The three discourses of Isaiah (xxix., xxx., xxxi.-ii.) which have
now been reviewed, are amongst his most characteristic which
we possess. The line pursued in each is similar, though the
imagery and other details naturally differ; hence they mutually
illustrate one another, and place us in a position to grasp more
completely the prophet's mind. All show how deeply he felt upon
the great political question of the day—the alliance with Egypt,
and its necessary correlative, the rupture with Assyria. He sees
what the issue of the alliance will be. Egypt will disappoint
the hopes that are placed in her; the vengeance of Assyria will
be certain and complete. The outlook for Judah is as dark as
can well be imagined; if salvation is to accrue for her, it will
arise from a wholly unexpected quarter; it will *not* accrue
through the exertions of her own political leaders, whose fall,

CHAPTER VII.

THE GREAT DELIVERANCE.

Sennacherib's campaign of 701—Its four stages : (1) against the cities of Phœnicia ; (2 and 3) against the Philistine cities of Ashkelon and Ekron ; (4) against Judah—Isaiah's position at the crisis—The great deliverance (chaps. x. 5-xii. 6 ; xiv. 24-7 ; xvii. 12-14 ; chap. xviii. ; chap. xxxiii. ; 2 Kings xviii. 13b-16 ; xviii. 17-xix. 36 [= Isa. xxxvi. 1b-xxxvii. 37]).

WE reach the critical year of Isaiah's life, the year 701 B.C. The forebodings which had found expression in the prophecies of the past year were only too surely to be verified ; and in the spring or early summer of 701 Sennacherib marches his forces westwards for the purpose of reducing his rebellious vassals to submission. We possess in duplicate,[1] on the Taylor Cylinder, found at Nineveh in 1830, and now in the British Museum, and on the Bull-inscription of Kouyunjik, Sennacherib's own account of the stages of his campaign. Sidon and the cities of Phœnicia were the first to be attacked ; and, after reducing these, and receiving homage from several of the kings of the countries bordering on Palestine,[2] who apparently were not this time implicated in the

---

[1] Schrader, pp. 288, 301 ; "Records," i. p. 35, vii. p. 59.

[2] "In my third campaign [701 B.C.] to the land of the Hittites I went. Lulii [Elulæus], king of Sidon, the terror of the splendour of my sovereignty overwhelmed him ; and to a far-off spot [*in the parallel text:* from the midst of the West country, to the land of Cyprus] in the midst of the sea he fled ; his land I brought into subjection. Great Sidon [Josh. xix. 28], Little Sidon, Beth-Zitti, Zarephath [1 Kings xvii. 9], Machallib, Ushu, Achzib [Judges i. 31], Akko [*ib.*], his strong cities, the fortresses, the open and unoccupied (?) places (?), his garrisons (for the majesty of the weapons of Asshur, my lord, overwhelmed them) submit 'ed themselves to me. Tubal

plan of revolt, Sennacherib started southwards, aiming to recover similarly Ashkelon, Ekron, and Jerusalem. In Ashkelon he deprived Zedek of his crown, which he bestowed upon Sarludâri, the son of a former king, doubtless on the ground that he was friendly to Assyrian interests :[1] at the same time four subject-cities belonging to Zedek, Beth-dagon, Joppa, Benē-Barak, and Azuru were captured and plundered.[2] Sennacherib next proceeds to deal with Ekron. The people of Ekron, in order to carry through their plan for the recovery of independence without hindrance, had deposed their king Padi, who remained loyal to Assyria, and sent him bound in chains to Hezekiah. Upon news of the approach of the Assyrians, they had summoned the Egyptians to their aid ; they arrive now " with forces innumerable ;" the encounter takes place at Altakû (probably not far from Ekron) ; victory declares for the Assyrian.[3]

[Ithobaal ; cf. 1 Kings xvi. 31] I seated upon the royal throne over them ; and the payment of the tribute of my sovereignty every year, without fail, I laid upon him. Menahem of Samsimuruna, Tubalu of Sidon, Abdiliti of Arvad [Ezek. xxvii. 8], Urumilki of Gebal [*ib. v.* 9], Mitinti of Ashdod, Puduil of Ammon, Chemoshnadab of Moab, Malikram of Edom, all the kings of the West country, all the coast-lands together brought to me their rich presents and utensils, and kissed my feet " (Taylor Cylinder, col. ii. lines 34-57). In 711 Edom and Moab are described by Sargon (above, p. 45) as " speaking treason " in concert with Judah ; and Ashdod was at that time the head-quarters of revolt : now, their rulers come forward to court the favour of his successor.

and the Egyptians retire without effecting the desired relief.
After this Sennacherib soon reduces Ekron ; he obtains,
moreover, the surrender of Padi from Jerusalem, and restores
him to his throne.[1]   Now follows the account of the aggressive
measures adopted by him against Judah and Jerusalem.   "And
Hezekiah of Judah, who had not submitted to my yoke, forty-six
of his strong cities, fortresses and smaller towns round about
their border without number, with laying low of the walls, and
with open (?) attack, with battle . . . . of feet, ... hewing
about and trampling down (?), I besieged, I took.   200,150
people, small and great, male and female, horses, mules, asses,
camels, oxen, and sheep without number, from the midst of them
I brought out, and I counted them as spoil.   Himself, as a bird
in a cage, in the midst of Jerusalem, his royal city, I shut up.
Siege-works against him I erected, and the exit of the great gate
of his city I blocked up.   His cities which I had plundered, from
his domain I cut off ; and to Mitinti, king of Ashdod, to Padi,
king of Ekron, and to Zilbel, king of Gaza, I gave them ; I
diminished his territory.   To the former payment of their yearly
tribute, the tribute of subjection to my sovereignty I added ; I
laid it upon them.   Himself, Hezekiah, the terror of the splendour

chariots, the horses of the king of Miluchchi [probably Ethiopia], forces
innumerable they summoned together, and they came to their aid.   In
front of Altakû [Eltekeh, Josh. xix. 44] they drew up before me their battle
array ; they called forward their troops.   In reliance upon Asshur, my lord,
I fought with them, and effected their defeat.   The charioteers, and the
sons of the kings of Egypt, together with the charioteers of the king of
Miluchchi, my hands captured alive in the midst of the battle.   The cities of
Altakû and Tamna [Timnath, Josh. xv. 10] I besieged, I took, I carried off
their spoil" (*Ib.*, lines 69–83).   The mention of Padi makes plain what does
not appear from the Biblical account, viz., that there was an understanding
between Hezekiah and the rebellious Philistine cities.   From Josh. xix.
43 sq., both Timnah and Eltekeh appear to have been in the neighbourhood
of Ekron.

---

[1] "Then I drew near to the city of Ekron.   The commanders, the nobles,
who had been guilty of rebellion, I put to death ; on stakes round about the
city I impaled their corpses.   Those inhabitants of the city who had committed mischief and wrong I counted as spoil ; to the rest of them, who had
not been guilty of rebellion and of execrable deeds, and had not committed
the same crimes, I proclaimed amnesty.   Padi, their king, from the midst
of Jerusalem I brought out ; I seated him on the throne of his sovereignty
over them ; and the tribute of my sovereignty I laid upon him" (*Ib.*,
col. iii. lines 1-11).

of my sovereignty overwhelmed : the Arabians and his dependents, whom he had introduced,[1] for the defence[1] of Jerusalem,
his royal city, and to whom he had granted pay, together with
30 talents of gold, 800 talents of silver, bullion (?) . . . . .
precious (?) stones of large size, couches of ivory, lofty thrones
of ivory, elephant-skins, ivory, . . . wood, ... woods of every
kind, an abundant treasure, and, in addition, his daughters, the
women of his palace, his male and female harem(?)-attendants
unto Nineveh, my royal city, he caused to be brought after me.
For the payment of tribute, and the rendering of homage,
he sent his envoy."[2]   Here the account on the Inscription
closes, the lines which follow relating to the campaign of the
subsequent year.

Such was the course of external events as told by the contemporary Assyrian annalist.   How, meanwhile, stood feeling
in Jerusalem, and how did Isaiah face the crisis?   Tidings of
Sennacherib's movements would, as we may be sure, be received
in Jerusalem with anxiety ; nor would the alarm be diminished
when it became known how rapidly one success had followed
another among the Phœnician cities, and when the report arrived
that his vast army was preparing for the march southwards.
The politicians, who a year before (p. 56 f.) had derided the idea of
an attack upon Jerusalem as beyond the limits of practical possibility, must have begun now to experience misgivings.   Still
Hezekiah had considerably strengthened his fortifications ;
according to the Book of Chronicles (II. xxxii. 2–5) he put in force
every necessary precaution for enabling the capital to resist a
siege ; and messages, we may suppose, would be sent to the
Egyptians, acquainting them with the situation and urging them
to hold their troops in readiness.   Now Isaiah steps forward in

Certainly he does not conceal from his countrymen that a time of suffering and anxiety is in store for them ; but the ultimate issue is painted by him more brightly than ever. Is Jerusalem to perish, and is the theocracy to be no more ? To Isaiah the answer is not doubtful : and as Sennacherib's army starts from Phœnicia for the south, it is greeted by him with a prophecy, which not less for grandeur of conception than for beauty of artistic form is, perhaps, the most remarkable which he has bequeathed to us—the prophecy x. 5—xii. 6. Isaiah here seizes the idea that there are bounds which even a despot cannot overstep with impunity. Sennacherib, like Napoleon in that terrible Russian expedition of 1812, had essayed a task which he was unable to complete. The Assyrians had no conception of benefiting or civilizing the nations which they conquered : their activity was a purely destructive one ; their only motive was ambition and lust of dominion. And now, in pursuing the same objectless career, they were meditating the extermination of a nation whose preservation was vital to the future of humanity. But the Assyrian, though he knows it not, is an instrument in the hand of Providence ; he has a mission to execute by the limits of which his pretensions must be bounded. And so Isaiah, describing first how the Assyrian fails to recognize this truth, and repeating his proud, yet true boast that the nations of the earth were, so far as hitherto appeared,[1] powerless before him, announces boldly his failure in

---

[1] The significance of v. 9 appears when the dates of the events alluded to are considered. Hamath was taken by Sargon in 720 ; Arpad by Tiglath-Pileser in 740 ; Samaria by Sargon in 722 ; Damascus by Tiglath-Pileser in 732 ; the city attacked last, then, succumbed not less easily than the one attacked earlier. The application to Jerusalem is obvious. (Carchemish was taken by Sargon in 717 ; when Calno was taken is not known—by analogy from the other instances it will have been at some subsequent date.)

It is true the conquests alluded to in v. 9–11 are not those of Sennacherib, and v. 13 f. would be in his mouth an exaggeration ; and hence the prophecy has been referred by some to the period of Sargon. But the subject in v. 7–11 is " Assyria " (see v. 5), and though Isaiah may have regarded the king (v. 12) as being here the speaker, yet v. 5 f. show that he speaks, not with reference to his personal achievements, but as an impersonation of the policy of his nation. And this policy Sennacherib in 701 was truly maintaining. The language of these verses does not therefore in reality militate against a date which in other respects is in entire accordance with the contents of the prophecy

his present enterprise. "For he hath said, By the strength of
my hand I have done it, and by my wisdom; for I am prudent:
and I have removed the bounds of the peoples, and have robbed
their treasures, and I have brought down as a valiant man them
that sit on thrones: and my hand hath found as a nest the riches
of the peoples; and as one gathereth eggs that are forsaken,
have I gathered all the earth; and there was none that moved
the wing, or that opened the mouth or chirped." This wonderful image of helplessness is followed by the defiant challenge,
"Shall the axe boast itself against him that heweth therewith? shall the saw magnify itself against him that shaketh
it? as if a rod should shake him that lifteth it up, or as if a
staff should lift up him that is not wood!" Isaiah's genius now
supplies him with a splendid figure under which to depict the
collapse of the Assyrian enterprise. The serried battalions of
Assyria appear to his imagination as the trees of some huge
forest, irresistible in their strength and countless in their
number: but the Light of Israel kindles majestically into a
flame; and at the end of a single day a child may count them!
(*v.* 17-19). For a moment the prophet turns aside in order to
trace the purifying effect of the judgment upon Judah (*v.* 20-23).
Never again will the remnant of Israel that escapes be
tempted to rely, like Ahaz, upon the Assyrian, who, though he
brought relief at the time, involved Judah in subsequent trouble;
for those who emerge from the crisis, though but a remnant,
will have their understanding enlightened, and will look to
none save Jehovah alone (cf. xvii. 7). But, for the present, "a
consumption is determined, overflowing with righteousness,"—
i.e. an exterminating judgment, giving effect with a torrent's
force to God's righteous purpose, is decreed to be enacted
upon the earth. Therefore, though Assyria menace, let not
Judah fear: ere long the yoke of the oppressor will torment
no more![1] There follows a passage of astonishing power, in
which the prophet, conscious of his strength, resorts to the use
of a species of irony. He knows that Sennacherib, having
completed his vengeance on the cities of Phœnicia, is on the
way, prepared to do the same upon Jerusalem; and he draws
accordingly an imaginary picture of the concluding stages of

---

[1] *V.* 27*b*, "And the yoke shall be broken by reason of fatness." Judah

his march. He is already at Aiath (Ai), nine miles north of
Jerusalem ; he advances rapidly to Michmash ; the deep gorge
of the Wady Suweinit[1] is no obstacle to his progress, for he
has seized Migron, south of the pass (1 Sam. xiv. 3), by a
coup-de-main,[2] and his army now crosses it, and is quartered
securely at Geba (*Jeba*). The inhabitants of the neighbouring
villages—Ramah, for instance, west of Geba, and Gibeah of
Saul (*Tell-el-Fûl*), three miles north of Jerusalem—are in consternation and flight ; he is now at Nob, within sight of the
capital itself, and swinging his hand audaciously against the
citadel of Zion ; the prize, as it seems, is within his grasp, when
suddenly, by an unseen stroke, his arm is paralyzed, and the
pride of his strength laid low :—" Behold, the Lord, Jehovah of
hosts, lops off the mass of boughs with a crash of terror ; and
the high of stature are felled, and the lofty are brought low ;
and He shall cut down the thickets of the forest with iron, and
Lebanon shall fall through a Glorious One." [3]

And thus, against hope, Judah will be rescued. But, as elsewhere—notably in the great prophecy uttered a generation
before, chap. ix. 4 f., 6 f.—the downfall of the Assyrian is the
signal for the commencement of a new era for Judah. The
house of Jesse, though humbled[4] (comp. x. 20 f.), has not lost
its recuperative power ; there emerges from the ancient stock a
shoot endued with new life ; and the stormy scene of tumult
and destruction is succeeded by Isaiah's marvellous picture of
the just and perfect rule of the ideal Prince (xi. 1–10), who will
tranquillize and transfigure human nature and diffuse a blessing
to the ends of the earth. Then will Israel's exiled citizens
return triumphantly ; seas and rivers will oppose no barrier to
their progress ;[5] Ephraim and Judah, no longer envious of each

---

[1] The "pass" (*v.* 29), the same deep defile, with precipitous sides, in
parts 600 feet high, which was the scene of Jonathan's exploit, 1 Sam. xiv.
1–16 (who, of course, traversed it in the opposite direction, from Geba to
Michmash). See Dean Stanley's "Sinai and Palestine," chap. iv.

[2] See W. R. Smith, *ap.* Cheyne (ed. 3) ii. p. 146.

[3] The "forest," as in *vv.* 17–19, a figure of the Assyrian host ; similarly
"Lebanon," from its cedars and pines (xxxvii. 24 ; lx. 13). For the
expression "Glorious One" compare xxxiii. 21.

[4] The "stock " (*v.* 1), *lit.* the hewn stump.

[5] *V.* 15, the "tongue," *i.e.*, bay (cf. Josh. xv. 2) of the Red Sea (the Gulf
of Suez) will be "banned," *i.e.* rendered harmless to those who would
cross it, by being dried up ; "the River," (the Euphrates), swift and too

other, will unite in friendly consort, and defend their common country from its common foes (*v.* 13 f.). Nor will the nation, thus wonderfully restored, be unmindful of its benefactor ; like Israel after the Exodus (Exod. xv.), it will give utterance to its gratitude in a hymn of thanksgiving and praise (chap. xii. ; with *v.* 2, cf. Exod. xv. 2).

The route imagined by Isaiah for Sennacherib's approach does not, however, appear to have been the one actually taken by him. To be sure, the danger, as Isaiah wrote, loomed upon Jerusalem from the north, and hence the prophet represents it as advancing from that direction ; there was further a dramatic propriety in exhibiting the Great King as bringing his army without difficulty over defiles and mountain ranges : but, in point of fact, Sennacherib followed the safer, if more prosaic, route through the Maritime Plain,[1] by the road leading straight down past the south-east foot of Carmel, into the heart of the Philistine country; and it was from Lachish, on the south-west, that the Rabshakeh, "with a great force," appeared ultimately before Jerusalem (2 Kings xviii. 17 ; cf. *v.* 14.). Arrived in the south, the Assyrian king, in the first instance, directed his attack upon the disloyal Philistine cities ; and the successes obtained by him against Ashkelon, against the Ekronites, with their allies, the "kings of Egypt," at Altakû, and Ekron itself, have been related (p. 67 f.). It was doubtless in consequence of the defeat of his allies—perhaps of his own troops as well—at Altakû that Hezekiah was obliged to surrender Padi (p. 68) to Sennacherib. At the same time Judah was overrun by the Assyrian soldiery ; forty-six strong cities and many smaller places were captured ; more than 200,000 inhabitants, with their possessions, carried off

offer of submission recorded in 2 Kings xviii. 14, " I have of-
fended ; return from me : that which thou puttest upon me I
will bear," accompanied doubtless by promises of obedience for
the future.   The offer was accepted: according to the Inscription, an immense and, in some items, hardly credible tribute
was imposed, consisting not merely in a heavy payment of gold
and silver, but in an enormous amount of other valuables as
well.   It is even added that Hezekiah's daughters and the
women of his palace were sent after the Great King to Nineveh.
However, in all its main features the statement of Sennacherib is
in entire agreement with the narrative in 2 Kings xviii. 13b–16,
which describes (1) the capture of the fenced cities ; (2) the
heavy tribute exacted—three hundred talents of silver and
thirty talents of gold ;[1] (3) the means to which Hezekiah was
compelled to resort for the purpose of satisfying the demands of
Sennacherib—not merely emptying all the royal treasuries, but
even stripping the gold off the doors and posts of the Temple.[2]

[1] The amount of gold agrees exactly with that specified by Sennacherib.
The quantity of silver named on the Inscription is eight hundred talents,
but it has been maintained, on independent grounds, that the silver talent of
Palestine was heavier than that of Babylon in the proportion of eight to
three.   If this be correct, the amounts named will agree in the case of
both metals.

[2] 2 Kings xviii. 14–16 are not in Isaiah, and are derived almost certainly
from a different source from that which has been followed by the compiler
in the ensuing prophetical narrative. (They differ in style, and the name
Hezekiah is spelt in them in a different way.)   The narratives which now
occupy Isa. xxxvi.-xxxix. are probably in their more original place in the
Book of Kings, whence they were excerpted (with a few slight abridg-
ments and alterations, and with one addition, viz., the Song of Hezekiah)
by the compiler of the Book of Isaiah on account of the important materials
contained in them relating to Isaiah's prophetical work.   It may be convenient to note here that (verbal differences being disregarded)—

2 Kings xviii. 13	= Isaiah xxxvi. 1.
,, xviii. 14-16	= * * *
,, xviii. 17—xix. 37	= ,, xxxvi. 2—xxxvii. 38.
xx. 1-6	= ,, xxxviii. 1-6 ($vv.$ 4-6 abridged).
,, ,, 7-8	= ,, ,, 21-22 (out of place).
,, ,, 9-11	= ,, ,, 7-8 (abridged).
* * *	= ,, ,, 9-20 (Hezekiah's song).
,, ,, 12-19	= ,, xxxix. (Merodach-Baladan's embassy).

The superior originality of 2 Kings xx. 4, 9-11 to Isa. xxxviii. 4, 7-8 is

Of Sennacherib's presence at Lachish (*v.* 14) an interesting
independent monument has been preserved in the form of a
bas-relief, now in the British Museum, which represents the
Assyrian king seated upon a throne, attended by his warriors in
their chariots, and receiving the submission of Jewish captives,
with the inscription : " Sennacherib, king of multitudes, king of
Assyria, seats himself upon a lofty throne and receives the spoil
of the city of Lachish." [1]   Doubtless Lachish was one of the
forty-six "strong cities" (cf. 2 Chron. xi. 5-10), the capture of
which is recorded on the Taylor Cylinder.

It may have been after the invasion of Judæan territory had
thus actually commenced, and while the main army of the
enemy was hourly expected at the gates of Jerusalem itself,
that Isaiah uttered the two brief, but artistically finished, prophecies, xiv. 24-27 and xvii. 12-14.   In the first of these
prophecies, with allusion, we may suppose, to the hills of Judah,
now overrun by the Assyrian soldiery, Isaiah asserts with
emphasis Jehovah's irrevocable purpose, that " I will break the

especially evident.   In Isa. xxxviii. 21 the rendering " Now Isaiah had
said," is ungrammatical, and is adopted in R. V. merely for the purpose of
affording the English reader a consistent and intelligible narrative.   The
only legitimate version is " And Isaiah said," which at once shows that the
words are in their proper position in 2 Kings xx. 7.   The only part of
2 Kings xviii. 13—xix. 37, which is undoubtedly from Isaiah's hand, is the
prophecy xix. 21 ff.   The origin of the narrative in which this prophecy is
embedded is doubtful.   A contemporary would hardly have attributed the
conquest of Hamath, Arpad, and Samaria (xviii. 34 ; see p. 70, note) to
Sennacherib (Isa. x. 9-11 is not parallel ; for here Sennacherib speaks in his
own person), or have so worded xix. 37, as to leave the reader without any
indication that Sennacherib's assassination occurred as long as twenty years
after the close of his expedition against Judah (*v.* 36).   Chap. xviii. 14-16
may be based upon the State annals ; the rest of the narrative, as in
other cases (*e.g.*, 2 Kings ix.-x.), has been incorporated by the compiler of
the Kings in his work from some earlier prophetical source, with occasional
additions and amplifications.   Traces of the compiler's hand are noticeable,
in particular, in the form in which Hezekiah's prayer is cast, xix. 15-19,
and in chap. xx. (*e.g.*, *v.* 1 ; cf. x. 32 ; xv. 37 ; *v.* 3, "a perfect heart ;"
cf. 1 Kings viii. 61 ; xi. 4 ; xv. 3, 14 [elsewhere, only in Chron.] ; *v.* 12 ;
cf. 1 Kings xiv. 1 ; 2 Kings xvi. 6 ; xviii. 16 ; xxiv. 10).   On the "fourteenth

Assyrian in my land, and upon my mountains tread him under foot;" and repeats the promise of x. 27, that his "yoke" will then depart from off the shoulder of Judah. In the second prophecy (to quote the words of Professor Cheyne), "Isaiah in his watch-tower hears, and we seem to hear with him, the ocean-like roar of the advancing Assyrian hosts:" but destruction, the prophet declares, awaits their vast array—like chaff from a threshing-floor upon the mountains, like a whirling eddy of dust before the wind, it vanishes before the Divine rebuke ; a single night effects its ruin—"At eventide, behold terror ! before morning it is not ! "

To the same period may be assigned chap. xviii. The king of Ethiopia, alarmed by the intelligence of the approach of the Assyrians, is sending messengers by the light river-vessels in use upon the Nile, for the purpose of summoning troops from the different parts of his empire (v. 1-2). Isaiah, as it were, intercepts the messengers on their route ; and substitutes for the instructions to arm which they carry with them, the invitation contained in v. 3 : "All ye inhabitants of the world, and ye dwellers on the earth : when a signal is lifted up on the mountains, see ye ! when the trumpet is blown, hear ye !" The anxiety displayed by the Ethiopians is needless : the prophet, in imagination, sees the signal given for the overthrow of the Assyrian host : let Ethiopia assist, not as a combatant, but as a spectator ! For at the moment when the Assyrian plans mature, under apparently the most favourable conditions, they will be suddenly, but effectually, intercepted ;[1] and the Assyrians themselves will be left a prey to beasts and birds upon the mountains.

But the end was not yet. Some circumstance occurred either arousing Sennacherib's suspicion, or making him dissatisfied with the engagement which he had concluded. It may be that news reached him of warlike preparations being still carried on in Jerusalem, or he may have heard of a fresh movement on the part of the Egyptian forces (which, in fact, soon actually took place—chap. xxxvii. 9), and may have begun to feel that he had

---

[1] This is the meaning of the figure in v. 4-5. The ripening crops represent the maturing plans of the Assyrians : Jehovah looks on, and in appearance promotes them, as a favourable sun and sky advances the grape ; but, just before maturity is reached, fruit and branch alike are violently cut away, i.e., the enemy's plans are abruptly intercepted.

been guilty of a strategical error in leaving a strong fortress like Jerusalem unreduced in his rear : whatever the motive,[1] a fresh demand was now made by him for the unconditional sur‑ render of the capital. Negotiations were at once commenced for the purpose of obtaining more favourable terms, but the messengers sent to Lachish returned with the disheartening news that their endeavours had been ineffectual, and that the Assyrian king remained obdurate. The dismay in Jerusalem must have been intense ; for the city was now not only cut off from its allies, but stripped of its resources, and so practically defenceless: how Isaiah seeks to allay it we read in chap. xxxiii., " the most beautiful of Isaiah's discourses," in which " the long conflict of Israel's sin with Jehovah's righteousness is left behind, and the dark colours of present and past distress serve only as a foil to the assured felicity that is ready to dawn on Jehovah's land."[2]

The nation which has dealt out, unchecked, a barbarous de‑ struction to so many, will at length, the prophet exclaims, suffer violence itself. For a moment he concentrates himself in prayer : " O Lord, be gracious unto us ; we have waited for Thee: be Thou their arm [3] every morning, yea, our salvation in the time of trouble." Hardly has Isaiah uttered his petition when he is conscious that it is answered : the " multitudes " of whom Sennacherib at Lachish boasted himself the king (p. 75) are in flight ; the Jews are eagerly seizing the spoil—

" At the noise of a tumult, the peoples are fled,
At the lifting up of thyself the nations are scattered.
And your spoil shall be gathered as the caterpillar gathereth ;
As locusts leap, shall they leap upon it. "

Nor is Jerusalem merely secure : it is also, in the prophet's vision, filled already with spiritual blessings (*v.* 5, 6). But he again reverts to the present ; the disconsolate envoys (the "ambassadors of peace ") have just returned from Lachish ; the country districts are beset by the foe, and impassable ;[4] the

[1] It is implied by Isaiah ("he hath broken the covenant," xxxiii. 8), that the demand involved a breach of faith.

[2] W. R. Smith, " Prophets of Israel," p. 354.

land "mourneth and languisheth," in sympathy with its suffering inhabitants. "Now will I arise, saith Jehovah, now will I lift up myself, now will I be exalted." He turns next to the proud invader, and in two expressive images declares that his plan is both futile and will defeat itself: "Ye conceive hay, ye shall bring forth stubble : your breath is a fire which shall devour you"; and the multifarious hosts of Assyria will be seized, and rapidly consumed, in the devouring flame (v. 11–12).

The prophet pauses, impressed by the magnitude of this great act, and invites all nations to recognize its far-reaching consequences (v. 13). But when the Divine judgment is thus near, even the Israelite cannot contemplate it unmoved : how, asks the unbeliever, when he sees the day approach at which he once scoffed (v. 19; xxviii. 14, 22), how is he to abide in the presence of such "perpetual burnings"? In two beautiful verses Isaiah gives the answer, and sketches the portrait of the man who, even in that appalling time, may deem himself secure (v. 15 f.). And thus his thoughts are brought back again to the people, and he pictures them in the age when the judgment has passed—

> " Thine eyes shall see the king in his beauty,
> They shall behold a far-stretching land : " [1]

the terror of the present will be "mused on" only as something which is past ; the hated Assyrian officials, who exacted the tribute and reconnoitred suspiciously the fortifications, will be no more : "Thine eye shall muse on the terror (saying), Where is he that counted, where is he that weighed the tribute? where is he that counted the towers?" Zion at length is at peace,—secure like a tent which no blast of wind or weather can overturn ; safe from the assaults of foes, like a city encircled by a broad protecting stream. For a while, indeed, it may seem otherwise ; and Zion, as the prophet speaks, may rather by a spectator be compared to a ship, shattered by wind and wave ; but, shattered though she be, she will yet gain the victory ; nay, so abundant will be the spoil that even the lame, even those who arrive last at the scene of the encounter—will not fail to secure their share. And then no sickness, and no sin, will mar the felicity

---

[1] *I.e.*, a land no longer "diminished" (to use Sennacherib's own expression, p. 68) by spoliation or hemmed in by foes (cf. xxvi. 15, R.V.).

which her citizens will henceforth enjoy (the same thought as iv. 3 ; xxix. 18–20 ; xxxii. 1–8).

Sennacherib, meanwhile, loses no time in taking steps for the purpose of enforcing his demand. He sends his officer, the Rabshakeh, from Lachish, accompanied by a " great army," to claim the surrender of Jerusalem. The Rabshakeh's harangue, the object of which is, partly to intimidate the people, partly to beguile them by false promises to rise up against Hezekiah, and compel him to open the gates to the Assyrians, is recorded in Isa. xxxvi. (esp. *v.* 12–21).[1] The alarm both of Hezekiah and his ministers is great : but the king's faith does not desert him, and he sends to Isaiah to crave his intercession (xxxvii. 1–4).[2] The prophet's reply is promptly given : he assures Hezekiah that he has no cause for alarm ; Sennacherib will be compelled by unexpected tidings to return to his own land (*v.* 6–7).[3]

Isaiah's answer inspired confidence in both king and people ; and the measures of the Rabshakeh were entirely ineffectual. The troops at his disposal were apparently not sufficiently numerous to enforce submission, and he was obliged to return to his royal master with the report that his mission had proved unsuccessful. Sennacherib was no longer at Lachish : he had advanced to Libnah (Josh. x. 29 ; xv. 42)—about twelve miles nearer to Jerusalem than Lachish [4]—which his army was now besieging. Here news reached him that the Egyptian general was marching against him in person [5] (xxxvii. 9) ; and alarmed

---

[1] In his estimate of the Egyptian promises, *v.* 6, the Rabshakeh agrees with Isaiah himself (*e.g.*, xxx. 6, 7). Comp. also the expression used of Egypt by Sargon in 711 (p. 45). In *v.* 11 the representatives of Hezekiah desire the Rabshakeh to speak in Aramaic, the language of commerce, and probably also of diplomacy, in the East. But his aim is to produce an impression upon the multitude, and accordingly he insists upon using Hebrew.

[2] "The remnant that is left " : comp. Sennacherib's account of the conquests won by him from Judah (p. 68).

[3] " I will place a spirit in him," &c., *i.e.* (as we should say), an unexplained impulse (see Numb. v. 14) will seize him, which, combining with the "tidings " (whether of the advance of Tirhakah, or of an insurrection in some part of his own dominions), will alter his intention, and bring about his retreat.

at last in his own turn at the possible consequences if the forces
of Tirhakah should succeed in uniting with those of Judah, he
sent yet a second message to Jerusalem, repeating his previous
demand. As before (xxxvi. 19-20), the argument urged by
the Great King turns upon the past successes of the Assyrians,
and the inability of any nation which they have hitherto
attacked, even with the presumed assistance of its gods,
effectually to resist them (xxxvii. 10-13). Hezekiah spreads
the taunting, defiant letter before Jehovah, and concentrates
his spirit in prayer (v. 14-20).

The crisis was indeed a real one. The reiterated demand for
the surrender of Jerusalem could only mean that, if it were not
complied with, Sennacherib would himself advance against the
city, and bring to bear upon it those formidable engines of attack
which made the name of Assyria dreaded in antiquity. The
boast of Sennacherib was a true one: Arpad, Damascus, Samaria,
the Phœnician and Philistine cities, which he, or his predecessors on the throne, had attacked, had, one after the other,
succumbed : Jerusalem was stripped of her allies, Isaiah himself
reposed no confidence in the relief to be expected from Egypt ;
even if news of the movement of Tirhakah had reached Jerusalem, the hopes which some might have been disposed to place
in it must have been sorely damped by the recent defeat at
Altakû. No fewer than forty-six of the fortified cities of Judah
had been captured, her territory was at the mercy of the enemy,
who was already dividing it among his vassal subjects, Judah's
ancient foes. Must not resistance have seemed desperate?
Were not the chances incalculably against Jerusalem's escape?
The prostration of Hezekiah and his nobles is manifest on both
occasions, when the messengers of Sennacherib are before the
gates ; and though the pen of the historian has not recorded it,
we may be sure that the agony and despair of the populace
generally (whose numbers would be augmented by refugees from
the country districts) could have known no limit. To the human
eye the fate of the city must have appeared sealed. And it was

(p. 67). "Ethiopia" here denotes, not Ethiopia proper, but the Ethiopian dynasty, founded by Sabako, and now ruling over Egypt (p. 43).
According to Egyptologists, the chronology of this dynasty was as follows :
Sabako, 725-712 ; Shabatok, 712-698 ; Tirhakah 698-672. It is supposed that Tirhakah is called "king of Ethiopia" in 701 by anticipation,
and that he was really in command as representing his father.

history can see, something more turned than the future of a single nation. The issue was as momentous as any that have been determined by the " decisive battles of the world." It was a crisis as grave as when Persia threatened to intercept the rising civilization of Greece, or Vandal and Moor to destroy the Christianity of Europe. Isaiah did not see it in its full dimensions ; but to him also the crisis must have seemed a real one : "The fate of the new world which lay in germ in his teaching must have seemed to tremble in the balance." But he never wavered. From the first he had seen distinctly ; and though the people were in terror, the messengers of peace " weeping bitterly," the king and his advisers helpless, the friends of Egypt of course disgraced, his confidence never forsook him ; his calmness and self-control are unperturbed. The more closely the toils seemed drawn about Jerusalem, the more boldly he announces his nation's deliverance, the brighter are his visions of its future glory (see esp. chap. xxxiii.). At the time of the Rabshakeh's mission, he is appealed to as a matter of course ; upon the present occasion (unless the narrative be curtailed), he volunteers himself a message to the king. His message consists of the fine prophecy (xxxvii. 22–35) in which the " virgin " stronghold of Jerusalem is represented as disdainfully mocking her proud assailant in his defeat, and watching derisively his retreating footsteps. The skilled strategy of the Assyrian will avail him no more ; his past career has been in accordance with the purposes of Providence ; but his appointed bound has at length been reached. Hope still remains for the " remnant " of Judah. " By the way that he came, by the same shall he return ; and into this city he shall not come, saith Jehovah." That night the long series of Isaiah's predictions received its fulfilment : the flower of the Assyrian army was cut off ;[1] and the Assyrian monarch " heard the rumour " which impelled his return to his own land. Sennacherib himself does not even claim to have captured Jerusalem ; and though he survived this expedition

[1] The locality of the disaster is uncertain. The Egyptian tradition recorded by Herodotus (ii. 141) describes Sennacherib, " king of Arabians

twenty years, and was engaged subsequently in numerous military undertakings, he never renewed the attempt against it.[1]

⸱ Never, it has been justly remarked, had a prophet predicted
more boldly, never was a prediction more brilliantly fulfilled.
Whether the blow which fell upon Sennacherib's army was due to
a supernatural interposition, or resulted from natural causes,[2] its
occurrence in time to save the Jewish state was a *coincidence*
which no political forecast could have anticipated, no estimate
of probabilities calculated. Yet Isaiah's foreknowledge of it was
of long standing, certain, and precise. Not once, but repeatedly,
even before Sennacherib's army had appeared on the north of
Palestine, and while all seemed calm on the political horizon,
he had announced, not merely the distress in which before long
Jerusalem would find herself, but the unexpected and startling
interposition by which she would be released from it. The very
first utterance, in the parable of God's lion (xxix. 1–8) speaks
as distinctly as any: Zion is represented as closely besieged—

shields, rendering them useless. If any confidence may be placed in this
tradition, Sennacherib had left Libnah, and was encamped at Pelusium,
amid the marshes at the mouth of the eastern-most end of the Nile. Isa.
xxxvii. 25 (R.V.) implies that it was part of Sennacherib's plan to press
forward into Egypt: his movement on this occasion from Libnah may have
been accelerated by a desire, if possible, to intercept the advance of Tirhakah (p. 79).

[1] The Biblical and the Assyrian accounts of Sennacherib's campaign, while
in substantial agreement, are both imperfect, and may be combined in
different ways. The essential difference between them is that while the
one narrates the *entire* campaign (viz.: (1) The subjection of the Phœnician
cities ; (2) the conquest of Ashkelon ; (3) the successes against Ekron and
the Egyptian forces ; (4) the hostilities against Judah), the other deals only
with the stage affecting Judah, and dwells principally upon two episodes (2
Kings xviii. 17–xix. 7 ; xix. 8–36), belonging in fact to a *fifth* and subsequent
stage, upon which the Assyrian account is silent. The combination given
in the text rests upon the close general coincidence of the fourth stage in the
Assyrian account with the verses 2 Kings xviii. 13*b*–16. Schrader combines
differently, supposing that in the Assyrian account the order of events has
been altered, that the concluding stage (the tribute of Hezekiah) might give
the appearance of an issue favourable to Assyria. There seems, however,
to be no necessity for such a supposition.

[2] The form in which the tradition of the occurrence reached Herodotus
(that the reverse resulted from a plague of field-mice) supports the view that
the immediate cause of the disaster was a pestilence, of which elsewhere
the mouse appears as a symbol. For the angel as the agent in a pestilence,
comp. 2 Sam. xxiv. 15, 16.

"But the multitude of thy enemies shall become as small dust, and as the flitting chaff the multitude of the terrible ones ; and it shall come to pass in a moment, suddenly." In xxx. 28, 30, 31, the terms are more general ; but afterwards we have the series, xxxi. 8 ; x. 33 f. ; xiv. 25 ; xvii. 13 f. ; xviii. 5 f. ; xxxiii. 3, 10–12 ; all, under different imagery, describing a stroke, dealt instantaneously by an unseen hand, and scattering or annihilating the Assyrian hosts. In chap. xxxvii. 7, 29, 33, 34, which are Isaiah's latest utterances, the language is less figurative, and also more definite : the prophecy of xvii. 14, for instance, is not reaffirmed to the letter ; Jerusalem will remain unharmed, but Sennacherib (with, presumably, other survivors) will return to his own land. Between these predictions, taken in their entirety, and the fulfilment, there is a consistency which could in no way have been suggested by the known circumstances of the case, and which is too striking and complete to be reasonably attributed to chance.

CHAPTER VIII.

THE OCCASIONAL PROPHECIES OF ISAIAH

(Chapters xiii.–xxiii.)

IT will be convenient to designate by this name the group of prophecies now occupying chaps. xiii.–xxiii. of the Book of Isaiah. In chaps. i.–xii., as also in chaps. xxviii.–xxxiii., xxxvi.–vii., the centre of interest is almost entirely the prophet's own country Judah, whether regarded in itself (as in chaps. i., ii.–v.), or in its relation to the combination of Syria and Ephraim (vii. 1–ix. 7), or to its great Assyrian antagonist (as in most of the remaining chapters). The prophecies of the present group, on the contrary, are as a rule concerned only indirectly with either Judah or Israel. Their interest centres in the particular country which they respectively concern. The prophets observed closely the movements of history : they saw in the rise and fall of nations the exhibition of a Divine purpose ; and hence it was natural to them to embrace within their survey of the future the destiny of the nations forming part of the same world to which their own people belonged. These nations were related to Israel and Judah in different ways. Politically, for example, they sometimes viewed one another with mutual jealousy and distrust : at other times, common interests united them together by the ties of sympathy or alliance. How intimately the prosperity of both Israel and Judah depended upon the relations maintained by them with such neighbours as Damascus, Moab and Ammon, or Edom, the historical books abundantly exemplify. And in addition to the relations grounded upon political antipathies and sympathies, mutual intercourse for commercial or social purposes was also, it is probable, not unfrequent. Nations thus variously related, and all familiarly known, to their own people, could not be left unnoticed by the Hebrew prophets. Amos opens his prophetic book by an enumeration of the specific sins of Damascus, Gaza, and other neighbouring principalities, and by an announcement of the judgment which each may expect (i. 2–ii. 3), deducing the conclusion that Israel and Judah, so far from being dealt with more leniently, as members of a chosen race, will be judged by precisely the same standard (ii. 4–16) ; and a century after Isaiah, Jeremiah (chaps. xlvii.-li.) and Ezekiel (chaps. xxv.–xxxii.) pass also in review the destinies of the foreign nations prominent in their age.

The occasional prophecies of Isaiah are distinguished by great individuality of character. The prophet displays a singular familiarity with the condition, social or physical, as the case may be, of the different countries with which he deals; and seizes in each instance some characteristic aspect, or feature, for notice. The haughty independence for which Moab was notorious, the tall and handsome physique of the Ethiopians, the manners and habits peculiar to Egypt, the careless gaiety of the Babylonians, the commercial enterprise and wide colonial relations of Tyre,—are brought before us one after another with picturesqueness of detail and great variety of literary form. The ancient Hebrews were keen observers of national character ; and Isaiah is true to the genius of his nation. Theologically these prophecies are of interest as exemplifying Isaiah's views of the future of the heathen world. The prophet applies the thought of ii. 2–4 to individual cases, and by typical instances represents the nations as incorporated ultimately in the kingdom of God.

The first of these prophecies is one on Babylon (xiii. 2–xiv. 23), which differs from all the other prophecies of Isaiah which have been hitherto reviewed in the remarkable circumstance that it stands *unrelated to Isaiah's own age.* The Jews are not

about to be delivered from it (xiv. 1-2).[1] It is of the very
essence of prophecy to address itself to the needs of the prophet's own age ; it was the prophet's office to preach to his
own contemporaries, to announce to them the judgments, or
the consolations, which arose out of the circumstances of
their own time, to interpret for them their own history.
As far as we have hitherto gone, this is what Isaiah has
uniformly done.   His prophecies have been replete with
allusions to contemporary history, to Ephraim, Damascus, and
the Assyrians ; that history is the foundation upon which
his grandest predictions rest. Here, on the other hand, the
allusions are not to Assyria, but to *Babylon*, not the Babylon
of Merodach-Baladan who sought (p. 49) Hezekiah's friendship,
which was known to Isaiah (chap. xxxix.), but the Babylon of
the exile, which held the Jews in cruel bondage (xiv. 2, 3), and
was shortly to be destroyed by the Medes (xiii. 17). To base
a promise upon a condition of things *not yet existent*, and
without any point of contact with the circumstances or situation of those to whom it is addressed, is alien to the genius of
prophecy.   Hence upon grounds of analogy and probability it
is reasonable to conclude that we really have here before us
the prophecy of a later writer, living in the exile, and writing
from the same position as Jer. l., li.   With the long invective
against Babylon contained in these chapters of Jeremiah, the
present prophecy is, indeed, in temper and spirit, remarkably
akin ; whilst, on the other hand, it exhibits few or none of the
accustomed marks of Isaiah's style.   The compiler of the Book
of Isaiah (who cannot have lived *earlier* than the exile,[2] and
may have lived much later), supposing it (upon what grounds
we know not) to be Isaiah's, inserted it amongst his prophecies,
assigning to it the first position among those dealing with foreign
nations, on account, probably, of the prominence assumed by
Babylon in the later centuries of Jewish history.   A closer study
of this prophecy is accordingly reserved for Part II.

[1] " For Jehovah will have compassion on Jacob, and *will yet choose Israel,*
and set them in their own land. . . . And the peoples shall take them and bring
them to their place ; . . . and they shall take them captive, whose captives
they were ; and they shall rule over their oppressors."

[2] For (p. 74) he excerpted chaps. xxxvi.–xxxix. from the Book of Kings,
the composition of which evidently cannot be earlier than the close of the
monarchy.

Chap. xiv. 24–27.—This prophecy, announcing the overthrow of the Assyrian hosts upon the mountains of Judah, has been noticed already (p. 75).

Chap. xiv. 28–32, on Philistia. The Philistines are in exultation at the fall of some dreaded foe : Isaiah warns them that their rejoicing is premature, that the power which they dreaded, though broken, will recover itself, and prove indeed far more formidable than before.[1] But while Philistia may expect to suffer severely at its hands, the faithful in Judah need not fear (v. 30). In a succeeding short strophe, the prophet repeats his cry of warning :—"Howl, O gate ; cry, O city ; thou art melted away [Exod. xv. 15], O Philistia, all of thee ; for out of the north a smoke cometh, and there is no straggler in his ranks." It is the Assyrian whose approach the prophet thus discerns,—the smoke marking either his camp-fires or the burnt villages along his line of march ; his ranks are broken by no loiterers or stragglers, every one is at his appointed post (cf. v. 27). A second time the prophet turns aside to address a word of consolation to his own people ; in the strength of its God, Jerusalem will yet be secure. The title suggests that "the rod which smote" Philistia is Ahaz ; and in this case, the more formidable power, represented by the " flying serpent," will be naturally Hezekiah. And it is true that the Philistines suffered at Hezekiah's hands (2 Kings xviii. 8), though he appears, both in 711 (p. 45) and in 701 (p. 67), to have been on friendly terms with them. But the connection of thought in the prophecy appears to require that the foe alluded to in v. 29 shall be identical with the foe alluded to, more directly, in v. 31. As the latter is plainly the Assyrian, the former will be the Assyrian likewise. The prophecy belongs, in all probability, to 705 or 704 B.C., Sargon being the " snake," and Sennacherib the more terrible " serpent flying about." The Philistines might well feel elated upon receiving news of

the murder of Sargon, who had ruinously defeated Hanno or
Gaza, at Raphia, in 720, and had captured Ashdod in 711 ;
and the alliance in 701 between Hezekiah and Padi (p. 67)
lends probability to the conjecture that the occasion of the
prophecy was the presence in Jerusalem of an embassy from
Philistia (the "messengers of the nation "), inviting the co-opera-
tion of Judah in the plan of revolt. Isaiah, of course, would
be strongly averse to such an invitation being accepted. His
prophecy did not long remain unfulfilled ; for Sennacherib,
before four years had elapsed, wreaked severe vengeance upon
both Ashkelon and the party opposed to him in Ekron (p. 68). It
may be observed that the teaching of the prophecy is in accordance with that adopted by the prophet at the period in question
(with *v.* 30*a*, cf. xxix. 19 ; xxxii. 18 : with *v.* 32*b*, cf. xxxi. 5 ;
xxxiii. 20).

Chaps. xv.-xvi., on Moab. The territory occupied by Moab
was the elevated and rich plateau [1] on the east of the Dead
Sea. Technically the steep defile of the torrent Arnon was
regarded as the northern limit of Moab, the country to
the north of this being assigned to the pastoral tribe of
Reuben (Numb. xxxii. ; Josh. xiii. 15–21). Reuben, however,
was not strong enough permanently to retain possession of the
district allotted to it ; and hence many of the cities mentioned
in Josh. xiii. 15–21, as part of the inheritance of Reuben, are
named by Isaiah as in the occupation of Moab. At times
relations of friendliness subsisted between Moab and Israel,[2]
but more usually Moab held aloof in haughty independence, or
was reduced temporarily to a condition of reluctant subjection.[3] The prophets allude frequently to the arrogant and
encroaching temper which Moab displayed in its dealings with
Judah.[4] From the Inscription of Mesha (*c.* 900 B.C.), found
at Dibon in 1869, and commonly known as the "Moabite
stone," [5] we learn that the Moabites spoke a language differing

---

[1] The *Mishor*, or "plain" (R.V.), Deut. iii. 10 (p. 11).

[2] Cf. 1 Sam. xxii. 3, 4 ; and in Uzziah's time, 2 Chron. xxvi. 10.

[3] To David, 2 Sam. viii. 1, 2 ; to Israel, reduced, as we now know from
Mesha's Inscription, by Omri. Mesha's annual tribute to Israel, prior to
his revolt, is attested by 2 Kings iii. 4.

[4] See (besides Isa. xvi. 6) chap. xxv. 11 ; Zeph. ii. 10 ; Jer. xlviii. 29, 42.

[5] The Inscription gives particulars respecting the revolt recorded briefly
in 2 Kings i. 1, and iii. 5. See Sayce, "Fresh Light from the Ancient
Monuments," p. 87 ff.

only dialectically from Hebrew ; and it is probable also that, in matters of material prosperity and civilization, Moab stood hardly upon an inferior level to Israel itself. Such was the nation whose approaching disaster is described by Isaiah with such vivid details and with evident sympathy.

A great catastrophe has befallen the two principal cities of Moab ; and the population crowd in terror to the temple—not improbably that " House of High Places " mentioned by Mesha —to invoke the aid of their god.[1] The streets and market-places are filled with signs of mourning; from Heshbon and Elealch, in the far north, the cry of agony penetrates into the very heart of the country. Moab is beset on all sides ; the pastures are ruined, for the waters upon which their fertility depends have been stopped at their sources by the enemy (xv. 8) :[2] there is no resource left for the inhabitants, except to seek refuge in flight, carrying what they can save of their possessions with them (v. 9). And now the cry of destruction has circled round the entire land ; it reaches equally Eglaim in the south, and Beer-Elim in the north. But still the vista of trouble does not end for Moab : for those who escape the prophet discerns worse evils in store (v. 9).

Meanwhile the fugitives are supposed to have found a temporary home in Edom. Here a voice addresses them (xvi. 1),[3] exhorting them to seek safety in the protection of the house of David, and to send a tribute of lambs[4] to Jerusalem, in token of their allegiance. The scene again changes. The prophet transports us back to Moab itself: at the fords of Arnon we see another band of fugitives prepared for flight in the opposite direction. They address themselves to the community of Zion (v. 3-4a), appealing to it to interpose on their behalf, to act the part of an arbitrator, to shelter the exiles. The appeal is a reasonable one ; for, as Isaiah well knows, in Judah the violence of the Assyrian aggressor will soon be stilled, and a king,

---

[1] Viz., Chemosh (Numb. xxi. 29, &c.), whom Mesha names repeatedly in his Inscription.

[2] As had been done before, at Elisha's suggestion, by the Israelites and

earnest in the execution of justice and prompt in righteousness, will be sitting upon David's throne (*v.* 4*b*–5). The passage
is Messianic, and is a counterpart to ix. 5–7. The advent
of the Messianic age follows immediately on the judgment upon
Assyria ; and the Messianic king protects his land henceforth
from all intruders.[1] And Moab also, the prophet freely admits,
if it will accept the needful conditions, may share the same
blessings as the chosen nation.

But there is an obstacle still unremoved. The haughty and
pretentious temper which Moab had already too often displayed, precludes the hope that these conditions will be at
present accepted. The judgment, therefore, must run its
course unchecked ; and the prophet, not without a deep thrill
of sympathy (*v.* 9, 11),[2] pictures in succession the ruined
vineyards,[3] the wasted orchards, the deserted winepresses,
closing with the figure of Moab exerting himself in vain at his
sanctuary to obtain the favourable intervention of his god
(*v.* 12). "This is the word which Jehovah spake concerning
Moab in time past. But now Jehovah hath spoken, saying,
In three years, as the years of an hireling, shall the glory of
Moab be brought into contempt, with all his great multitude ;
and the remnant shall be very small, and not many." These
two verses form an epilogue. The prophecy, as a whole, had
been delivered originally on some previous occasion ; but it
was now solemnly reiterated by Isaiah. The expression used
is an indefinite one : it may denote a comparatively short interval of time (2 Sam. xv. 34), or may be applied to a much longer
period (Ps. xciii. 2). The epilogue may be assigned with some
plausibility to a period shortly before Sargon's campaign against
Ashdod in 711, when Moab is mentioned (p. 45) as engaged in
treasonable negotiations with Philistia and Egypt, such as would

---

Micah v. 6 (p. 42). With *v.* 4*b* compare chap. xxix. 20.

[2] *V.* 11. The "bowels," in Hebrew psychology, are the seat of deep-
felt emotion or affection (cf. lxiii. 15 ; Jer. xxxi. 20 ; Cant. v. 4) ; and the
prophet, therefore, means to say that his inmost being vibrates to the
impression produced by the scene of woe, as the lute responds to the
touch.

[3] In *v.* 9 *end* there is an oxymoron. Not the joyous *huzzah* with which
the vintagers pressed out the juice of the grape (which the word properly
denotes, Jer. xxv. 30), but the *huzzah* of the fierce Assyrian soldiery, is
heard among the vineyards. See Jer. xlviii. 33.

naturally arouse the displeasure of the Assyrian king. There exists, however, no evidence showing that Moab was actually invaded then by Sargon.[1] But to what date the body of the prophecy is to be assigned is altogether uncertain. Perhaps it was written by Isaiah, twenty-four or twenty-five years before, in anticipation of the foray made by Tiglath-Pileser upon the districts east of Jordan in 734. This, according to 1 Chron. v. 26, extended as far south as the territory of Reuben ; and Tiglath-Pileser at least mentions receiving tribute from "Salman of Moab" on the occasion (as it would appear[2]) of his march southwards from Syria and Phœnicia to Gaza. Whether, how-ever, this tribute was the result of an appeal to arms, we do not know. If not, the fulfilment of the prophecy may have re-mained in suspense until it was reaffirmed by Isaiah shortly before 711. It will be noticed that the disaster does not annihilate Moab : as in the case of Judah (vi. 13 and often), Israel (xvii. 6), Egypt (xix. 18), a "remnant," however small, escapes—a remnant, doubtless, though that is not here ex-pressly stated, worthy to inherit a better future and to share the blessings of the Messianic age.

Chap. xvii. 1–11 and 12–14 have been noticed before (pp. 75, 76).

Chap. xviii., on Ethiopia. The sudden destruction of the Assyrians and the homage of Ethiopia to Jehovah form here Isaiah's theme, which is worked out by him in a picturesque and dramatic way. Ethiopia [in Hebrew, *Cush*] was the region to the south of Egypt, beginning at Syene, and corresponding generally to what is now known as the *Soudân* (*i.e.*, the land of the Blacks), which the earlier Egyptian kings often on their monuments describe themselves as invading. The country is traversed by the Nile, which in its turn is fed by numerous tributaries, to both of which Isaiah in his first verse alludes.[3] Its capital was Napata, situated in a great bend of the Nile, be-tween lat. 18° and 19° North. By the ancients the character of the Ethiopians was almost idealized : they were imperfectly known to them, and yet report told that they controlled, in their distant home, an extensive empire. Homer applies to them the

---

[1] This date is, however, preferable to 701, for Moab seems at this time to have been friendly to Sennacherib, and renders him homage (p. 67).

epithet "spotless," alluding probably to their physical beauty ; and Herodotus calls them "the tallest and handsomest of men." Isaiah notices their personal physique ("tall and smooth "), but he emphasizes more particularly their martial qualities—the capacities which they possessed for subjugation and conquest. Isaiah's words may here reflect the memory of recent events ; for Sabako, an Ethiopian prince, had not long since (p. 43) acquired dominion over Egypt, and his son now occupied the throne of the Pharaohs.   The country, however, which is the subject of the present prophecy, is not Egypt, albeit still ruled by an Ethiopian monarch,[1] but Ethiopia properly so called. The scope of the prophecy, regarded historically, has been explained previously (p. 76).   In the last verse Isaiah dwells upon the moral effects which may be expected to ensue from the promised deliverance.   Ethiopia, in gratitude, will own the power of Israel's God : and the ancient and mighty nation, in token of its faith, will send a "present" (Ps. lxviii. 29, cf. 31) to " the place of the name (1 Kings viii. 17) of Jehovah of hosts, the mount Zion."

Chap. xix., on Egypt, one of the most noteworthy and characteristic of Isaiah's foreign prophecies.   A period of unexampled collapse and decay, affecting every grade and class of society, is about to commence for Egypt, to be succeeded, however, ultimately, by the nation's conversion and spiritual renovation. The spell which Egypt cast around Judah, and the unbounded confidence which she there inspired, have been repeatedly noticed in these pages ; and no doubt one motive prompting Isaiah to draw this picture of Egyptian weakness was the desire to point a moral for his own countrymen, and to show how unreasonable it was to look for aid from such a source. The figure used in the opening verse is applied effectively by the prophet.   At the approach of Israel's God, riding—as in the imagery of the Psalmist, Ps. xviii. 9—upon a cloud, the idol-gods of Egypt totter upon their pedestals, and the heart of the entire nation "melts " within it (Josh. ii. 11, &c.) in dismay.   The immediate result is that the hand of government is paralyzed : the country is distracted by dissensions and party conflict ; city contending with city, and "kingdom (i.e., nome-principality)

---

[1] The Ethiopian dynasty held Egypt from 725 to 672 (p. 80), when Esarhaddon expelled Tirhakah, and reduced Egypt to the condition of an Assyrian province.

with kingdom."[1] The power of cool and rational deliberation
ceases : advice is sought by recourse to those magical arts for
which in antiquity Egypt was celebrated. But the issue is disastrous : "I will deliver Egypt into the hand of a hard lord, and
a fierce king shall rule over them" (v. 4).

In a second strophe the prophet describes, under its most
characteristic traits, the period of material and social decay
which will then begin for Egypt. The traits which he notices are
just those which are the common accompaniments in this country
of civil disorder. From lack of regular attention to reservoirs
and dykes, the supply of water, upon which the soil of Egypt
was dependent for its fertility, will fail: vegetation will be
parched : one class after another of the population will find its
occupation gone (v. 5–10). The counsellors of Egypt, in spite
of their boasted possession of a traditional lore, will be in
perplexity and dismay: a spirit of infatuation will seize them :
no plan that may be proposed will succeed. And, the prophet
adds, reverting to the thought of v. 1, the mere mention of the
name of Judah, whose God Jehovah is, will strike terror in
Egypt into all that hear it (v. 11–17).

At this point an abrupt transition follows. The prophet interrupts his main theme, the description of Egyptian disorder
and collapse, to contemplate the happier future, when a remnant,
at least, of those who survive the approaching troubles will have
learnt to own the God of Israel as their Saviour. "In that
day," among the innumerable cities of the populous nation,
there will be just "five"[2] speaking the language of Canaan,
and swearing to Jehovah of Hosts, i.e., using the Hebrew
language in their religious rites, in token of their loyalty to
Israel's faith : "one of them shall be called the city of destruction"—with Heliopolis, the city devoted to the worship of
the sun, in his mind, and playing upon the name which it might

---

[1] From 725, Egypt, as has been just observed, was under the sway of
an Ethiopian dynasty ; but the country was, for administrative purposes,
divided into forty-four provinces or districts, called technically "nomes"
(νομοί), the governors of which attained often to the dignity and importance
of sub-kings. A spirit of local jealousy prevailed in these "nomes" ; and
when the central authority was weakened, the tendency was for Egypt to be

have borne in Hebrew, Isaiah says, that it will be no more
'*îr ha-chéres,* "the city of the *sun,*" but '*îr ha-héres,* "the city of
destruction," the city in which the sun-worship has been destroyed.[1] In lieu of the obelisks and other heathen emblems with
which Egypt abounded, there will henceforward be the tokens
that it is a land devoted to Jehovah—an altar in its midst, and
a pillar, symbolizing the same truth to all who enter it, upon its
border. The people will be zealous and prompt in the performance of their religious duties (*v.* 21). Egypt and Assyria, implacable at present in their enmity, will then unite har-
moniously in the common service of Jehovah (*v.* 23); more
than this, they will hold a position not inferior to Israel itself,
and will share the same privileges and the same honourable
titles which have been hitherto reserved for the chosen nation
alone (*v.* 25).

The expressions in *v.* 18–25 are of course figurative, and are
not to be understood literally any more than, *e.g.,* the expressions
in xi. 15 f. The prophet, desiring to express the truth that the day
will come when Egypt will recognize the God of Israel, clothes
his idea in the religious forms with which his own age was
familar—the altar,[2] the pillar,[2] the vow. But we are impressed
by the width and catholicity of Isaiah's view : not merely Egypt,
the nation which more than any other he himself mistrusted,
but Assyria, the power which he saw from the first was destined to be his people's oppressor (vii. 18 ff.), are treated by
him as incorporated in the ideal kingdom of God. "Never had
the faith of prophet soared so high, or approached so near to the
conception of a universal religion, set free from every trammel
of national individuality."[3] "He rises far above the strife of
party and the war of nations, and points to that golden age in
which all strife and war will cease : when Egypt and Assyria

---

[1] The best explanation of the verse is Jer. xliii. 13, where Beth-shemesh
(*i.e.,* "House of the Sun") alludes to the great Temple of Tum (*i.e.,* the sun)
in the same city. The site of Heliopolis is near Cairo, on the north-east.
In ancient times the city was full of obelisks, dedicated to the sun, of which
now only one remains erect. "Cleopatra's needle" was one of two erected
by Thothmes III. (of the 18th dynasty), in front of the Temple of Tum
(Ebers, "Egypt," i. 186–8).

[2] It may not be superfluous to remark that these terms cannot denote a
pyramid, as has been oddly supposed.

[3] W. R. Smith, "Prophets of Israel," p. 336.

and Israel will all be one people, sharing the sacred names that are the peculiar inheritance of Israel."[1] True : such an era never dawned for Assyria or for Egypt. But these nations represent to the prophet the heathen world which was "eventually to be incorporated in the kingdom of God. The prediction can never be realized for those nations, because they have ceased to exist ; but it will yet be realized in that great peace of the world, which is the hope of all the nations of mankind."[2]

The date of the prophecy is uncertain, as it is not clear who is alluded to by the expression in v. 4, a "cruel lord," and a "fierce king." On the whole, the opinion of Prof. Cheyne is as plausible as any, that it was written in 720 upon the occasion of the defeat of the Egyptians by Sargon at Raphia. It is true that Sargon did not actually enter and "rule over" Egypt ; it was reserved for Esarhaddon to take that step, many years later, in 672 : but it is not necessary to suppose that Isaiah had any individual definitely in view in v. 4—what he rather means to express is his sense that, owing to its inherent political incapacity, the whole country will fall a prey to the first ambitious and determined man who invaded it. And this actually happened. Already Sábako had acquired an over-lordship over Egypt ; her armies were defeated by both Sargon (in 720 and 711) and Sennacherib (in 701) ; Esarhaddon penetrated as far as Thebes, breaking up the country into twenty governments, and reducing it to the condition of an Assyrian dependency, which with some interruption was maintained till another foreigner, a Libyan named Psammetichus, made himself master of the country about 660, and inaugurated a new era in Egyptian history by opening it, for the first time, to the Greeks.[3] Thus, once and again, Egyptian nationality showed itself unable to hold its ground. That Isaiah as early as 720 had begun to view Egypt with distrust, appears plainly from chap. xxviii. (p. 51), and this date has more to recommend it than 703-2 (which has also been suggested), when Isaiah would, perhaps, be less disposed to view with such a favourable eye the future prospects of Assyria.

This prophecy is remarkable for the acquaintance which it shows with the local peculiarities of Egypt (v. 2, 6, 7, &c.)

On chap. xx. (the siege of Ashdod), see p. 53.

Chap. xxi. 1–10 on Babylon. The prophet in imagination
sees Babylon besieged by an eager and impetuous foe : the
vision, as he gazes at it, agitates and appals him (*v.* 3–4) ;
and he announces the issue, as a duty imposed upon him,
but with no sense of satisfaction or relief (*v.* 10). The prophecy
has been commonly referred to the capture of Babylon by the
Medes and Persians under Cyrus in 538. This view, however,
is not free from objection ; for, firstly, no intelligible purpose
would be subserved by Isaiah's announcing to the generation of
Hezekiah an occurrence lying like this in the distant future
and having no bearing on contemporary interests : and, secondly,
it does not account for the attitude of alarm and aversion with
which the prophet contemplates the issue (*v.* 3, 4, 10), so different
from the strain of exuberant exultation with which elsewhere
the prophets always announce the fall of the great oppressing
city (chap. xiii. 2–xiv. 23 ; chaps. xl.–lxvi. ; Jer. l.–li.). It is
probable therefore that Prof. Cheyne is right in following the
view proposed by a German scholar, Dr. Kleinert, in 1877, and
in referring it to a siege of Babylon by the *Assyrians* in Isaiah's
own time. As we now know (p. 45), Merodach-Baladan sought
indefatigably to free his native city Babylon from its condition of
unwilling subjection to Assyria ; and prior to his revolt of the
year 710 had " for twelve years " been " sending ambassadors."
The embassy to Hezekiah, narrated in Isa. xxxix., was in all
probability one of those thus undertaken by Merodach-Baladan
for the purpose of providing himself with allies. Inasmuch
now as there was at this time in Judah a party straining its
utmost to combine all elements antagonistic to Assyria, there is
nothing unreasonable in supposing that some understanding
was arrived at between the ambassadors from Babylon and
Judah. Upon this view of the circumstances of the occasion,
Hezekiah's motive in displaying his treasures will have been to
satisfy the embassy that he had resources at his disposal ; and
Isaiah's rebuke (xxxix. 6 f.) gains in significance and force. If, now,
such an understanding subsisted, when the Assyrians entered
upon the task of reducing the rebellious city to submission, the
issue of the struggle would be awaited with eagerness in Judah :
for their success would of course mean not only the failure of
the combination against Assyria, but the prompt and condign
punishment of those who were suspected of being implicated

in it. This success Isaiah finds it his duty to announce. His human sympathies are with his own people : he foresees the sufferings which, sooner or later, the present triumph of Assyria will entail upon them ; nevertheless he delivers his message faithfully, though he betrays by his accents and tone that it is one which does not fall readily from his lips.[1]

The mode in which Isaiah conveys the announcement to his people forms the most striking scene which the volume of his prophecies contains. "As tempests in the South sweeping along" —as the whirlwinds, that is, rising rapidly with tempestuous violence (Job i. 19), in the south land (the "Negeb") of Judah —"it cometh from the wilderness, from a terrible land" : the prophet is sensible of some mysterious agency borne along irresistibly from the Arabian desert towards Babylon. A "hard" vision unfolds itself next before his gaze, overwhelming him with anguish and alarm (v. 2-5). He sees the enemy— who is denoted by the same characteristic terms[2] which he uses in xxxiii. 1 to designate the Assyrian—storming the Babylonian capital, and hears him in spirit exhorting his forces to commence the assault : "Go up, O Elam ; besiege, O Media." The fated city is only too confident and unprepared ; its generals and officers are revelling at a banquet (v. 5a), when suddenly the loud call to arms interrupts the feast : "Arise, O princes, anoint the shield ! "[3] But how has Isaiah been assured of the issue ? In the next verses he explains this. He describes how in spirit he had ascended his prophet's watch-tower,[4] with instructions : "should he see a troop, horsemen in pairs, a troop of asses, a troop of camels "—i.e., a long military train moving along—"let him hearken diligently with much heed," to discover, if possible, the message which they bear. For a while, eagerly as his attention was fixed, he saw and heard nothing ; and his long

---

[1] Comp. Jer. xvii. 16 ; xx. 7-9 ; Ezek. xxiv. 15-18, passages which exemplify the distinction between the human interests of the prophet and the Divine impulse actuating him.

[2] The "treacherous dealer "—i.e., the barbarous warrior, who "has no regard for the law of humanity" (Cheyne)—and the "devastator." "Elam" and "Media" are named (like Elam and Kir, in xxii. 6) as contingents in the assailing army.

and fruitless watch wrung from him a cry of impatience [1] (*v.* 8).
Even as he speaks, however, his inner eye descries "a troop of
men, horsemen by pairs " : silently, like the figures in a *camera
obscura*, they move in the distance over the plain : at first,
apparently, he does not perceive their significance ; he pauses
for a moment, and it flashes across him—they are the messengers
bringing tidings of what has occurred ; and he answers forthwith, "Fallen, fallen is Babylon ; and all the images of its
gods he hath broken to the ground." The second part of this
answer is a rebuke aimed indirectly at those in his own country
who had been tempted to rest their hopes upon an alliance with
the idolatrous power. "O thou my threshing, and child of my
floor "—*i.e.*, Judah hardly treated by the merciless Assyrian—
"that which I have heard from Jehovah of Hosts, the God of
Israel, have I declared unto you."

Though the scene in *v.* 6–9 is an ideal one, it is pourtrayed
with all the vividness of real life ; and we can see in imagination the prophet—like the watchman "on the roof of the gate,"
for whose report David listened so intently (2 Sam. xviii. 24
ff.), or like that other watchman, standing upon "the tower in
Jezreel," spying afar off a company of horsemen, but uncertain
for a while what it signified (2 Kings ix. 17–20)—eagerly scan-
ning the horizon, his eye fixed, his mind intent, the disappointment visible on his countenance transformed to hope, the hope
changing into sadness, until finally, with grave and solemn
earnestness, he delivers the message which he has "heard."
Whether Babylon was actually upon this occasion taken under
the circumstances described by the prophet, cannot be said :
probably, as in other cases (*e.g.*, x. 28–32 ; xxx. 33), the details
are merely the drapery in which Isaiah clothes his idea ; but
it is certain that the Assyrian attack was successful, and
Sargon relates (p. 45 f.) how he triumphantly entered Merodach-
Baladan's capital, and re-established the Assyrian power over
Babylonia.

Chap. xxi. 11–12, on Dumah. Neither the Dumah of Gen.
xxv. 14, nor that of Josh. xv. 52, can be here intended by Isaiah ;
and as the prophecy plainly relates to Seir (*i.e.*, Edom), it is
probable that the name, which signifies *silence* (Ps. xciv. 17), is
an anagram (though not an exact one) of Edom, with an allu-

---

[1] Such appears to be the sense of the comparison, "cried as a lion."

sion to the "silence" which the prophet sees is reserved for it.
Edom was celebrated for its "wisdom" (Obad. 8; Jer. xlix. 7),
i.e., for shrewdness in discovery (1 Kings iii. 28; x. 3, 4, 8;
Prov. i. 6) or device (2 Sam. xiv. 2; xx. 16); and Isaiah, as it
seems, adapts this prophecy to the character of the nation which
it concerns, casting it into a dark, enigmatic form, with the
view of stimulating their interest. A call of inquiry seems to
reach him from Edom, "Watchman,[1] what hour of the night?"
The call is repeated, in token of the anxiety with which it is
asked. He replies, "Morning cometh, and also night: if ye
would inquire, inquire; return, come (*or*, turn, *viz.*, to God,
come);" *i.e.* (if the "dark speech" be rightly interpreted),
"Edom may see the dawn of brighter days, but it will be but
the dawn, a night of trouble will quickly follow. If ye would
have fuller information, ye may come and ask again"—with an
allusion, perhaps, to the other sense of the word rendered *return*,
viz., "turn" to Jehovah (x. 21), as the condition of a more satisfying reply. The prophet has nothing hopeful to communicate to
Edom; and purposely gives his answer indirectly.

Chap. xxi. 13-17, on Arabia. The term "Arabia," in the
Old Testament, is not used in such a wide sense as in modern
English, and denotes merely a particular tribe, having its home
in the northern part of what is now known as the Arabian
peninsula, and mentioned in Ezek. xxvii. 20-21 by the side of
Dedan and Kedar as engaged in commerce with Tyre. Isaiah
sees a tide of invasion about to overflow the region inhabited by
these tribes, and addresses the Dedanite caravans, warning them
that they will have to turn aside from their customary routes
and seek concealment in the "forest." In *v.* 14 he sees in
imagination the natives of Tema bringing food and water to the
fugitive traders.[2] Tema was the name of a tribe settled in the
same neighbourhood, about 250 miles south-east of Edom, on
the route between Damascus and Mecca,[3] in a locality in which
some interesting inscriptions have recently been discovered.
Within a year, the prophet concludes, the glory of the wealthy

---

[1] A different word from that in *v.* 6, and signifying not one who *spies* or
looks out, but one who *guards* or *keeps* (Ps. cxxx. 6).

pastoral (ch. lx. 7) tribe of Kedar—here used so as to include by implication its less influential neighbours—will be past, and of its warriors only an insignificant remnant will survive.

Sargon names "Samsieh, queen of the land of Aribu," as paying him tribute, both in 720, after the battle of Raphia, and in 715[1] (though it does not appear that he conducted in this year any expedition into these parts); and in 711 he mentions (p. 45) Edom as concerned in a treasonable conspiracy with Judah and other nations. It may be conjectured that these two prophecies were delivered in view of an expected campaign of Sargon in one of these years—probably either in 720 or in 711, when his troops are known to have been engaged in the district south of Palestine.

Chap. xxii. contains the only two strictly domestic prophecies which have found a place in the present group. The aim of the first of these, v. 1–14, is to administer a rebuke to the inhabitants of the capital, on account of the undignified temper exhibited by them upon an occasion when their city was threatened with an assault by the foe. The prophecy is a difficult one, but the situation, so far as the allusions enable us to judge, is apparently as follows. The Assyrians are outside the city: an encounter has already taken place; and many of the Judæans have fallen dishonourably (v. 2, 3). The occasion, however, is treated by the people at large partly with indifference, partly with the forced gaiety of despair (v. 1). The prophet, on the other hand, is overwhelmed with grief and shame; yet so little are his emotions in harmony with the feeling prevalent about him that the attempt is even made to calm and console him (v. 4, 5). Isaiah now goes back to describe more particularly what has occurred. When the Assyrian troops were actually at the gates (v. 6, 7), hasty measures of defence were taken—the armoury in "the house of the forest of Lebanon"[2] was examined, the fortifications were repaired, provision was made to ensure a supply of water in the event of a siege (v. 8–11a); yet no thought was directed to Jehovah who alone could ensure the safety of the city (v. 11b). The call had been to humiliation and seriousness (v. 12); but there had been no response; and when the moment of danger came, it found the people so unprepared

---

[1] Schrader, p. 397, 404; "Records," ix., p. 5; vii., p. 34.
[2] Comp. 1 Kings vii. 2 with 1 Kings x. 17.

that not only was an ignominious disaster the result, but the survivors were demoralized, and abandoned themselves to despair, heedless of the future—"Let us eat and drink ; for tomorrow we shall die " (*v.* 13). It is the discreditable temper thus exhibited, that is the occasion of the prophecy, and evokes from Isaiah the severe rebuke with which it ends (*v.* 14).

But what is the invasion to which Isaiah here alludes? The measures described in *v.* 6-11 agree generally with those attributed in 2 Chron. xxxii. 3-6 to Hezekiah upon news of the approach of Sennacherib's forces in 701. The objection to referring the prophecy to that date arises from the contrast of tone which it displays, as compared with the other prophecies belonging to the same period ; in these (see Chap. VII.) he exerts himself uniformly to encourage and sustain, whereas here the language is minatory to a degree unparalleled in any other part of his writings. Ewald was so impressed by the difference of tone distinguishing this prophecy from others belonging to the period of Sennacherib's invasion, that he postulated for it a different occasion, which he himself assigned conjecturally to the reign of Shalmaneser. Since Ewald wrote, however, Assyriology has brought to light abundant particulars relating to Sargon's reign, and the text has been already quoted (p. 49), in which that monarch styles himself " subjecter of the land of Judah.' It is considered that this text confirms the justice of Ewald's view, and gives the occasion which Ewald could only supply by conjecture. The prophecy, it is supposed, alludes to one of the successes by which Sargon won that title ; and it is referred to the year 711, when he mentions Judah (p. 45) as "speaking treason " against him—a circumstance which would form a sufficient pretext for a body of troops being detached from the siege of Ashdod and despatched against it. That is not impossible. There may have been at this time some collision with Sargon's soldiery, resulting in a defeat of the forces of Judah, such as Isaiah describes. It is, however, too bold to assume (as has been done [1]) that Sargon gained a series of successes

---

[1] The writer regrets on this point to be unable to yield assent to the conclusions of his friend, Professor Cheyne. He has never been able to satisfy himself either that sufficient *data* exist to support such a hypothesis, or that the facts require it. He agrees with the criticisms of W. R. Smith, "Prophets of Israel," p. 296 f., though the view expressed in the text was reached by him independently and prior to the appearance of Dr. Smith's volume.

against Judah, and even ended by capturing Jerusalem [1]; more
probably immediate submission was tendered, with offer of tribute, which satisfied his demands.[2]   It is however possible that
the prophecy may refer to an *episode* in the invasion of Sennacherib—to the first alarm, for instance, which the sight of his
troops inspired.   There may easily have been at such a crisis
fluctuations of feeling which our authorities do not notice ; and
for a time the temper of the capital may have been such as to
merit the rebuke administered by the prophet, though afterwards
the panic was allayed, and discipline restored.[3]

Chap. xxii. 15-25, on Shebna.   This prophecy illustrates
the influence wielded by Isaiah in the domestic politics
of Judah.   Shebna was a minister holding an important
office in Jerusalem, and no doubt representing a policy
obnoxious to Isaiah—probably one of the friends of Egypt :
and the prophet exerts himself here to secure his overthrow.   The office that Shebna filled was that of Governor
or Comptroller of the Palace, an office dating from the time
when Solomon completed the organization of the monarchy,[4]
and, owing to the duties and privileges attached to it, a post of
authority and influence.   From the terms used in *v.* 16, it may
be inferred that Shebna was not a native of Jerusalem ; to judge
from the form of his name, he was probably a Syrian.   Isaiah
accosts him as an ostentatious foreigner, presuming to treat
Jerusalem as though it were his native home, and parading its
streets in state ("the chariots of thy glory," *v.* 18).   He declares
to him, in no measured terms, that he will assuredly be hurled
ere long from his office, and banished from the country in dis-
grace (*v.* 17-19).   Eliakim, a man of approved views, will be
invested as his successor with the robes of office, and will be
entrusted with the "key of the house of David," *i.e.*, will
receive the authority peculiar to his office, and delegated to the
holder of it by the king.   His tenure of office will be assured ;

---

[1] Sayce, "Fresh Light," &c., pp. 137, 157.

[2] The term *mushacnish* ("subjecter") need not apparently imply more
than this.   Ramman-nirar is said to have "*subjected* to his yoke" the land
of Israel (Schrader, p. 213, l. 19), viz., by imposing tribute upon it (*Ib.*
p. 216).   The notice is, moreover, an isolated one (see the context in
Oppert, *Inscriptions des Sargonides*, 1862, p. 34) : in the *continuous* annals
of Sargon's reign, no mention is made of an invasion of Judah.

[3] So W. R. Smith, "Prophets of Israel," p. 346.

[4] 1 Kings iv. 6 ; 2 Kings xv. 5 ; in Israel, 1 Kings xvi. 9 ; xviii. 3.

and his elevation, the prophet adds, in language betraying, apparently, a touch of satire, will redound to the honour and advantage of his relations.[1]

This prophecy must be prior to 701,—for in that year (chap. xxxvi. 3 ; xxxvii. 2) Eliakim is mentioned as holding the office here promised to him by Isaiah ; and Shebna occupies the subordinate position of " scribe," or secretary. Perhaps Shebna had been degraded, when events in 701 made it plain how gravely the friends of Egypt were jeopardizing the State. Whether after the triumph of Isaiah and his party, which that year subsequently saw, his prediction was more completely fulfilled by Shebna's banishment, we have no means of knowing.

Chap. xxiii., the last of Isaiah's foreign prophecies, on Tyre. The Phœnicians were conspicuous in antiquity for enterprise and activity ; and Tyre, their chief city, was the pioneer of commerce, the parent of colonies, the mistress of the sea. Tyrian merchants were the first who ventured to navigate the Mediterranean waters ; and they founded their colonies on the coasts and neighbouring islands of the Ægean Sea, in Greece, on the north coast of Africa, at Carthage and other places, in Sicily and Corsica, in Spain at Tartessus, and even beyond the pillars of Hercules, at Gadeira (Cadiz). The Phœnicians exerted an important influence upon the early development of Greece, by acting as a channel of civilization and art,[2] and the nations of Europe are indebted to them for their knowledge of that greatest of all inventions, the alphabet.[3] A graphic picture of the extent and variety of Tyrian commerce is drawn by Ezekiel, writing about 588 B.C., in the twenty-seventh chapter of his

---

[1] The vessels, large and small, in *v.* 24, are figures of the various members of Eliakim's family. As vessels of every kind are suspended upon a nail, so will Eliakim's connexions, rich and poor alike, support themselves upon him in his new dignity. Verse 25 is difficult. It is generally understood to refer to Eliakim, who the prophet foresees will misuse his position in favour of his many relatives, and meet in consequence with the usual fate which attends nepotism. But this comes strangely after the laudatory terms that have been applied to Eliakim, and perhaps Gesenius and Ewald are right in supposing that Isaiah in this verse reverts to the fall of Shebna.

[2] See the luminous study of Lenormant, " Les premières Civilisations," ii. p. 313 ff. ; or Sayce, in *The Contemporary Review*, Dec., 1878.

[3] The characters in old Greek inscriptions are scarcely distinguishable from Phœnician, and are even written similarly from right to left, or indiscriminately, in opposite directions in alternate lines.

Book. The oldest Phœnician city was Sidon (Gen. **x.** 15) : but Tyre had a longer and more illustrious history. In Isaiah's time Tyre consisted of two parts, a rock fortress, forming the older city, built on the mainland, and an island, situate about half a mile distant. This island was strongly fortified : it was taken by Alexander the Great after a siege of seven months, by an enormous mole being thrown across to it from the main-land ; the mole still remaining, what was formerly an island is now a peninsula. This, however, was not the only memorable siege which the city sustained. Josephus relates, or the authority of the Tyrian historian, Menander, that the island city held out against a combined attack of Shalmaneser and of Phœnicians of the mainland who assisted him for five years ; but he does not state how the struggle terminated. Owing, however, to the failure, in the reign of Shalmaneser, of Assyrian sources (p. 44), this statement of Josephus cannot be controlled. Nebuchadnezzar also besieged it,—according to Josephus, for thirteen years ; but again there is uncertainty whether he succeeded in taking it. Ezekiel, from the manner of his allusion in xxix. 18, implies apparently that he did not. Both Tiglath-Pileser and Sargon mention tribute being paid by Tyre ; but there is no statement that either besieged it. After all these sieges Tyre recovered, though it ceased to be a place of the same political and commercial importance. The last blow was given to it A.D. 1291, when it was taken by the Saracens, and its entire population expelled.

The prophecy is artistically constructed, and may be divided into four strophes.

Ships returning from Tarshish, the Phœnician emporium in Spain, are greeted upon their arrival at Cyprus[1] with the unexpected tidings that the great merchant city has fallen, Her populous quays are empty and deserted, and the island fortress is compared in her desolation to a woman passionately be-wailing her childlessness (_v._ 1–5). There is no hope left for Tyre where she is ; let the ancient proud city find herself a home elsewhere ; let her emigrate, and take refuge in her colonies ! But who, the prophet here asks, has purposed this against Tyre, "the crowning[2] city, whose merchants are

---

[1] Kittim (Gen. x. 4), _i.e._, Kition, the capital of Cyprus.
[2] Alluding to the kings ruling in the Tyrian colonies.

princes, whose traffickers are the honourable of the earth"?
It is Jehovah's purpose, is the answer, "to profane the
pride of all glory, to bring into contempt all the honourable of the earth" (v. 6-9). But further humiliation yet
awaits Tyre. The fall of the mother city is the signal for
the emancipation of her colonies : Tarshish may now "overflow" its "land as the Nile," fearless of restraint ; even therefore, should Tyre follow Isaiah's advice and emigrate, her
colonies would be free to repel her:—"Arise, pass over to
Kittim : even there thou shalt have no rest!" The next verse
is difficult and uncertain : as rendered in the R.V., it describes
the punishment recently inflicted upon the land of Chaldea and
its capital, Babylon, by the Assyrians, to which the prophet
ominously points as an example of what Tyre may expect, when
her turn comes to be attacked by Assyria. The third strophe
ends as the first had begun, with the same ominous cry :—
"Howl, ye ships of Tarshish ; for your stronghold is laid waste."
In the fourth and last strophe, the prophet dwells upon the
revival of Tyre in the ideal future. After seventy years of
enforced retirement and quiescence, Tyre will resume her
previous activity, but with the significant change that her gains
will now be consecrated to Jehovah, supplying food and stately
clothing to the people of Israel who dwell in His immediate
presence (v. 18). The figure under which Isaiah expresses
this thought, appears to us a strange one ; but it is suggested
by the reflection that devotion to gain as such, unrelieved by
any ennobling principle, is an unworthy occupation, which may
easily degenerate into spiritual prostitution.[1] The prophet
having once made use of the figure retains it to the end. Dis-
engaged from its singular garb, the truth which he enunciates
is an important one. Tyre was pre-eminently, in Isaiah's day,
the representative of the spirit of commerce : and the prophet
here anticipates the time when this spirit may be elevated
and purified. Isaiah, as we have seen, pictures to himself the
future growth of religion among the different nations with which
he was acquainted under figures consonant to the peculiarities
of each : in the case of Tyre, it takes the form of a purification
of the base spirit of commerce ; the old occupation of Tyre is
not discarded, it is only purged of its worldliness, and ennobled.
If verse 13 be rightly interpreted, the event alluded to will

[1] Comp. Nahum iii. 4 (of Nineveh).

fix, at least as a *terminus a quo*, the date of the prophecy. Babylonia was ravaged, and Babylon itself entered, by the Assyrians, more than once during Isaiah's lifetime,—by Sargon in 709; by Sennacherib in 703, and again in 696-5. The language of *v.* 13 is most exactly applicable to the third of these occasions, when Sennacherib relates, "The city and houses from its foundation to the upper chambers I destroyed, I dug up, in the fire I burnt."[1] The successes gained by him in 703 (above, p. 55) would, however, be hardly exaggerated by the terms of Isaiah's description. The criteria are insufficient to enable us to fix the date absolutely. If the prophecy were written between 703 and 701, Isaiah may have anticipated in it the attack made by the Assyrians upon Phœnicia in 701, when Sidon was indeed taken by Sennacherib, though his inscription (p. 66) is silent with regard to Tyre. But at whatever period in Isaiah's life the prophecy was written, there is no evidence that it was fulfilled, either at once or subsequently, *in accordance with the details of his description.* Tyre indeed was shorn in the end of her former glory, but the process was a gradual one. As in so many other cases, the prophecy is fulfilled only in its main conception, and the details are but the poetical form in which this is presented, and are unessential.[2]

[1] " Records," ix. p. 28.

[2] The "seventy years " of *v.* 18, must also, as it would seem, be symbolical. At least, it is arbitrary to identify them with the period of Babylonian supremacy, B.C. 604-538. There is nothing to authorize the inference that either 604 or 538 marked an epoch in the history of Tyre ; and the siege by Nebuchadnezzar must (Ezek. xxvi. 1 compared with xxix. 17) have fallen between 588 and 572.

CHAPTER IX.

ISAIAH'S CHARACTER AND GENIUS.

Isaiah as a statesman and social reformer—His most characteristic theological doctrines—The figure of the Messiah—Isaiah's literary and
poetical genius.

OUR study of Isaiah, as a prophet interested in the hopes and
fears, the projects and the disappointments, of the age of Ahaz
and Hezekiah, is concluded. The parts of his book which remain to be noticed stand unrelated to the period of his lifetime,
and contribute no fresh features to the picture which we have
formed of his character and personality. The present will therefore be a convenient occasion for a review of the position occupied by him in his own age. We may consider him under the
four aspects of statesman, reformer, theologian, and poet.

The position taken by Isaiah as a statesman has been so
abundantly illustrated in these pages, that little need be here

her action should be guided. In the panic caused by the Syro-Ephraimitic invasion, Isaiah alone (so far as appears) retained the power of sober reflection, estimated the danger at its just proportions, and saw that no stress of circumstances could justify the abandonment of principle, or neutralize the consequences in case it should be resorted to (viii. 12–15). Isaiah, then, discountenanced the application to Assyria ; when, however, it was made, and the Assyrian protectorate had become a *fait accompli*, he acquiesces ; and all his efforts are directed towards averting a rupture. From the first he saw the hollowness of Egyptian promises ; and it was doubtless owing chiefly to his exertions and influence that the alliance with Egypt was deferred for so many years. The soundness of his judgment was shown by the event. Again and again, when it came to a contest of strength, Egypt was defeated by Assyria ; neither to Samaria, nor to the Philistines, nor to Judah, did she render any effectual aid ; and Jerusalem was only rescued from destruction by an occurrence which could not have been calculated upon, and which was the termination of a crisis, that (so far as we can judge) would itself not have arisen had Isaiah's counsels been listened to. And the strength and support which in that crisis Isaiah proved himself to be, in the midst of the distracted capital, we have seen in Chapter VII.

As a reformer Isaiah laboured to correct all political and social abuses. To elevate statesmanship, to purify justice, to reform religion, to fight against inconsistency, to redress social wrongs, was the aim which he set himself in life ; and his book discloses to us the persistency and uncompromising earnestness with which he pursued it. No rank escapes his censure. The soothsayers, and other professors of occult arts, who found in Judah an only too ready welcome ; the men of wealth and influence, who ignored the responsibilities of office or position ; the leaders of opinion, who possessed weight in the government, or gave a tone to society ; the irreligious, short-sighted politicians, who nevertheless knew how to put forward their views in an attractive and plausible guise ; a powerful minister, whose policy he saw was calculated to jeopardize the State ; the women, whose frivolity and thoughtlessness on two distinct occasions suggested to him his darkest apprehensions for the future ; the masses, whom he saw sunk in indifference or formalism ; the king himself, whether it were Ahaz, in his wilfulness and insincerity, or Hezekiah listening incautiously to the overtures of a foreign potentate—all in turn receive his bold and fearless rebuke. True, this aspect of a prophet's work, to enforce a proper standard of action, to remind a nation of the moral obligations which its professions of religion impose upon it, was in no way peculiar to Isaiah : it is common more or less to all the prophets ; but it is exemplified by Isaiah with singular completeness and force in the course of his lifelong conflict with the dominant tendencies of his age.

Theologically, there is, of course, much that is common to Isaiah with other prophets ; we must look the more attentively in order to ascertain what is distinctive or new. As has been remarked (p. 18), the aspects of the Divine nature most prominent in Isaiah's writings are those of majesty and holiness. The attribute of majesty is effectively represented in the picture of Jehovah's " Day " (ii. 10-21) ; it is conspicuous also in the figures of a manifestation of Divine power, which shape themselves in the prophet's imagination (*e.g.*, v. 16; x. 17; 33 f. ; xxiii. 11 ; xxviii. 2, 21 ; xxix. 6 ; xxx. 27 f. 30) : it is embodied in the thought of the seraphs' hymn (vi. 3) that the world in all its parts is a reflection of the Divine glory. The attribute of holiness implies that upon occasion Jehovah will vindicate His holiness in an act of judgment (v. 16) ; it further demands as its correlative in those who are His people that they should act towards Him accordingly, or " sanctify " Him, *i.e.*, treat Him as holy, and regard Him with reverence and godly awe (viii. 13 ; xxix. 23). Idols and idolatrous rites are alluded to with contempt, as an unworthy substitute for Jehovah (ii. 8 ; xvii. 8), or as a source of disappointment to their worshippers (i. 29 ; ii. 18, 20 ; xvii. 10 f.).[1] Isaiah expects their spontaneous repudiation from the regenerated community of the future (xvii. 8 ; xxx. 22 ; xxxi. 7). There is, however, no formal polemic against idolatry, such as meets us in Jer. x., or in the second part of this book (chaps. xl.–xlviii). Like his predecessors, Hosea (vi. 6), and especially Amos (v. 21–27), Isaiah denounces with impassioned eloquence the inutility, in the sight of God, of the external observances of religion (i. 10-17), and of a routine

---

[1] The favourite term which Isaiah uses to denote them is *elīlīm*, *i.e.* (apparently), *nothingnesses* (ii. 8, 18, 20 ; x. 11 ; xix. 1, 3 ; xxxi. 7) ; in the

ceremonial (xxix. 13 f.), when not accompanied by sincerity of
heart, and a consistent discharge of the duties of social life.[1]

Isaiah's most characteristic doctrine is the idea of a judgment
imminent upon the nation, accompanied by the preservation of
a faithful remnant, for whom a new and blissful era will then
immediately begin. This doctrine is first adumbrated at the
time of Isaiah's call (vi. 13) : it is soon afterwards embodied by
him in the name of his son, "Shear-jashub," *i.e.*, *A remnant
shall return* (viz., to God) ; it appears subsequently under many
different figures and in different contexts,[2] and holds its place in
his last recorded utterance (B.C. 701), chap. xxxvii. 31 f. The
significance of this doctrine to Isaiah has been indicated before
(p. 21 f.). The chosen nation is imperishable ; but Divine
justice requires that its unworthy members should be swept
away : the rest, purged and renovated, will then form the foundation of a new community, exhibiting the *ideal* character of
the people (Exod. xix. 6, "an *holy* nation "). The thought of the
security and permanence of Zion, in spite of the distress and
peril which may befall her (xiv. 32 ; xxviii. 16 ; xxix. 5 ; xxxiii.
5), is evidently merely the same idea under another form. The
ideal is nobly and attractively delineated by the prophet : he
grasps it firmly ; and the preceding pages will have shown what
power it held over him, and how constantly he reverts to it.
In the darkest times it is his consolation and support. The
approach of trouble or danger throws him back upon the
thought of the permanence of the nation, and intensifies his
faith in a blissful future reserved for it. The series of passages
belonging to the Assyrian crisis (xxix. 17-24 ; xxx. 20-26 ; xxxii.
1-8, 15-18 ; xxxiii. 5-6) will be a sufficient illustration of what
has been said.

But how was Isaiah's ideal to be realized? It is by himself
always closely connected with the end of the Assyrian troubles,
and is apparently to commence as soon as they are passed.
The turning point in the history of the people is the overthrow
of the Assyrian power, which is to mark the inauguration of the
new era.[3] This, certainly, never so happened. No such trans-

---

[1] Comp. iii. 14 f. v. 7 ("And he looked for justice, but behold oppression ; for righteousness, but behold a cry ") : xxxiii. 14-16, &c.

[2] *E.g.*, i. 27 ("those who *return* of her ") ; iv. 2 ; x. 21, 22, R.V. ; xxviii.
5 (primarily, of Samaria) ; and elsewhere by implication.

[3] See xvi. 4-5 ; xxix. 17 ("a very little while "), and comp., *e.g.*, xxx. 20,
ff. with xxx. 18 f., or xxxii. 1 with xxxi. 8 f.

the world's civilization and industry ; there are no Philistines or Ammonites (xi. 14), to own the suzerainty of restored Israel : there is no sanctuary on Zion (John iv. 21) privileged to witness the adoration of the converted Ethiopians (chap. xviii. 7).[1] Isaiah's genius enabled him to clothe his ideas in noble imagery ; and a gallery of gorgeous pictures, the delight and wonder of the ages, but significant often *symbolically*, rather than literally, is his legacy to humanity. When, however, we divest Isaiah's thought—for instance, his faith in the permanence and future renovation of the nation—of the form in which he presents it, we can see that it has not remained wholly unrealized. For, in process of time, and after a far more complex series of events than Isaiah imagined, there were brought into operation, within the Jewish people, new forces, which exhibiting themselves in a minority of the entire nation, invested it with new possibilities, and laid the basis for a further progress in the future. The purification and perfection of society, as a whole, is indeed a consummation which Christ Himself has taught us not to expect till the end of all things ; but in the Christian dispensation the goal of Jewish history was reached, and that transformation of the individual and of society which Isaiah first sketched in such brilliant colours, was made potentially a reality.

A frequent, but not a constant, figure in Isaiah's picture of purified and renovated society, is the ideal king, commonly known as the Messiah.[2] The development which this idea received at his hands has been alluded to already (p. 42). In place of the permanence of David's dynasty, which is the substance of Nathan's prophecy, or of the bare representative,

---

[1] Comp. also xxiii. 18 (p. 105), xxx. 33 (p. 61), &c.

[2] *I.e.*, the *anointed one*. The "anointed" (same word) "of Jehovah" is a standing designation of the chief ruler of Israel (1 Sam. xvi. 6 ; xxiv. 7, 11 ; Ps. xx. 6, &c.) ; and starting from this usage the later Jews designated the future ideal ruler of the prophets by the title, "the King Messiah." Hence "Messiah."

ceremonial (xxix. 13, of David's house, which is all that is offered heart, and a crea (iii. 5), Isaiah delineates a concrete, individual Isaiah's my, whose birth, under remarkable circumstances, he immineunces, whom he represents (viii. 8) as the owner and a fauardian of the land, and whom he views afterwards, when arrived at years of discretion, as the capable reformer and administrator of David's realm (ix. 6 f.; xvi. 5), as endued for his office with divine graces (xi. 1–4), and as extending far and wide the blessings of a peaceful and equitable rule (xi. 5–10). Similar representations, though not so fully developed, appear in Isaiah's contemporary, Micah (v. 2–6), as well as in Zechariah (ix. 9 f.), and Jeremiah (xxiii. 5 f.) ; but the portrait is essentially the creation of Isaiah, and even later prophets do not contribute to it any substantially fresh features.

But here, also, as in the previous cases, the fulfilment was no literal one. Like the prophets generally, Isaiah (cf. p. 94) views the future through the forms of the social and religious orga ization under which he lived ; his own times, his own surroundings, supply the figures under which he represents it. For centuries the monarchy had been the centre and pivot of the Jewish constitution ; and accordingly one prominent feature in the delineations of the future sketched by the prophets is the figure of the ideal king, who will realize the highest possibilities of earthly monarchy, governing Israel with perfect justice and perfect wisdom, and securing for his subjects perfect peace.[1]

[1] Observe, the virtues delineated in xi. 2–4 are those of a *ruler* and *judge* (the two functions united, as in 1 Sam. viii. 5, 20 ; 2 Sam. viii. 15, &c.), competent alike to defend his country from its foes (cf. Mic. v. 6), and to secure justice for his subjects. The foundation of the character of the ideal prince is the "spirit of Jehovah" resting upon him ; this displays itself in (1) "wisdom and understanding," *i.e.*, the faculty of clear perception leading him aright in matters whether of intellectual or moral interest (1 Kings x 8 ; Job xxviii. 28) ; (2) "counsel and might," *i.e.*, sagacity in conceiving a course of action, and firmness and courage in carrying it out (cf. xxxvi. 5) ; (3) the "knowledge and fear of Jehovah," *i.e.*, a full apprehension of what Jehovah demands, and the inclination to act accordingly. This fixes the ideal prince's character as such : *v.* 3–4 show next how his character thus fixed will operate by guiding him in the practical work of government. An instructive commentary on both this passage and chap. ix. 6–7 is Jer. xxii. 1–xxiii. 8, where the character of the Messiah (xxiii. 5, 6) is in evident contrast to the imperfect rulers of Jeremiah's own time, described in chap. xxii. Ps. lxxii. is a poetical development of the same theme (*v.* 8 from Zech. ix. 10).

But *in this form* their visions were never realized. The deliverer
promised by Isaiah was to appear speedily (vii. 16) : he was to
free his nation not from their foes generally, but from the *Assy-*
rians. For though Assyria is not actually named in ix. 4, or
x. 33, yet parallel passages (such as x. 12, 24 ; xxx. 31 ;
xxxi. 8) make it plain that Assyria is intended ; and it is quite
without warrant in Biblical usage to suppose the Romans, or
other representatives or successors of the Assyrians, to be included in the terms used by the prophet. We must read such
prophecies as Isaiah's contemporaries would read them : it is
not permissible to impose upon them arbitrary senses in imaginary accordance with the necessities of the fulfilment. Isaiah's
view does not reach into the distant future : it is fixed in vii.
14-16 on the immediate future, in chaps. ix. and xi. on a future
not indeed, perhaps, quite so near, but still not remote. At the
same time, the fact that, in chap. xi., uttered a generation after
his first Messianic prophecies (chaps. vii. and ix.), when his hopes
of a literal fulfilment (if such were cherished by him) must
have been disappointed, the vision reappears, as distinct and
brilliant as ever, shows that in truth his conceptions are *inde-*
pendent of time. They are ideal creations, projected, as has been
said (p. 41), upon the shifting future. By Isaiah himself they
are, indeed, localized always within the Assyrian period ; but
the postponement of their realization, so far from extinguishing
his hopes, invigorates and renews them. They are thus capable
of being detached from the occasion or circumstance with which
originally they were associated. The empire of Assyria passed
away, yielding to the superior forces of a better organized
nationality : no Messiah or ideal ruler provided Israel with the
means of repelling its attacks (Mic. v. 6), or marked by his just
administration its abandonment of jurisdiction over Palestine
(Isa. xvi. 4-5). But Isaiah's ideal remained ; and, judging from
the example of consistency which has been quoted, it is not too
bold to conclude, that however often his hopes of an immediate
fulfilment might have met with disappointment, he would not
have abandoned it. He would have transferred it, as Jeremiah
did (xxiii. 5-6), to a new point of contact in the future. But
even though thus independent of time, the visions of Isaiah, as
of the other prophets, have still not been realized in the form in
which they conceived them. Christ, it is true, summed up in
Himself the perfections of which Isaiah writes and founded a

kingdom : but the kingdom of the prophets is *transformed :* the glorified earthly kingdom, with a visible centre at Zion (Isa. ii. 2), has given place to a spiritual " Kingdom of Heaven " with no local centre (John iv. 21); and the material blessings which their ideal king was to secure for the nations owning his sway are replaced by the empire of Christ exercised over the minds of men. A too literal interpretation of prophetic imagery opens the door to great misunderstandings ; and hence the importance of noting the conditions by which its application is limited.

Thirdly, Isaiah gives clear expression to the ultimate scope of Israel's religion. The future establishment of a blessed relationship between Israel and the Gentiles is probably hinted at in Gen. xii. 3 ; but it is for the first time exhibited distinctly by Isaiah — or, at least, by the prophet whose words he adopts in ii. 2–4 (p. 23) ; and, after him, is met with frequently in later prophets. This thought is foreign to Hosea ; Amos (ix. 11 f.) anticipates merely the enforced re-subjection of the nations conquered by David to the yoke of his successors ; Isaiah conceives the relation as a *voluntary* one : the nations stream spontaneously (ii. 3) to Zion as their spiritual metropolis ; in xi. 10, the future scion of David's house appears as the ensign, or banner, riveting their gaze ; afterwards, Ethiopia, Egypt, Assyria, Tyre, are represented as rendering their willing tribute to Israel's God. The vow, and still more the performance of it (xix. 21), is an especial mark of voluntary service (Deut. xxiii. 21, 22). As before, the figurative character of much of Isaiah's language will not be overlooked : the physical elevation of the Temple hill (ii. 2), the pilgrimage to it, the " altar " and " pillar " in the land of Egypt, the " highway " between Egypt and Assyria (xix. 19, 23) are, it is evident, merely *emblems* representing the truths which he seeks to express under forms suggestive and significant to his hearers.

On Isaiah, as an orator or poet, our remarks must be brief. Ewald has pointed to the discrimination shown by him in ever adapting his language to the occasion, and to the skill with which he secures that the development of the thought is always complete without being prolix ; the picture impressive, but never overdrawn. His literary style reflects the elevation and dignity of his thought. It is chaste and severe ; every sentence is compact and well rounded ; the movement of the periods is stately and measured. Thus his prophecies form artistic wholes, adequate to the effect intended, but not more. Then he always has at his command an apt figure or metaphor to bring his meaning home: for example, the scene depicted in iii. 6 f. or xviii. 5, the proverb in ix. 18, the child in x. 19 (cf. xi. 6), the uneasy couch, xxviii. 20, the disappointing dream, xxix. 8, the subtle flaw, spreading insidiously through a wall, xxx. 13 f. For the same purpose he avails himself of the methods which appeal to an Eastern people—the symbolical act (xx. 2), the enigmatic word (xxix. 1), and the significant name (viii. 1 ; xix. 18; xxx. 7). The capacity shown by him for seizing salient features of character has been observed before (p. 85).

His earliest prophecies already give evidence of his poetical power ; the " Day " against all that is high and lofty (ii. 12 ff.), the first description of the Assyrian armies (v. 26–30), the torrent overflowing its banks and inundating Judah (viii. 7 f.), the challenge to the nations (*ib.* 9 f.)—are worthy preludes of what he afterwards accomplished. For it is evident that the great Assyrian discourses exhibit him in the plenitude of his genius, and kindle his poetical inspiration to its greatest achievements. Perhaps, on the whole, the section x. 5–xii. 6 is the most powerful and original of his writings ; but opinions will differ on a point of this nature ; and ch. xxix.–xxxiii. contain passages singularly striking and fine.

Amongst all the prophets, Isaiah is pre-eminent, both for the variety of the images which he employs, and also for their grandeur. His imagination never fails him ; and the figures which it supplies him with are of astonishing brilliancy and force. Only a few examples can be cited. The signal is raised aloft upon the mountains, and we see it commanding the attention of distant peoples (v. 26 ; xi. 12 ; xviii. 3) ; we see it again the terribly suggestive symbol of the sparseness and isolation of his nation's survivors (xxx. 17). The huge forest consumed rapidly by fire, or deprived of its luxuriant foliage by the axe, wielded by an invisible hand, represents the collapse of the hosts of Assyria (x. 16 f. 33). Images borrowed from the country life of Palestine are often effectively employed by him. The Divine protection is a canopy or shade (iv. 6*a*), a rock in a thirsty land (xxxii. 2), under the burning Oriental noon ; or again, it is a covert from the rain-storm, a refuge from the tempest, such as are apt to burst in Palestine with appalling violence (iv. 6*b*). The *wadys*, dry or nearly so, in summer, swelling in the winter time to impetuous torrents, suggest to him some of his grandest pictures—the waters mounting up, and all but submerging Judah (viii. 7 f.), judgment advancing irresistibly as a surging tide (x. 22), the rising current washing away the fortress of Samaria (xxviii. 2), the "overflowing scourge" drowning all that it encounters (xxviii. 18 ; xxx. 28), the indescribably grand storm by which Assyria is finally panic-stricken (xxx. 30). Or, again, to illustrate the fewness of the survivors after the judgment upon Ephraim, he brings us to the valley of Rephaim, white with an abundant harvest, and shows us the reaper busy at his work ; he takes us to an olive garden, on the day when the berries have been beaten off, and we descry in the uppermost branches the few which have escaped the beaters' staves (xvii. 5 f.).

Lastly, Isaiah delights in sudden contrasts. The gathering clouds, which no ray of light seemed able to pierce, are succeeded by a brilliant day (viii. 22–ix. 1) ; the foes pressing impetuously round the prostrate "daughter of Zion" are transformed in an instant into clouds of vanishing dust (xxix. 5) ; the surging multitudes are scattered and disappear in a single night (xvii. 14) ; the waste and uncultivated ruins are supernaturally clothed with a rich and abundant verdure (iv. 2) ; the scene of confusion and destruction, x. 33 f., is succeeded by the marvellous picture of serenity and peace in xi. 1–9 (cf. p. 71, 72). In conclusion, two examples of bold, but effective, change of image may be cited ; one (xxxi. 4 f.), in which the comparison of Jehovah, advancing against Zion, to a lion descending from the mountains, and undismayed by the multitude of shepherds called together to defend the flock against him, is abruptly followed by the simile of the birds hovering over their nest and shielding it against its assailants ; the other, from xxxiii. 20 ff., where Isaiah surpasses himself in his description of the free and triumphant Jerusalem of the future. The image with which he begins is that of a tent, securely pitched, which can defy the stress of wind and weather. But the vision changes, and we see the broad stream encircling and protecting Jerusalem ; it changes again, and the State is now a ship, disabled and distressed ; another image rapidly follows, the victory has been won, and the crew are dividing a superabundant spoil.

PART II.

———◆———

CHAPTER I.

ISRAEL'S TRIBULATION AND SUBSEQUENT REDEMPTION.

(Chapters xxiv.-xxvii.)

THE prophecy, chaps. xxiv.-xxvii., stands by itself in the Book of Isaiah, and, indeed, in the Old Testament. In its general drift, it is the description of a great catastrophe about to fall upon the earth—specially, as it appears, upon the land of Judah —to be followed by the overthrow of some great power (the name of which is not stated) hostile to the theocracy, and the consequent triumph of the people of God. No event of Isaiah's

Isaiah never connects either the aggressions or the ruin of the Assyrian power with movements of the dimensions here contemplated. The Assyrian *army* is annihilated, the plans of the Assyrian *king* are defeated : but the earth generally is untouched. Here, on the contrary (chap. xxiv.), desolation overtakes land and city alike (*v.* 1-12), and words are insufficient to paint the confusion which is to prevail far and near (*v.* 17-20). Again, Isaiah always speaks of the *army*, or *king*, of Assyria ; here the oppressing power is throughout some great *city* (compare xxv. 2-3 ; xxvi. 5). In Isaiah, the "remnant" which escapes is saved in Judah or Jerusalem (iv. 3 ; xxxvii. 32 ; cf. xiv. 32 ; xxviii. 16) : here the voices of the redeemed are first heard from distant quarters of the earth (xxiv. 14-16). Further, the literary treatment (in spite of the occurrence of certain more or less characteristic words, which Isaiah also uses) is, as a whole, unlike Isaiah's : the prophecy contains many peculiar expressions, and the prevailing type of representation is not that of Isaiah. For these reasons, and especially for the first, the absence of any *occasion* in Isaiah's lifetime sufficient to explain or account for the language here used by the prophet, the author can hardly be Isaiah. We seem to have before us the work of some other prophet, not, indeed, devoid of originality, but gifted with an originality different from Isaiah's ; and we must have recourse to a different period of Jewish history for the purpose of explaining it. It is, however, not impossible that it may rest upon an Isaianic basis, and that its author may have availed himself sometimes of phrases and verses written by Isaiah : to this circumstance may perhaps be attributed its incorporation in the Book of Isaiah, where, moreover, it occupies a suitable position after the completion of the prophecies dealing with particular foreign nations (chaps. xiii.-xxiii.). That it was no unfamiliar custom with the prophets to borrow from the writings of their predecessors can be demonstrated in the case of Jeremiah, who (to take but one example) in his prophecy on Moab (chap. xlviii.) adopts some of the most remarkable and striking expressions occurring in Isaiah's prophecy on the same nation (chaps. xv.-xvi.).[1] Verses here which, in particular, recall the style or thought of Isaiah, are, for instance, xxiv. 13, 16*b*, 23 ; xxv. 6-8, 10-11 ; xxvii. 9-13.

---

[1] See the references in the margin of R.V. on Jer. xlviii. Comp. also Jer. xlix. 7-16 with Obadiah ; and Isa. ii. 2-4 with Mic. iv. 1-3.

The positive data which exist for fixing the occasion of the prophecy do not, however, speak decidedly. Moab is named in xxv. 10, 11 ; in xxvii. 1, Babylon *seems* to be alluded to, as well as Assyria and Egypt, as a power to be smitten by Jehovah. The oppressing city, as has been remarked, is not mentioned by name. The introduction of Moab is abrupt ; and the unity of the prophecy would, no doubt, be more complete if the oppressing city could be identified with the Moabite capital. But the hostile city seems to be represented as a power too great and formidable to allow of this identification, so that the allusion to Moab must be attributed to some incident—probably some act of insolence or aggression on the part of the Moabites—of recent occurrence when the prophecy was written.[1] The unnamed city is, in all probability, Babylon, according to the representation usually given of this power (Jeremiah, *passim*). We may suppose the prophecy to have been written on the eve of the Babylonian captivity. Though the terms are general, the part of the " earth " which the author has chiefly in view in xxiv. 1–13 is apparently Palestine. The great political upheaval produced by Nebuchadnezzar (the magnitude of which may be inferred from the terms in which Jeremiah speaks, xxv. 15–31) seems to form the historical basis of chap. xxiv. ; only, since this, as the prophet writes, is still *future*, he gives the reins to his imagination, and its effects are described in ideal colours. The insolent language of Moab, noticed in Ezek. xxv. 8–11 (dating shortly afterwards), would explain the reference to that country in xxv. 10 f. But, as the prophet looks out into the future, the conquests of Nebuchadnezzar, and the ultimate fall of his empire, and accompanying deliverance of the Jewish exiles, foretold by Jeremiah (xxv. 12 ; xxix. 10), are not always clearly separated from one another ; he passes rapidly from the approaching troubles to the future deliverance, and back again to the intervening period of difficulty and suspense. That his representations do not accord exactly with the event is no ground of surprise ; like other prophets, the author speaks figuratively : in some of Isaiah's predictions of the ruin of the Assyrian army (*e.g.*, xxx. 30–33), it would be difficult to recognize the disaster which actually befell it. It is an imaginative picture

---

[1] It is against the usage of the prophets to regard Moab here as typical of Israel's foes in general : Moab, in the Old Testament, is always mentioned in a strictly literal sense.

of the future, which the prophet here draws, embodying through-out true ideas, but (like many of Isaiah's) not designed to receive a *literal* fulfilment. There seems no difficulty in supposing that such a picture might have been drawn by a contemporary of Jeremiah's, developing, in view of the troubles imminent upon Judah, that prophet's conception of the future restoration of his nation. Of course, the *mode* in which the subject is developed is not that which would be followed by Jeremiah, any more than it is one which Isaiah would have chosen. It is peculiar to the author of the prophecy, and in many particulars is original and uncommon.

The prophet sees a great convulsion about [1] to overwhelm the land, obliterating (*v.* 2) every distinction of class, and spreading ruin and desolation far and wide. In *v.* 4–12 the scene is painted with terrible completeness : clause follows clause in long succession, each adding some fresh trait to the dark dicture, or describing the cessation, one after another, of the delights and satisfactions of life. "For thus shall it be in the midst of the earth among the peoples, as at the beating of the olive, as at the grape-gleaning when the vintage is done." If we are right in supposing these verses to be prompted by the political and social changes which the prophet sees will be a consequence of Nebuchadnezzar's conquests (Jer. xxv. 15–31), the immediate reference will be to the approaching ruin of the land of Judah ; though, doubtless, other nations are not to be considered as exempted from the judgment, and the language of the prophecy soon becomes such (*v.* 17–22) as distinctly to include them. But first, for a moment, the vision of ruin is interrupted : borne from afar, over the Western waters, the chorus of praise rising from the lips of the redeemed falls upon the prophet's ear :—"*These* (*i.e.*, the escaped, implied in *v.* 13) lift up their voice, they shout : because of Jehovah's majesty they cry aloud from the sea." [2] Next, he hears in spirit the song celebrating the good fortune of the righteous : "From the skirt

---

[1] xxiv. 1, *lit.* "is making," *i.e.*, is on the point of making, as xvii. 1, &c.

[2] The word in *v.* 15 rendered in R.V. *east* is very uncertain : probably, it is best to follow Bp. Lowth and others in reading, with a slight change in one letter, "isles." The two clauses of the *v.* will then be parallel (cf. for the rhythm Ps. xxix. 5, 8). The "sea" is the Mediterranean : comp. chap. xi. 11 *end*, and Hos. xi. 10. The *majesty* of Jehovah is that shown in the deliverance of His people: cf. Exod. xv. 1 in the Hebrew.

of the earth we have heard songs : 'Honour (is come) for the righteous!'" but this, he feels, is premature : so speaking in the name of his fellow-countrymen in Judah, he replies, " Misery [1] to me ! misery [1] to me ! woe is me ! The barbarous deal barbarously, the barbarous deal very barbarously :" the period of trouble is not yet over : another scene in the drama of judgment has still to be enacted ; and how terrible that will be is shown by the imagery of the following verses, 17-20, which depicts shock following shock in succession, until finally even the earth itself totters in its place. So total, indeed, will be the ruin of nations, that not only their kings upon earth, but their guardian princes in heaven, will suffer with them, implicated in their guilt (*v.* 21 f.). In the end, however, Zion will emerge triumphant : and the reign of her Divine king will then begin, in splendour such as to put to shame the natural luminaries of day and night (*v.* 23 ; cf. xxx. 26).

Here the prophet transports himself to the period after the deliverance has been consummated ; and identifying himself with the redeemed community, utters in their name a hymn (xxv. 1-5), expressing their thankfulness for the mercies vouchsafed to them. God's ancient purposes, they exclaim, have been fulfilled : the oppressing city has at length been overthrown, even the remnant of their oppressors now own Jehovah's might (*v.* 3), who has proved Himself a shelter to the needy, when the blast threatened to sweep them away (*v.* 4), and a screen protecting them from the consuming violence of the foe (*v.* 5[2]).

The hymn of thanksgiving ended, the prophet returns to his own standpoint (using *future* tenses), to dwell on the blessedness, of which Zion, at the time imagined, will become the centre. A rich banquet—a figure at once of spiritual [3] and

in this beautiful vision are similar to those which we have met
in Isaiah : the nations admitted in the future to the privileges
of Israel (ii. 2–4, &c.), and a state of ideal felicity to be enjoyed
by the redeemed and transfigured nation (i. 26 ; iv. 2–6 ; xxxiii.
17, 24). The abolition of the power of death is a new feature :
the curse pronounced upon man in Eden is hereby annulled.
In a second short strain of thanksgiving, the redeemed nation
again declares its gratitude (*v.* 9). For "upon *this* mountain
(Zion) shall rest" the protecting hand of Jehovah : but haughty
Moab will be humbled, and humbled ignominiously (*v.* 10–11¹).

A third hymn now follows. It is the prophet's effective method
of depicting vividly the feeling of the redeemed community of
the future. The nation glories (*v.* 1) in the strength of its city
—a strength, consisting not in material bulwarks, but in "salvation," *i.e.*, in freedom² and safety, assured by God, and the
guarantee of continued spiritual blessedness. Let the gates be
opened wide, that those who are worthy to be its citizens—those,
viz., who possess the steadfast, unwavering spirit, which is the
mark of faith—may enter in (*v.* 2–4³) ! The hostile city is humbled to the dust ; and the poor may now walk unhindered over
its ruins (*v.* 5–6). Henceforth, the way of the just will be free
from trouble or difficulty (*v.* 7⁴) : the prayer, or aspiration, so
often uttered by Psalmists (v. 8 ; xxvi. 12 ; xxvii. 11), will now
become a reality. A retrospect here follows which may be thus
paraphrased : "How long and earnestly," the redeemed Israelites
exclaim, " did we desire to witness this consummation of Divine
judgment which is at length accomplished ! (*v.* 8–10). Thy
hand, Lord ! has been lifted up ; there have been some who see
it not ; but they must see it now, they must learn Thy zeal for
Thy people. It is Thou, Lord, who wilt assure us peace ; it is

---

¹ In *v.* 11*a* the figure is of Moab vainly struggling to save himself
in the water of the dungpit : in 11*b* "he" is, of course, Jehovah, who
frustrates the efforts made by Moab.

² The original sense of the word rendered *salvation* (as Arabic shows) is
breadth, largeness, absence of constraint.

³ *V.* 3 (see R.V. *marg.*) states the conditions of membership in the ideal
Zion ; a "steadfast mind" may share the "peace" which the ideal city is
to enjoy.

⁴ "The way of the just is a right way ; the path of the just thou directest
aright" (R.V. *marg.*). The verse does not describe the condition of things
in the prophet's own present, but is part of the song (see *v.* 1) describing
the ideal condition of the future.

through Thee alone that we are alive this day to celebrate Thy name (*v.* 11–13).   Our oppressors are dead : they are forgotten in the shadowy world below : they will rise no more : but as for *us*, our nation is increased, its strength replenished, its territory enlarged l (*v.* 14–15 [1]).   In our trouble, ere deliverance reached us, we sought Jehovah ; we addressed to Him the faintly-whispered prayer, while His chastening was upon us (*v.* 16). We cherished hopes (*v.* 17) : but disappointment overtook us ; we could achieve no effectual deliverance, we could not re-people our desolated land (*v.* 18 [2]).   We turned to God : ' Let Thy dead live ! let my dead bodies arise ! ' " and here the prophet himself, interrupting the retrospect, joins in with the jubilant reply : " Awake and shout, ye that dwell in the dust : for thy dew is as the dew of herbs,[3] and the earth shall cast forth the Shades " (*v.* 19).   The two next verses (*v.* 20–21) are spoken from the prophet's own present ; he bids his people withdraw into the privacy of communion with God, whilst the judgment—that, viz., described in xxiv. 1–12, 17–20—visits those who are doomed to perish by it.

Throughout the whole of the first eighteen verses of this chapter, it must be recollected, the prophet has spoken not from his own standpoint, but from that of the redeemed nation in the future, expressing in its name the feelings of gratitude and devotion which he imagines that it will naturally entertain, and confessing the disappointment which the failure of its own exertions had brought upon it.   The thought that Israel can only be finally restored by the agency of a *Resurrection* is an important one.   In the Old Testament the idea of a resurrection is rarely met with ; and even where it occurs, it is expressed as a hope rather than as a dogma, and it is, moreover, limited in its scope, being restricted to *Israel.*   That it is limited to Israel here is evident from the context ; in *v.* 14 it is expressly denied in the case of Israel's oppressors ; and it is denied similarly in Jer. li. 39, already cited.   There is the same limitation in the famous Vision in Ezekiel (chap. xxxvii.) of the Valley of Dry Bones

---

[1] *V.* 14 may be illustrated from Jer. li. 39 ; *v.* 15 from chap. xxxiii. 17 ; xlix. 19–20.   " Art glorified," rather, " hast gotten thee glory," viz., by our deliverance : cf. Exod. xiv. 4 (same word).

[2] Clause *b* : "We made not the land salvation, neither were inhabitants of the land produced " (Cheyne).

[3] *I.e.*, as the dew which revives the drooping plants.

(see *v.* 11 f.). The passage which speaks most explicitly in the Old Testament is in one of the latest prophets, Daniel (xii. 2) ; but even there, the terms are not universal. In fact, in the Old Testament, the dogma is not yet fully formed ; it is *nascent;* and we can trace the stages of its growth. The full revelation of this great truth was reserved for Jesus Christ in the gospel ; in the Old Testament the way was prepared for this ; and the passage before us shows that the idea, though not yet revealed as a *fact*, is a postulate involved in the complete restoration of the Jewish nation.

In chap xxvii. the prophet dwells upon particular aspects of the coming future—sometimes the judgment on Israel's foes being foremost in his thoughts, sometimes the period of felicity which is to ensue. *V.* 1, Israel's three great representative foes, Assyria, Babylon, and Egypt,[1] are depicted as finally overpowered and slain. In a fourth song of thankfulness (*v.* 2–5[2]), provided by the prophet, the redeemed nation expresses, under the figure of a vineyard, its sense of the Divine protection under which it rests. And thus cared for, the vine of Israel in the future will spread, and "fill the face of the world with fruit" (cf. Hos. xiv. 5–7). Israel, however, must suffer, before this consummation can be reached ; but how? "Hath Jehovah smitten Israel, as He smote those that smote it? Is Israel slain as Jehovah's slain ones are slain?" in other words, Is Israel exterminated? On the contrary, the prophet replies, "in exact measure," not in excess, has Jehovah "contended" (cf

---

[1] According to the most probable interpretation. "Leviathan," properly something *wreathed* or *coiled*, in Job xli. 1 of the crocodile ; in Ps. civ. 26 of a sea-monster ; in Job iii. 8 (R.V.) of a monster, supposed popularly to devour the sun at an eclipse. The "fleeing serpent" occurs in Job xxvi. 13 pretty clearly of a constellation, in allusion (it can hardly be doubted) to some popular belief of a dragon transfixed by Jehovah, and fastened in the sky : applied here as an emblem (probably) of Assyria. The "crooked" or "winding" serpent appears to represent Babylon. The "dragon" often symbolizes Egypt: see chap. li. 9, and especially Ezek. xxix. 3 ; xxxii. 2.

[2] *V.* 4. The figure being that of a *vineyard*, the foes who would vex and overrun Israel are denoted by "briers and thorns." Jehovah says, "Wrath have I none (against the vineyard): if only those who would assail it were before Me in battle ! I would speedily attack and destroy them—unless, indeed, they desisted from the attempt, and took refuge with Me ; for, if they were ready to make peace with Me, I would not repel them." (*Or else let him* = *unless he*, in accordance with an Arabic usage.)

'er. ii. 9) with His people, when He put it from Him : the "rough
blast" passed over the nation, but did not exterminate it : Israel
was banished, but not destroyed (*v.* 8). Jehovah has not yet
cast off His people ; repentance therefore will yet be accepted, if it be sincere, and if all idolatrous emblems be resolutely
discarded (*v.* 9). For then the hostile city [1] will be visited with
irretrievable disaster and ruin (*v.* 10, 11). Abruptly, in conclusion, the prophet sets before us two episodes of the restoration.
The land of Israel, to its ideal limits, from the Euphrates to the
torrent of Egypt,[2] will be repeopled, as quickly as if it were
the vast olive-garden, the olives being "beaten" (Deut. xxiv. 20)
from the trees, and picked up carefully, one by one, that none
be lost. Next, as soon as the signal (xviii. 3) is heard, the
exiles from Egypt and Assyria will prepare to start homewards ;
and will meet in Jerusalem ! (comp. xi. 11–16 ; Hos. xi. 11).

The prophecy is a striking one. We are impressed by the
width of area which the prophet's imagination traverses, by the
novelty and variety of the imagery which he employs. The
interspersed songs are even penetrated by a deeper and more
delicate vein of feeling than the one in chap. xii. ; they remind
us of the emotional tenderness of Hosea more than of the majesty
of Isaiah. A lively faith sustains the author : notwithstanding
the dark days which must be passed through first, his eye
reaches beyond, and lingers with delight upon the bright vision
which it there descries. In this he resembles Jeremiah, who
though repeatedly commissioned to declare to his people the
coming exile (*e.g.*, chaps. xv., xxi., xxv.), nevertheless anticipates confidently his people's return, and dwells upon the period
of ideal blessedness which will then begin (chaps. xxx.–xxxiii.).
The sequence of ideas is not so regular as it is in Jeremiah :
and hence the connection of thought is in parts difficult to seize :
but this appears to be due to the manner in which the prospect
presented by the future impresses the author ; the coming
troubles affect him so deeply that he reverts to them, directly
indirectly, again and again ; and his visions of the blessedness which is to follow are accordingly interrupted by abrupt
prospects and transitions.

CHAPTER II

BABYLON AND EDOM.

(Chapters xiii. 1-xiv. 23 ; xxxiv.-xxxv.)

THE first of these prophecies consists of an announcement of the approaching fall of *Babylon* (xiii. 19), and of the subsequent release of the Jews (xiv. 1-2) from the land of their exile. The reasons which forbid our attributing it to Isaiah have been stated briefly already (p. 86). The prophet is, in the first instance, *the teacher of his own generation :* hence it is a fundamental principle of prophecy that the historical situation of the prophet should be the basis of his prediction. Isaiah lived during the Assyrian supremacy : and it is the failure of *a particular Assyrian king*[1] to destroy or subjugate Judah which he uniformly foretells. In the present prophecy *Babylon* is represented as owning the empire of the world (xiii. 19 ; :, 6 f.), which it exercises in particular (xiv. 1-2) *by holding the Jews in exile;* and it is *the city and empire of Babylon* whose overthrow is announced in it. By analogy it will have been written during the period of the Babylonian supremacy. Hence it is arbitrary to suppose (as has been done) that Babylon may have been mentioned by Isaiah as the "representative" of Assyria : not only does Babylon appear here as the sole and supreme seat of the world-empire ; but Babylon, in Isaias's day, so far from being the representative of Assyria, was its antagonist, ever struggling to win independence (pp. 45, ; 96). Moreover the two empires of Assyria and Babylon are

---

[1] Isaiah never announces the fall of the Assyrian Empire generally, or the destruction of its capital Nineveh (which happened, p. 134, about a century after his time), but only, like Micah (p. 42), Judah's immunity from future oppression by it. The announcement of the final end of the Assyrian power was reserved for the subsequent prophets, Nahum and Zephaniah

quite distinct in the Old Testament : the *rôle* which they play in history is very different ; and they are never confused—still less, "identified"—by the prophets. The embassy of Mero-dach-Baladan, the temporary "king" of Babylon, to Hezekiah, afforded Isaiah a substantial motive for announcing (xxxix. 6) a future *exile* to Babylon : it could supply no motive for such a promise of a subsequent *return* from exile, as these chapters contain. The circumstances of the exile—while the Jews were yet in bondage and the power of Babylon seemed still unshaken —constitute a suitable and sufficient occasion for the present prophecy, an occasion of exactly the nature which the analogy of prophecy demands : on the other hand, the circumstances of Isaiah's age supply no such occasion. We have all along been guided by internal evidence in assigning the prophecies of Isaiah to the dates with which, severally, they seem best to accord ; and we shall scarcely be misled if we follow the same guidance here. It only remains to add (for the purpose of obviating misconception[1]) that in assigning the prophecy to a date during the exile, we do not divest it of its *predictive* character : it becomes no "vaticinium ex eventu;" the language of chap. xiii. makes it certain that it was written *prior* to the actual capture of Babylon by the Medes in 538. Written some few years before this event,[2] it would be as fully and truly pre-dictive as were Isaiah's prophecies of the failure of Sennacherib (chap. xxix.–xxxii.), which indeed, as we have seen, preceded the event by not more than a single year.

The time is approaching for Babylon to fall ; and the prophet imagines poetically the command to be given for a signal to be raised aloft, that the foes of Babylon, in all quarters,

[1] Which has led astray even Dean Plumptre in his Commentary on this prophecy. The question at issue is not the possibility or impossibility of prediction (which must be determined by the testimony of accredited history), but whether or not the historical situation during Isaiah's lifetime was such as to explain the tenor of the present prophecy. Undoubtedly Babylon came within Isaiah's "historical horizon ;" but in order to vindicate Isaiah's authorship, it must be shown that it came within it in a manner suited to form the occasion for *this particular prophecy*, viz., as the power which held the Jews in the thraldom of *exile*, and was destined ere long to be destroyed. It is evident that this was not the position which Babylon occupied in Isaiah's day.

[2] As the prophecy contains no allusion to Cyrus or the Persians, it is probable that it was written in fact before 549 (see p. 136).

may see it, and advance to the attack. Jehovah's warriors, consecrated (Mic. iii. 5 ; Jer. vi. 4) for battle, are ready : and already among the mountains—those, namely, which skirted Babylonia on the north-east—he hears in spirit the thronging hosts assemble. The judgment itself is first depicted under the form of a " Day of Jehovah " (*v.* 6-10) : " Howl ye : for the day of Jehovah is near ; as destruction from the Almighty shall it come." The idea of the " Day" has occurred before (chap. ii. 12 ff. ; p. 27 f.) : but it is worked out here with different imagery, which recalls rather Zeph. i. 14-18 or Joel ii. 1-2, 10. The prophet proceeds to describe more particularly the capture of the city : the fewness of the survivors (*v.* 12 : " I will make a man more rare than fine gold, even a man than the pure gold of Ophir "), the hurried flight of the multitudes, who for purposes of commerce (Ezek. xvii. 4 ; cf. Jer. l. 16 ; li. 9) had made Babylon their home (*v.* 14), the carnage and rapine of which its streets will then become the scene (*v.* 16). Next, he specifies the captors, a people who know no pity, and who will be pacified by no bribe (*v.* 17 [1] f.),—the Medes, whose home was in the mountains (cf. *v.* 4) north-east of Babylonia, who were consolidated and organized by their ruler Cyaxares (633-593 B.C.), and who afterwards, amalgamating with the Persians under Cyrus, captured Babylon in 538. And thus " Babylon, the glory of kingdoms, the proud ornament of Chaldea, shall be as when God overthrew Sodom and Gomorrah." The busy and populous city " shall never be inhabited, neither shall it be dwelt in from generation to generation : " its castles and palaces of luxury will become the resort of wolves and jackals. And why is all this? The prophet supplies the answer (xiv. 1-2), *Because the time has come for Israel to be released from exile :* " For Jehovah will have compassion upon Jacob, *and will again choose Israel,* and settle them in their own land : " they will return to Palestine, under such changed conditions that foreigners will now claim eagerly the privilege of incorporation in their community, and the nations will press forward to offer them an honourable escort upon their journey.

Here the prophet provides Israel with an Ode of triumph, which he imagines it to sing in the day of its deliverance. This ode, if it is to be admired as it deserves, must be read as a whole : its perfection as a work of art, its picturesque

---

[1] *Lit.,* Behold, *I am stirring up,* of the imminent future, as xvii. 1, &c.

imagery, the delicate and subtle vein of irony by which it is penetrated—it is called a " taunt-song," *v.* 4—will not endure partial quotation or paraphrase. The line of thought is as follows. In the first strophe (*v.* 4–8), the prophet declares exultingly how at length the tyrant is stilled,[1] the earth is at peace ; only the sound of rejoicing is heard. In the second (*v.* 9–11), he accompanies in thought the Shade of the King of Babylon as it journeys to the Underworld, and imagines the ironical greeting which there meets it from the lips of the other kings—still, as on earth, supposed to be invested with the panoply of state.[2] The third strophe (*v.* 12–15) depicts the abasement of the Babylonian monarch in its full magnitude : he who would have joined the ranks of the gods, is cast down to the inmost recesses of the pit.[3] In the fourth and last strophe (*v.* 16–20), the prophet's thought passes to the battle-field—from the feeble Shade, to the unburied, dishonoured corpse · the passers-by express their amazement at the contrast which its fate presents to that of other kings after their death : it is excluded from the royal burial-place, flung aside as a worthless bough, hidden amongst the bodies of slain common soldiers.[4] The prophet concludes with an epilogue, spoken in his own person, and reasserting emphatically the final and irretrievable ruin of the great city (*v.* 21–23).[5]

The best commentary on this prophecy is Jeremiah's long and impassioned invective against Babylon (l. 1—li. 58), which must belong quite to the close of that prophet's life, and which is written from the same standpoint. By Jeremiah the judgment upon Babylon is developed in greater detail; but both prophecies view the impending future similarly, both contemplate with manifest gratification (chap. xiii. 15–22; xiv. 21) the fall of the oppressing city, both name the Medes as its captors, and both expect with equal confidence the approaching release of the Jews. The thoughts of the two verses xiv. 1, 2 recur often in chaps. xl.–lxvi. The introduction into a prophecy of a lyrical ode we have seen recently exemplified in chaps. xxiv.–xxvii. : the ode in chap. xiv. differs, however, widely in character from those in these chapters, for while the latter are hymns of thanksgiving to God, this is secular in character—an ode of worldly triumph sung by Israel over the fall of its oppressor.

Chap. xxxiv.–v., on Edom. Edom, Israel's "brother," appears to have been an older nation than Israel, and attained earlier than Israel the stage of settled government (Gen. xxxvi. 31) : but it was outstripped by the younger nation ; and great jealousy and rivalry prevailed between them. By David, Edom was forced to own the suzerainty of Judah (2 Sam. viii. 13, R.V. *marg.* 14), and this relation continued till, under Jehoram, it successfully revolted (2 Kings viii. 20-22). Amaziah, the predecessor of Uzziah, inflicted upon Edom a severe defeat (*ib.* xiv. 7), though we do not know the circumstances which led to it. Allusions in the prophets illustrate the feeling which subsisted between the two nations. Amos (i. 6) charges Edom with receiving as slaves Jewish captives, who had been taken by the Philistines of Gaza ; and in *v.* 11 speaks bitterly of the implacable animosity cherished by Edom against his "brother." According to 2 Chron. xxviii. 17, the Edomites in the reign of Ahaz "smote Judah and carried away captives"; and when Rezin expelled the Jews from the port of Elath, it was at once occupied by Edomite settlers (p. 30). But the day of Edom's triumph was when Jerusalem was entered by the Chaldeans in 588 : then their exultation knew no bounds (Obad. 10–16 ; Ezek. xxxv. 10-15) ; then, as a Psalmist, writing long after, has not forgotten, they eagerly assisted at the demolition of the walls :

"Remember, Jehovah, against the children of Edom the day of Jerusalem ·
Who said, Rase it, rase it, even to the foundation therein" (Ps. cxxxvii. 7).

Jeremiah (xlix. 7–22), and the Book of Lamentations (iv. 21 f.),

as well as the passages just referred to, testify how keenly this
outbreak of malicious delight on the part of Edom was resented
by the Jews; and the strong vein of feeling which pervades chap.
xxxiv. makes it probable that this outbreak was the historical
occasion of the prophecy.   Isaiah, it will be recollected,
addresses Edom (xxi. 11 f.) in a very different strain : if the
"watchman's" answer be no encouraging one, it is at least
uttered in tones of commiseration and sympathy, as far as
possible removed from the glow of passion which animates the
present prophecy.[1]   Under what circumstances the prophecy
was fulfilled we do not know.   In, and after, the captivity, the
Edomites encroached upon the territory of Judah ; and ultimately an Edomite family, the most famous name of which
was that of Herod the Great, acquired rule over Judæa.
Malachi, however (*c.* 400 B.C.), describes Edom Proper as already
desolate (i. 3).   A century later it appears in the possession of
the Nabatæans, an Arabian tribe (called Nebaioth in the Old
Testament, Gen. xxv. 13), though how they secured it is not
known.   There this thriving commercial nation maintained itself
for many centuries, until, after the Mohammedan conquest,
in the seventh century, A.D., the cities of Edom fell to ruin, and
the country became a desert.   It is to be observed that the
prophecy opens with an announcement of judgment against
"*all* the nations" (*v.* 2 ; comp. Jer. xxv. 31–33), though Edom
is speedily singled out as the one whose fate would be viewed
with the greatest interest by the Jews.

Universal nature is summoned to hear the prophet's declaration : for a judgment is imminent which will embrace all
nations ; and slaughter and carnage will shortly encircle the
entire earth (*v.* 1–4).   Specially upon Edom will the Divine
sword descend ; for Jehovah is preparing "a great sacrifice" in
Bozrah, and all classes of Edom, chiefs and common people[2]
indiscriminately, will be struck down into the slaughtering
trough.   "For unto Jehovah belongeth a day of vengeance, and
a year of recompence for the quarrel[3] of Zion."   The inhabitants being all slain, desolation will henceforth be the fate of

---

[1] Observe also that in xi. 14 it is the re-subjugation of Edom, not its
destruction, which Isaiah expects from the future.

[2] Figured by the wild oxen, &c., of *v.* 7 and the smaller cattle of *v.* 6.

[3] Compare the charges brought against Edom in Ezek. xxxv. (where also

Edom; its castles and fortresses will become the resort of desert creatures, which will haunt its ruins for ever.

Far different will be the lot of the ransomed Jews. For them the wilderness and the parched land will rejoice, and the desert burst forth into a brilliant and abundant bloom. Let the timid, therefore, take courage, and the weak feel strong : a Divine Avenger is at hand to save them. Then human infirmities will cease to vex, and nature will co-operate spontaneously in the relief of human needs. "For waters shall break out in the wilderness, and streams in the desert," yielding grateful refreshment to the returning exiles : the mirage, or "phantom-lake," which so often deludes the caravans, shall become a reality, and the thirsty land shall send forth springs of water. More than this, the prophet imagines in the desert a raised way leading to Zion : only those who are worthy will be admitted upon it ; but it will be so broad and plain that even the simplest will not lose their track upon it, so elevated and well-protected that no dangerous beast will be able to climb up and molest the pilgrims journeying along it. And thus "the freed ones of Jehovah shall return, and come with singing unto Zion ; and everlasting joy shall be upon their heads : they shall overtake gladness and joy, and sorrow and sighing shall flee away." Many of the figures in this beautiful prophecy of Israel's restoration recur in the course of chaps. xl.–lxvi.—*v.* 10, for instance, is repeated *verbatim* in li. 11 : here it forms a finely-conceived contrast to the scene of carnage, desolation, and abandonment anticipated in chap. xxxiv. for Edom.

CHAPTER III.

THE GREAT PROPHECY OF ISRAEL'S RESTORATION.

(Chapters xl.-lxvi.)

Circumstances which led to the Babylonian captivity— Condition and prospects of the Jews during the exile—Standpoint of the author of chaps.
xl.-lxvi., and exposition of his argument.

IN passing from chaps. xxxvi.-xxxix. to chap. xl. we find ourselves introduced into a new world. The persons whom the
prophet addresses, the people amongst whom he lives and
moves, whose feelings he pourtrays, whose doubts he dispels,
whose faith he confirms, are not the inhabitants of Jerusalem
under Ahaz, or Hezekiah, or Manasseh, but the *Jewish exiles in
Babylonia.* Jerusalem and the Temple are in ruins (lxiv. 10), and
have been so for long (lviii. 12 ; lxi. 4—"the old waste places") :
the proud and imposing Babylonian Empire is to all appearance
as secure as ever ; the exiles are in despair or indifferent ; they
think that God has forgotten them, and have ceased to expect,
or desire, their release (xl. 27 ; xlix. 14, 24). To arouse the
indifferent, to reassure the wavering, to expostulate with the
doubting, to announce with triumphant confidence the certainty
of the approaching restoration, is the aim of the great prophecy
which now occupies the last twenty-seven chapters of the Book
of Isaiah. The arguments which combine with singular cogency
to show that it is not the work of Isaiah himself will be stated
in Chap. V. : the scope and meaning of the prophecy are of
greater importance than the question of its authorship, and claim
therefore our first consideration.

In order to understand the prophecy, it will be necessary to

sketch in outline the course of history, in so far as it affected
Judah, since the period of Isaiah's lifetime. Sennacherib was
succeeded in 681 by Esarhaddon ; Esarhaddon by Asshurbanipal in 668, under whose reign of forty-three years the literature
and art of ancient Assyria reached their greatest perfection. But
after the death of Asshurbanipal in 626, Assyria rapidly declined : in 625 the great rival of Nineveh, Babylon, through the
enterprise of Nabopolassar, emerged finally from dependence ;
and in or about 607 [1] Nabopolassar, allying with the Medes
under Cyaxares (p. 128), laid the proud capital of Sargon and
Sennacherib in ruins. The supremacy exercised hitherto by
Assyria now passed to Babylon, and was retained by it till 538.
Nabopolassar was succeeded by Nebuchadnezzar (606–561), who
greatly strengthened and extended the Babylonian Empire, and
beautified and largely rebuilt his capital, Babylon. In the
history of Judah, the great turning point was *Jehoiakim's fourth
year*, 604 B.C., the year in which Nebuchadnezzar won his
decisive victory over Egypt at Carchemish, on the upper course
of the Euphrates (Jer. xlvi. 2). The prophet Jeremiah at once
perceived the political significance of this victory ; and comes
forward to advise his countrymen on the course to be adopted
by them. He greets the conqueror with an ode of triumph
(chap. xlvi.), he promises him further victories ; he forms the
conception of a great plan or purpose being enacted in history ;
Nebuchadnezzar is Jehovah's "servant," into whose hand all
countries will fall for seventy years (chap. xxv.), and the safety
of Judah is to be sought in recognizing this, and in submitting
to his dominion accordingly. Jeremiah here occupies the same
position as political adviser of his nation, which Isaiah assumed
a century before : his advice differs from that of Isaiah, simply
because circumstances had changed, and the political situation
was different. But Egypt had not lost its old power of fascina-
tion for Judah : Jeremiah's warnings were ineffectual ; and after
submitting to the Chaldeans for three years, Jehoiakim rebelled.
The Jews went into exile in two detachments : the flower of the
nation (including, amongst others, the prophet Ezekiel), under
Jehoiakim's son, Jehoiachin (2 Kings xxiv. 12–16 ; Jer. xxiv. 1)
in 599 ; the rest, after the revolt of Zedekiah, in 588, when the
city was taken, the Temple burnt, and its vessels carried away
to Babylon (2 Kings xxv.).

On this date, see Schrader, pp. 358–61.

The exiles must have formed a considerable community in Babylonia. The texts which speak of the numbers of those carried
into captivity (2 Kings xxiv. 14-16 ; Jer. lii. 28-30) are indeed
imperfect, and apparently also in some disorder [1] ; but that they
formed a numerous body is evident from the fact that upwards
of forty-two thousand males, irrespective of women and dependents, returned with Zerubbabel (Ezra ii. 2, 64 f.), and
many, as we know, remained behind. In a community as large
as this the life and society of Judah would in great measure be
perpetuated ; some kind of organization would be needed ; and
the moral and religious condition of the exiles would be substantially what it had been in the closing years of the monarchy.
Thus Ezekiel refers to the " elders " in exile with him as still
forming a distinct class (viii. 1 ; xiv. 1 ; xx. 1), and alludes
to the idolatrous tendencies still prevalent in their midst
(xx. 38, 39). At first the exiles were unsettled by prophets,
who raised their hopes by delusive promises of a speedy
return to Palestine : Jeremiah shortly after 599 addresses to
them a letter (chap. xxix.), in which he assures them that the
seventy years of Babylonian dominion must expire before their
hopes can be realized, and exhorts them to rest satisfied meanwhile with their condition, to " build houses and dwell in them,
and plant gardens, and eat the fruit of them," in the land of
their captivity. Circumstances left the exiles no option but to
follow the advice of Jeremiah (cf. Ezek. viii. 1 ; xxxiii. 30,
" houses ") ; and many, in consequence, grew so attached to their
new home, that when, sixty years afterwards, permission was
granted to leave it, they did not care to avail themselves of it.

Nebuchadnezzar was succeeded in 561 by his son Evil-Merodach, who " lifted up the head " of Jehoiachin, king of Judah,
releasing him from the prison in which he had for thirty-seven
years been confined, and granting him a continual allowance
from the royal table. After a reign of two years, Evil-Merodach
was followed on the throne by Neriglissar (559-555), and Neriglissar by Nabo-nahid (555-538). Meanwhile, Cyrus, heir of a
branch of the royal house of Persia, which had established itself
in Elam or Susiana (on the west of Persia proper), had already
begun to give proof of those abilities as a conqueror, and com-

had passed away, would have absorbed even the nations of Europe, had not Athenian patriotism, at Marathon and Salamis, rolled back the threatening tide. Uniting and organizing the different tribes of Persian origin, Cyrus overthrew the Median empire of Astyages, Cyaxares' (p. 128) successor, in 549;[1] the Medes themselves amalgamated rapidly with their Persian conquerors—they were both of Aryan origin—and at the head of the combined armies of both nations Cyrus advanced to further conquests. One of his first successes was obtained against Crœsus, the wealthy and powerful king of Lydia, in Asia Minor, whose capital city, Sardis, he took (Herod. i. 73–84). Leaving his general Harpagus to complete the subjugation of Asia Minor (including the Greek cities on the west coast), Cyrus next (Herod. i. 177) reduced one after another the tribes of Upper (or Inner) Asia, and ultimately prepared to attack Babylon. His own inscription narrates the result.[2] Nabo-nahid had neglected the worship of the gods of Babylon, especially of Merodach,[3] who accordingly were displeased with him, and though, when danger threatened, he had images of them brought in solemn state to Babylon, they refused to be conciliated, and transferred their favour to the invader. Cyrus attributes his success to the aid of Merodach. "The gods dwelling within them left their shrines in anger, when he (Nabo-nahid) brought them into Babylon. *Merodach . . .* appointed a king to guide aright in the heart what his hand upholds; *Cyrus, king of Elam, he proclaimed by name for the sovereignty. . . .* To his city of Babylon he summoned his march, and he bade him take the road to Babylon ; like a friend and a comrade, he went at his side. The weapons of his vast army, whose number, like the waters of a river, could not be known, he marshalled at his side. Without fighting or battle he caused him to enter into Babylon ; his city of Babylon feared ; in a place difficult of access, Nabo-nahid, the king who worshipped him not, he gave into his hand." After this Cyrus relates how he proceeded to honour the gods of Babylon, by restoring their shrines, and to crave

---

[1] The Inscription of Nabo-nahid, discovered in 1879, fixes the defeat of Astyages to Nabo-nahid's sixth year. See Sayce's "Fresh Light," &c., p. 168. Astyages was abandoned by his soldiers, who deserted *en masse* to Cyrus. [2] *Ibid.* pp. 172–4.

[3] The patron-god of the city of Babylon. See Sayce's "Hibbert Lectures," 1887, pp. 85–88, 91, 92, 96–98, 107 f.

their good-will : " In the goodness of their hearts may all the gods whom I have brought into their strong places *daily inter-cede before Bel and Nebo* that they may grant me length of days : may they bless my projects with prosperity, and may they say to *Merodach my lord* that Cyrus the king, thy worshipper, and Cambyses his son (deserve his favour)." Babylon fell in 538.

The precise moment at which the prophecy opens cannot be determined ; but it must, in any case, have been prior to 538, and, as xli. 25 implies a date subsequent to the union of the Medes with the Persians in 549 (p. 139 note), it will be limited to the interval between these years, during which Cyrus was pursuing his career of conquest in the north and north-west of Asia. The prophet's eye marks him in the distance as the coming deliverer of his nation : he stimulates the flagging courage of his people by pointing to his successes, and declares that he is God's appointed agent both for the overthrow of the Babylonian Empire, and for the restoration of the chosen people to Palestine.

The prophecy may be divided, for convenience, into three parts of nine chapters each. In the first of these parts, chaps. xl.–xlviii., the prophet's aim is to demonstrate *the certainty of the coming release,* which no opposition, or other contingencies, will avail to hinder. In the course of the argument, Israel and the heathen are represented dramatically as engaged in contro-versy ; Jehovah and the gods of the heathen are contrasted with one another, and the claims of each, as judged by the tribunal of reason, are compared.

The theme of the whole prophecy is stated in the opening verse : "Comfort ye, comfort ye, my people, saith your God." It is the volume of Israel's consolation and encouragement which here begins. The words are a reversal of the sad reality which had been expressed by the poet of the Lamentations forty years previously (i. 2, 9, 17) : "There is none to comfort her." Soon the prophet hears in imagination the voice of one calling—

> " In the wilderness clear ye Jehovah's way ;
> Make plain in the desert a highway for our God."

Let a way be prepared through the wilderness for the triumphal progress of Israel's King : let the mountains and valleys be made plain before Him : a revelation of His glory is to be made ; and all flesh shall see it together (xl. 3–5). A second

voice falls upon the prophet's ear, with the command, " Cry."
What is he to cry?   The answer expresses the fundamental
thought, which the following chapters expand : hence it is
introduced with peculiar solemnity :—

> " All flesh is grass ;
> And all the goodliness thereof is as the flower of the field.
> The grass withereth, the flower fadeth,
> If the breath of Jehovah [1] hath blown upon it :
> Surely the people is grass.
> The grass withereth, the flower fadeth ;
> But the word of our God shall stand for ever."

The words are of universal import : but the connection shows
the sense in which they are here used by the prophet. *Israel's
oppressors are mortal : the promise of Jehovah*—such a promise,
viz., as that contained in *v.* 4, 5—*remains sure.*   In a transport
of joy, the prophet forthwith bids ideal messengers bear the
glad news to Zion : Jehovah returns thither as a conqueror,
leading before Him His prize of war, the "reward" of His
battles—the recovered nation itself. Nor is the Deliverer strong
only ; He displays also towards His people the tender and dis-
criminating regard of a shepherd (*v.* 9–11).   In the next paragraph the prophet demonstrates at length the *power* of Israel's
Divine Deliverer : no finite spirit can be compared with Him
(*v.* 12–17) ; no human conception can express Him (*v.* 18–26) ;
He is incomparable and unique.   The argument in•this fine
passage is drawn principally from the great works of nature, in
contrast to the Being whose omnipotence and wisdom they
reflect.   The prophet points ironically to the idol-gods, manufactured as the means of their devotees, rich or poor, may
permit.   In the emphasis laid upon the insignificance of nations
and their rulers (*v.* 15, 23, 24), as well as in the sarcastic notice
of the idols, there is a side-reference to the imperial power and
gods of Babylon, which it is the prophet's aim to show cannot
thwart the Divine purpose for Israel's restoration,   The practical conclusion follows, *v.* 27–31. Israel had suffered in exile so
long that there were many who thought that their case had
escaped God's eye, and that their "judgment " (*i.e.,* their cause)
had passed beyond His notice : the prophet replies, Jehovah
is no local, limited God, as you imagine ; His power embraces
Babylon not less than Palestine ; His strength is not exhausted ;

[1] See Hos. xiii. 15.

"there is no searching of His understanding"—some inscrutable purpose must guide Him in delaying, if He do delay, the redemption of His people ; only continue to trust !

Here the prophet imagines a judgment scene. The nations are invited to come forward and plead their case with Jehovah. The question is, *Who has stirred up*[1] *the great conqueror, Cyrus ? Who has led him upon his career of victory ?* (xli. 2–3).[2] Only one answer is possible—Jehovah, the Creator of history, who preceded the generations of the past, and will abide through the generations of the future (*v.* 4). And with exquisite and well-timed irony, the prophet pauses to depict the nations of the earth, alarmed at the victories of Cyrus, engaged anxiously in the manufacture of fresh idols for the purpose of arresting his further advance ! (*v.* 5–7).

A digression follows (*v.* 8–20), designed for the encouragement of Israel. "But thou, Israel, my servant, Jacob whom I have chosen, the seed of Abraham who loved Me,—fear not, is the nations ; be not dismayed, for I am with thee : thou shalt conquer and overcome those who would oppose thee ;" and the thought of the caravans returning homewards through the thirsty desert suggests to the prophet an effective Image symbolizing the Divine care which will attend them : the ground at their side bursts into waterpools, and noble trees cast their shade about them !

The judgment scene, interrupted after *v.* 4, is now resumed. The second proof of Jehovah's godhead is adduced : *He alone knows the future.* The heathen gods are addressed : "Let us hear your arguments (*v.* 21) : can you either refer us to former predictions, which have been (or are now being) fulfilled, or can you announce to us things still future? (*v.* 22–23*a*)? Can you do anything whatever? can you give any proof at all of your existence?" (*v.* 23*b*).[3] They are silent ; and judgment accordingly goes against them by default (*v.* 24). "It is I, then,

---

[1] Not "raised up:" the sense is "*impelled into activity.*"

[2] *V.* 2, "from the east:" Cyrus's home, Susiania, being to the east of Babylonia. "From the north," in *v.* 25, alludes to the Medes, who united with the Persians under Cyrus (p. 136), and whose home was to the north or -north-east of Babylonia. "In righteousness"—Cyrus's career being a furtherance of God's righteous purpose for the government of the world (so xlv. 13).

[3] With the proverbial phrase here used, comp. Zeph. i. 12 ; Jer. x. 5.

who have 'stirred up' this conqueror ; and promised him his successes : but of the devotees, or prophets, of the false gods, if I look among them, there is not one who can give answer, or advise as to the future !" And so the idolaters, as before (*v.* 24) the idols, are dismissed as unworthy of serious attention (*v.* 25–29).

Jehovah's godhead having been thus demonstrated from nature (chap. xl.), and from the inability of the idol-worshippers to explain either the appearance of Cyrus or the phænomena of prediction (chap. xli.), the prophecy advances to a new stage. Jehovah's Servant appears again under a new aspect, and with new functions—no longer the historic nation of Israel (as in xli. 8 f.), but an *ideal figure*, reproducing in their perfection the best and truest attributes of the historic nation, and invested by the prophet with an august and world-wide mission. The significance of this remarkable creation of the prophet's inspired imagination will be considered subsequently (Chap. IV.) : here it will be sufficient to notice the general scope of the mission entrusted to him. It is twofold: *to teach the world true religion* (" to set judgment [1] in the earth," *v.* 4, to be " a light of the Gentiles," *v.* 6), and *to be the instrument of Israel's restoration* (to be " a covenant of the people," *v.* 6). The far-reaching prevision of the prophet deserves notice. Looking out into the future he associates the restoration of Israel with the extension of Israel's religion to the Gentiles. The epithets in *v.* 5 are also significant ; not only do they add solemnity to the announcement of the Servant's work in *v.* 6, but they imply that that work is part of God's plan as the creator and preserver of the human race. " Behold," the prophet exclaims (*v.* 9) in conclusion, "the former things are come to pass, and new things do I declare ; before they spring forth I tell you of them "—former prophecies[2] are fulfilled ; let this be the guarantee

---

[1] Or "right," *i.e.,* religion, viewed as an ordering of life : so Jer. v. 4.

[2] What the prophet here and xlviii. 3 means by the expression, "the former things," is not quite certain. His argument would be best satisfied by the supposition that he has in view prophecies relating to Cyrus's *first* appearance, and earliest successes, with which he contrasts the fresh announcements now made by himself relating to his *further* conquests, and the release of the Jews. xli. 2 f. appears to show that, as he writes, Cyrus is well advanced on his career of victory ; *what is still in the future* is his conquest of Babylon (xlv. 1–3).

to you that my present announcement will be fulfilled likewise. The prospect evokes from him a short lyric ode of thanksgiving (*v.* 10–12) ; after which he depicts, in splendid anthropomorphic imagery, Jehovah's approaching manifestation for the deliverance of His people, and the discomfiture of those (primarily the Babylonians) who trust to graven images to save them (*v.* 13–17).[1]

But some are blind and deaf ; Jehovah's " servant " (Israel, as xli. 8) has fallen short of the ideal which the titles bestowed upon it implied : it has failed to profit by the experience through which it has passed (*v.* 18–20). It was Jehovah's pleasure, for the sake of His righteousness, to "make instruction great and glorious"—to give Israel a succession of inspired teachers, from whom they might learn noble truths : yet so little did they heed them, that they are now "a people robbed and spoiled," held fast in bitter bondage. How were they reduced to this deplorable condition, and who placed them in it ? Was it not He against whom they sinned ? "Therefore He poured upon him in fury His anger, and the violence of war, and it set him on fire round about, but he took no notice, and kindled upon him, but he would not lay it to heart "[2] (*v.* 21–25). But now, Jehovah's wrath is for the time satisfied : "Fear not, O Israel ; thou shalt be free ; Egypt, Ethiopia and Seba, shall take thy place as Cyrus's vassals : from all quarters thy exiles shall return !" (xliii. 1–7).[3]

Another judgment scene is next imagined. "Let Israel appear on the one side, the host of heathen nations on the other." The question is the same as before (xli. 21–3) : Can the heathen offer now predictions such as these? or can they point to past events correctly foretold (the "former things")? If so, let them bring their witnesses, that they may be justified, and have the truth of their statements attested. Again, judgment goes by default ; and Jehovah appeals to *His* witnesses, viz., His servant Israel, which has had abundant proof of His predictive power

---

[1] With *v.* 15 f. cf. xl. 4 ; xli. 18. The "man of (many) wars," cf. Exod. xv. 3.

[2] Compare, especially, Lam. ii. 1–6 ; also Jer. x. 25 ; Ps. lxxix. 6–7.

[3] *V.* 3–4 the prophet poetically imagines that, on account of the favour with which Israel is regarded by Jehovah, it will be ransomed by other nations : compare, for the thought, Ezek. xxix. 18 f. Egypt was actually conquered by Cambyses, Cyrus's successor. By *Seba* (Ps. lxxii. 10) is meant Meroe, in Ethiopia.

(*v.* 8–13). "For *your* sake, the decree is gone forth ; and the might of Chaldea shall fall. Think no more of the past (*v.* 18) · look to the future, the glorious future, which is now promised to you" (*v.* 19–21). But this promise is not based upon anything that *Israel* has done : Israel's fealty has ever been imperfeet (cf. xlviii. 8) : even in exile, when released from the service of sacrifice, the only requital offered by it for this exemption has been to make God "serve" with its sins, and to "weary" Him with its iniquities. It is Jehovah, then, who alone, and for His own sake (xlviii. 11), blotteth out Israel's transgressions, and promises graciously to remember them no more. Has Israel aught to offer in its defence? (*v.* 26) can it urge any merit of its own? Nay, its whole history shows the stains of sin : its "first father" (Abraham, or Jacob) sinned ; its representatives, the prophets and priests, have transgressed against Jehovah. "So I profaned holy princes, and delivered up Jacob to the ban, and Israel to reproaches."[1] But *now* (xliv. 1) all this is past : God's pardon is freely granted ; and in acknowledgment of His ancient choice, He bestows anew upon His people the lavish tokens of His favour. A glorious and blessed future shall dawn upon it (*v.* 3) : a future in which the nations will press forward to dedicate themselves to Jehovah, and to claim the honour of membership in His people (*v.* 5).[2]

Here a fresh stage in the prophecy begins, extending to the end of chap. xlv. Again the prophet brings forth the evidence of Jehovah's godhead ; and the promises of deliverance given already are made more definite. Who, as Jehovah, can point to past predictions fulfilled ? Who, as He, can announce the future now ? It is the same double question that was asked before in the judgment scene, xli. 22 : and it is followed by the same appeal to the witness of Israel, as in xliii. 10–12. "Fear ye not," then, "neither be afraid," when ye see one nation after

---

[1] The allusion is, of course, to the destruction of Jerusalem (see Jer. lii. 24), and the context requires the past tense (as xlii. 25 ; xlvii. 6). So Sept., Vulg., Pesh. The Hebrew text is pointed wrongly in a future sense : there is a similar error in lxiii. 3, 6. "Holy princes" is an expression used—at least at a later time—of the chief priests, in 1 Chron. xxiv. 5.

[2] *V.* 5 *end, i.e.,* a name into which "Israel" enters —*e.g.,* "son of Israel"—will be regarded as the most honourable title that a man can bear.

another succumbing before Cyrus : " Have I not declared unto thee of old, and showed it ? " Is not the fall of the Babylonian power what Jeremiah long since gave you reason to expect (xxv. 12 ; xxix. 10) ? Or do you think that the idol-gods of Babylon, imposing as their temples and the ceremonial of their worship are, will avail to save their city? And the prophet points his question by proceeding at once to draw a satirical picture (*v.* 9–20) of the manner in which idols were manufactured in antiquity—the laboriousness of the work, the large number of human agents who co-operated in it, the strange blindness which hid from the worshipper the logical contradiction in which he was implicated. " He burneth part thereof in the fire : with part thereof he eateth flesh ; he roasteth roast, and is satisfied : yea, he warmeth himself, and saith, Aha, I am warm, I have seen the fire : and the remainder of it he maketh into a god, into his image : he falleth down unto it and worshippeth, and prayeth unto it, and saith, Rescue me, for thou art my god." " Remember these things, O Jacob " — take to heart the nature of idolatry : can idols made in this fashion impede thy freedom? Thou, on the contrary, art My " servant," nor canst thou, as thou vainly complainest (xl. 27 ; xlix. 14) be forgotten of Me. The only impediment to thy release has been removed by God's free grace : " I have blotted out, as a thick cloud, thy transgressions, and, as a cloud, thy sins " (cf. xliii. 25) : let the earth rejoice, then, for Israel is now free ; and in a majestic series of verses, the prophet describes the commission of Cyrus, culminating in the permission to be given by him for the rebuilding of the Temple (*v.* 24–28), and supported by the renewed assurance (xlv. 1–7) that he will triumphantly enter Babylon, and take possession of its treasures : [1] for Israel's sake he has been called and commissioned, even though he " knew not " God, and had no claim to be deemed worthy of such honour. [2] And the final aim of the work thus confided to Cyrus, it is added, is to produce through the world a general recognition that Jehovah is the true God—the absolute author of light and darkness, of welfare and calamity, [3] the maker

---

[1] " Treasures of darkness," &c., *i.e.*, the wealth stored in concealment in Babylon. Cf. Jer. l. 37 ; li. 13 ("abundant in treasures ").

[2] *V.* 4, " surnamed," or " titled " (as xliv. 5), *i.e.*, with such titles as

of all things. The thought of the blessings thus to be secured for
Israel suggests to the prophet one of the lyric interludes such
as he loves (xlii. 10–12 ; xliv. 23 ; xlix. 13) ; he poetically invites
heaven and earth to co-operate in the work, and by an expressive figure pictures the earth as blooming with the fruits of
righteousness and peace (*v.* 8). Turning aside for a moment to
rebuke the want of faith on the part of those who murmured at
the tardy advent of the deliverance, and questioned the Divine
power (*v.* 9–11), he reiterates the assurance respecting Cyrus's
future policy : It is I, who made the earth and created man upon
it, who have also " stirred up " Cyrus " in righteousness " (p. 139),
and will make plain all his ways : *he* shall build My city, and
let Mine exiles go free, not for price, and not for reward, saith
Jehovah of hosts ! He pauses, to express in one long verse the
unspeakable honour awaiting his people in the future, when the
most illustrious nations of antiquity will come over to Israel,
surrendering themselves and their wealth to its service, and confessing with adoration the God who is in its midst. And so the
paragraph ends, with a comparison of the alarm and confusion
which will be the fate of the idolaters, who now hold Israel enthralled, with the abiding salvation which Israel will enjoy
(*v.* 16 f.).

The prophet does not, however, rest here. He justifies anew
the promises which he has uttered ; and takes a still more comprehensive and penetrating glance into the future. He appeals
again to the certainty of Jehovah's predictions, emphasizing,
however, two fresh features in connection with them, *viz.*, that
(unlike the generality of heathen oracles) they were uttered
openly and in the light of day, and that He who gave them had
no intention of disappointing or misleading his worshippers. As
there was no uncertainty in their source, no ambiguity or indis-
tinctness as to their intention, their fulfilment might be confidently expected (*v.* 18–19). On the other hand, as before, no
proof is forthcoming of the divinity of the idols (*v.* 20–21). But
Jehovah is a *Saviour;* and boldly generalizing this truth, the
prophet apostrophizes the furthest quarters of the earth—

"Look unto Me, and be ye saved, all the ends of the earth :
For I am God, and there is none else—"

"evil " here. The word is the same as in xxxi. 2 ; for the thought, comp.
Amos iii. 6.

and declares forthwith, with peculiar solemnity, His irrevocable promise that in due time the whole world shall accept His sovereignty : " By Myself have I sworn, the word is gone forth from My mouth in righteousness, and shall not return, that unto Me every knee shall bow, every tongue shall swear." Unreservedly will those who thus confess Jehovah own that He is the source of their righteousness and strength; and the Israel of God, augmented now by those gathered in from the Gentiles, will glory in the consciousness of the state of grace in which they stand before Him. And so, in the prophet's vision of the future, the deliverance of Israel culminates in the salvation of the world at large.

The favourable light in which the prophet in this section views Cyrus is noticeable. The unselfish and generous character of the Persian king is indeed recognized by Greek writers ;[1] and is in harmony with the freedom from motives of worldly interest or gain (such as would generally operate with an Eastern conqueror), with which he is here described (xlv. 13) as granting the return of the Jews. From the Inscription referred to above (p. 136),[2] it would seem to follow, however, that this was no favour bestowed specially upon them, but was part of Cyrus's general policy in dealing with conquered nations. The same Inscription has also rendered it doubtful, whether (as used to be supposed) Cyrus was in reality a monotheist. Undoubtedly the Persians had strong monotheistic tendencies : Darius, for instance,[3] speaks of Ormazd as the creator of heaven and earth, and attributes to him his successes. Cyrus, however, was not a direct ancestor of Darius, but belonged to a collateral branch ; and in his Inscription he expressly ascribes his victories to Merodach, and relates how, after entering Babylon, he restored his shrines, as well as those of the other gods, and sought to win the favourable regard of Bel and Nebo. " It is clear, therefore, that Cyrus was a polytheist, who, like other polytheists in other ages, adopted the gods of the country he had conquered, from motives of State policy."[4] In xli. 25 the prophet apparently implies Cyrus's recognition of Jehovah's godhead, if not in the present, at least in the future. How far

[1] ὡς εὔφρων ἔφυ, Æsch. *Persae* 735.
[2] " All their peoples I assembled, and I restored their lands " (p. 174).
[3] " Records," v. 151 (on the Inscription of Naksh-i-rustam) ; cf. vii. 87 ff.
[4] Sayce, " Fresh Light," &c., p. 175.

this corresponded to the event is uncertain : the terms of the
edict in Ezra i. 2–4 are not necessarily an exact reproduction of
Cyrus's words . upon the general analogy of speeches and prophecies contained in the historical books, the form in which it
appears will be due rather to the compiler. On the whole, the
truth probably is that, as the instrument of the release of the
Jews, the character of Cyrus is, in this respect, *idealized* by
the prophet ; and he views the permission thus granted by him
as involving a more distinct recognition of the God of the Jews
than, perhaps, was actually the case. It appears further from
the Inscription, that Babylon opened its gates to Cyrus without
a siege—"without fighting or battle he [Merodach] caused him
to enter Babylon." This, however, is in no contradiction with the
language of the prophet : in fact, it agrees excellently with the
picture drawn by him in xlv. 1–2.

There follow two chapters (xlvi., xlvii.) in which the prophet,
having sufficiently established his main contention, dwells upon
the prospect of the fall of Babylon. In chap. xlvi. he thinks
principally of its humiliated idols : in chap. xlvii. he contemplates
the city itself, obliged to relinquish its proud position of imperial greatness, and impotent to avert the fate which threatens
it. "Bel[1] boweth down, Nebo stoopeth"—the supreme deities
of Babylon are humbled : and the prophet sees in imagination
a procession of idols moving along, not, as on some festal day,
amid marks of honour and rejoicing, but on the way from the
captured city into exile. The thought of the idols, borne labo-
riously by the wearied beasts, suggests to him by contrast the
thought of Israel, sustained through its long history by Jehovah
with an attention and affection which has never flagged. But
the prophet uses the opportunity afforded him by the spectacle
of the useless images of the Babylonians to emphasize once
again (xl. 18) the incomparableness of Jehovah. "Remember
this," take to heart the difference between an idol-god and

---

[1] *I.e.,* "lord," a title of Merodach, according to Prof. Sayce, "Hibbert
Lectures," p. 92. Nebo was Merodach's son, his "prophet," and pro-
claimer of his wishes (*ib.* 112 ff.). Nebuchadnezzar styles himself on
an Inscription, "Nebo's favourite" (Schrader, p. 413). The verses contain a signal warning against interpreting the prophetic imagery too
literally : in point of fact, the images of the Babylonian gods, so far from
being exiled by Cyrus, were reinstated by him in their places with honour
(p. 136) I The prophet, of course, merely seeks to show, by an effective
figure, the inability of the Babylonian gods to defend their city.

Jehovah : remember "the former things of old"—whether prophecies or other occurrences, which were evidence of the godhead of Jehovah, and proof that He could "declare the end from the beginning," *i.e.*, could declare at the beginning of a new phase or crisis of history its ultimate issue—as Isaiah, for instance, had foretold in 702 the issue of the revolt from Assyria, or Jeremiah the end of the empire of Nebuchadnezzar. The application at once follows. The declaration already made respecting the successful issue of Cyrus's advance upon Babylon will be confirmed. The word spoken will be accomplished. The exhortation is addressed specially to those among the exiles who were unspiritually minded, and "far from righteousness," *i.e.*, indifferent to the promised salvation, which here (as elsewhere in this prophecy, *e.g.*, li. 6, lvi. 1) is viewed as a manifestation of Divine righteousness. On their behalf, then, the assurance is repeated, that the deliverance will not be delayed beyond the appointed time.

Chap. xlvii. is an ode on the humiliation of Babylon. The city is addressed as a queen, who has boasted that she was the "lady of kingdoms:" but she is bidden to descend from her throne, and prepare in ignominy and shame to pass into exile. For Babylon had abused her position : in dealing with God's people she had shown no mercy, paid no regard to age or infirmity (comp. Lam. iv. 16; v. 12), heedless of the consequences ("the latter end thereof"), in which such heartlessness would ultimately involve her. Let Babylon, then, listen now to what she would not consider before, and hear her fate ! In spite of her imperial supremacy, in spite of the curious arts which made her name famous in antiquity, in spite of her assurance that there was no avenging God to behold her tyranny, the "childlessness" and "widowhood" to which she deemed herself superior will come upon her, with a suddenness that will make resistance futile, and evil will fall upon her, which her boasted skill in sorcery will be powerless to avert. Ironically, the prophet bids her make the attempt :—"Persist then in thy spells, and in the multitude of thy enchantments, wherein thou hast laboured from thy youth : perchance thou wilt be able to profit, perchance thou wilt strike terror i . . . Let the astrologers, the star-gazers, the monthly prognosticators, stand up and save thee from the things that shall come upon thee !" And the

frequented Babylon for purposes of trade (p. 128), fleeing each to his native country from the doomed city, eager to escape the impending disaster.

Chap. xlviii. is mainly a repetition and reinforcement of the arguments insisted on in the previous parts of the prophecy. The first paragraph is addressed in particular to those who, though nominally worshippers of Jehovah, had in reality no faith in Him ; and the prophet explains why, in some instances, predictions had been given long before the events to which they related (v. 3–6a), whilst in others they had been spoken only on the eve of their accomplishment (v. 6b–8). The former method had been adopted in order to preclude the possibility of the event, upon its occurrence, being attributed to some idol ; the latter method had been adopted, and was, in fact, the one followed now by the prophet, lest Israel, familiarized beforehand with the prediction, should plead forgetfulness of its source, and claim to know it as a matter of course.[1] A nation which needed to be dealt with in this way had no claim for mercy or regard ; but "for His own sake," that His name may be no more profaned among the heathen (Ezek. xx. 9), Jehovah spares it. "Listen, then, Israel to my words : He, who changes not, has spoken : one whom He favours is approaching : He has called him ; and his way will prosper. O that thou hadst hearkened to Him before ! then had thy peace already come, thy righteousness already been established ! then had old promises (Gen. xxii. 17 ; xxxii. 12) already been realized !" But the time is now not far off : and the first division of the prophecy ends with a jubilant cry, addressed to the exiles, bidding them depart from Babylon, and proclaim to the ends of the earth the wondrous story of their return.

In the second division of the prophecy, beginning with chap. xlix., there is an evident advance in the development of the author's theme. The controversial tone, the repeated comparisons between Jehovah and the idols, with the arguments based upon them, disappear ; the prophet feels that, as regards

---

[1] The same contrast between the "former things," i.e., former predictions, and "new things," now declared, as in xlii. 9 (p. 140). In v. 6b render, "Henceforth I show (not ' have showed ') thee new things "—not, as in the first case, announced some time before the event, but things revealed now, when they are on the point of being realized ("created," v. 7).

these points, he has made his position sufficiently secure. For the same reason, allusions to Cyrus and his conquest of Babylon cease also ; that, likewise, is now taken for granted. The prophet's thoughts are free to dwell more exclusively on the future in store for Israel ; in particular, fresh features are added to the portrait of Jehovah's ideal "Servant," who hitherto has been alluded to but once (xlii. 1–7) ; his character is further developed, and the functions to be discharged by him are more exactly defined.

Chap. xlix. opens with a dramatically conceived representation of Jehovah's ideal Servant, describing his person and experiences. The description should be compared with that in xlii. 1–7, to which it is partly parallel, partly supplementary. The speaker announces himself primarily as the medium of Israel's restoration : but he has besides a mission to the world ; and hence he begins by inviting distant nations to listen to his words. He has been called from his birth, guarded carefully, and trained for his work, given the sharp tongue to rebuke and to correct ; he is *Israel*, in whom Jehovah will glory [1] (*v.* 3). For a moment he had felt discouraged in the execution of his mission—like Elijah, dejected by want of success (*v.* 4) ; but he was reassured by the reflection that his cause was in God's hands, who would render him in due time the reward of his labour. And now a new and more honourable commission is confided to him : he had been predestined, indeed, to effect the restoration of the chosen nation ; but a wider and loftier mission is now opened before him : he is to be a "light of the Gentiles," in order to bring all mankind to the knowledge of the true God. Despised, indeed, and abhorred now, a very different future is in store for him : " Kings shall see and arise ; princes, and they shall worship ; " in the season of God's good pleasure, the strength needful for the completion of his task will be vouchsafed to him (*v.* 8) : he will be made the embodiment of a new covenant between Jehovah and His people (cf. xlii. 6) ; and Israel's exiles will triumphantly return (*v.* 8–13).

And does Zion yet think that she is forgotten ? Impossible ! " Can a woman forget her sucking child, that she

---

[1] *Lit.* deck himself: one of the words characteristic of the author of these chapters. See xliv. 23 ; lx. 21; lxi. 3 ; also lv. 5 ; lx. 7, 9, 13. " Be

should not have compassion on the son of her womb? **Yea,**
these may forget, but I will not forget thee. Behold, I have
graven thee upon the palms of My hands; thy walls are continually before Me." Art thou bereaved, barren, a homeless
exile? only look with thine eyes! already thy children are
clustering around thee! already they are more than the space
about thee can contain! Dost thou wonder whence they come?
The signal has been raised aloft to the nations: honourably,
and with tender regard to age, they are escorting back thy
children; and kings, and queens are vying with one another in
zeal to do thee service.[1] But the thought that there are those
among his hearers who are incredulous of such promises, and
question whether the strong grasp of the Babylonian despot will
ever be relaxed, recurs to the prophet, even in the moment of
his sublimest transport. "Shall the prey," he hears it objected,
"be taken from the mighty, or the captives of the terrible one [2]
escape?" Yes, the answer is, "Even the captives of the
mighty shall-be taken, and the prey of the terrible one shall
escape; for with him that contendeth with thee I will contend,"
and internecine conflicts (*v.* 26) will consume the strength of
thy foes. In conclusion, the prophet turns reassuringly to the
children. By two figures borrowed from legal phraseology, he
shows that there is no insuperable impediment to Israel's
restoration to favour. No formal evidence of their mother's
(Zion's) divorce from Jehovah exists; and no creditor can be
produced to whom (according to the custom of Hebrew parents,
when in debt, 2 Kings iv. 1) they were sold: thus no legal
impediment exists to their restoration; and the moral impediment, which alone stands in the way, will cease, so soon as the
Divine offer of pardon is met by the nation's penitence (l. 1-3).

At this point the ideal Servant is again dramatically introduced, soliloquizing in a strain not unlike that of xlix. 1-4. He
dwells however here, more particularly, on the manner in which
he fulfils his mission, and the trials which attend it. He is a
prophet: he has received the " disciples' tongue "—the tongue
skilled to reproduce its master's teaching; day by day his ear is
touched that it may appropriate its lesson from above: in the

---

[1] A famous verse: "And kings shall be thy nursing-[*rather*, foster-]
fathers (2 Kings x. 1), and their queens thy nursing-mothers "—implying
the *superior* royalty of Zion herself.

[2] Read, by a slight change, with the Vulg. and Syr., as on R.V. *marg.*

execution of the task entrusted to him, he shrinks from no reproach or humiliation which it may bring upon him ; the strength of Jehovah sustains him, for he knows that in the end he will prevail (*v.* 4-9). The soliloquy ended, the prophet resumes speaking in his own person. Addressing first those who fear and obey Jehovah, he exhorts such, if the way before them seems dark, or the prospect blank, not to lose their faith ; and turning afterwards to those who despise the Divine word, and arm themselves ("that gird yourselves about with fire-brands ") against the prophets who announce it, he bids them ironically walk into the flame that they have kindled : the weapons which they have forged against others, they will find recoil upon themselves (*v.* 10 f.).

In the section extending from li. 1 to lii. 12 the prospect of the approaching return is that which chiefly fills the prophet's thoughts ; and his confidence finds joyous expression in the thrice-repeated jubilant apostrophe li. 9, 17 ; lii. 1. He begins with a word of assurance addressed to those who, unlike the merely nominal Israelites of xlviii. 1 f., strove earnestly to lead a consistent life, and practised a religion of the heart (*v.* 1, 7). Let such review their past : let them look back to their origin, and reflect upon their wonderful gròwth from a single ancestor : let the blessing which thus visibly rested upon Abraham's seed be to them a source of encouragement in the present. Let them listen to what the prophet has now to tell them. A noble and august future is to be theirs ; for through Israel instruction will go forth to the nations, and the light of a Divine law will be revealed to the world (*v.* 1-8). "*Awake, awake,* put on strength, O arm of Jehovah : awake, as in the days of antiquity, the generations of old ": let the wonders of the Exodus be re-enacted,[1] that the freed ones of Jehovah may return exultingly to Zion. To the doubts of such as had still not overcome their dread of human opposition, the prophet replies by the same effective comparison ("grass ") as in xl. 6, and by pointing again, as in the same chapter, to the marks of Jehovah's power, and to His purpose of creating, through Israel's agency, a new moral world (*v.* 9-16). "*Wake thee up, wake thee up,* arise, O Jerusalem, which hast drunk at the hand of Jehovah the cup of

---

[1] *V.* 9, Rahab, and the "dragon" (or, sea-monster), of course symbolizing Egypt, as Ps. lxxxix. 10 ; lxxiv. 13.

His fury ; thou hast drunken the bowl of the cup of reeling '
and drained it." Jerusalem is pictured as a woman, prostrate
through misfortune, lying helplessly, as though drunken, on the
roadside, her sons unable to guide or assist her : but she is to
stand up ; the past is now solemnly reversed ; and the cup of
" reeling " which she has drunk is to be given to them that
afflicted her (*v.* 17–23). "*Awake, awake,* put on thy strength,
O Zion ; put on thy beautiful garments, O Jerusalem, the holy
city : for henceforth there shall no more come into thee the
uncircumcised and the unclean !" Let Zion prepare to lay aside
her captive's garb : for Israel has no longer any place in
Babylon : Jehovah will no longer endure to remain in banishment with His people. And now the prophet sees in imagination the messengers bearing the tidings of Israel's deliverance
arrive in the mountains of Judah, and hears the watchmen,
whom he pictures as looking out eagerly from the city walls,
exultingly announcing the joyous news.[2] More triumphantly
than ever he bids "the waste places of Jerusalem" rejoice ;
for Jehovah has comforted His people : His arm is bared for
action before the eyes of the nations, and all the world will now
witness the manifestation of His salvation (cf. xl. 5). "Depart
ye, depart ye ; go ye out from thence ; touch no unclean thing ;
go ye out of the midst of her ; purify yourselves, ye that bear
the vessels of Jehovah.[3] For ye shall not go out in haste,
neither shall ye go by flight : for Jehovah will go before you,
and the God of Israel will be your rearguard."

The section which now follows, lii. 13–liii. 12, deals again
with the figure of Jehovah's ideal Servant, and develops under

---

[1] *I.e.,* "the horror and bewilderment caused by some great calamity"
(Cheyne). For the figure of the " cup " comp. Ezek. xxiii. 32-4 ; Jer. xxv.
15–28 ; Lam. iv. 21. *V.* 20 may be illustrated from Lam. ii. 11, 19.

[2] *V.* 7, "Thy God reigneth !" rather, "is become King," the kingdom
having seemingly, while Israel was in exile, been in abeyance. Cf
Ps. xciii. 1 ; xcvii. 1 ; xcix. 1—psalms which (as well as Ps. xcvi., xcviii.
[cf. chap. xlii. 10]), reproduce, in a lyric form, the spirit of this part of
II. Isaiah, and are instinct with the same consciousness that a new epoch
of Divine revelation is beginning for the world.

[3] Or, perhaps, "ye *armour-bearers* of Jehovah." Jehovah, figured as a
warrior (xl. 10 ; xlii. 13 ; lix. 17), would be preceded, upon a solemn
occasion, by armour-bearers (cf. 1 Kings xiv. 28). "From thence," *i.e.,*
from Babylon, the prophet, from *v.* 7, having placed himself in spirit in
Jerusalem. In *v.* 5 "in Babylon" is *here.*

a new aspect his character and work. The division of chapters is singularly unfortunate : for lii. 13–15, describing the ideal Servant's exaltation, after an antecedent period of humiliation and distress, is just a summary or epitome of what is stated in greater detail in chap. liii. "Behold, My servant shall deal wisely (or, shall prosper[1]) :" he will in consequence be "high, and exalted, and lofty exceedingly"; and the heathen, who were for the time astonished at the spectacle of his misfortune, will afterwards be correspondingly amazed by his new and unexpected greatness (lii. 13–15).[2]

The contrast here expressed is developed in chap. liii. The first three paragraphs (*v.* 1–3, *v.* 4–6, *v.* 7–9), dwell on three several stages in the ideal Servant's humiliation : the persons speaking are the *Israelites*, represented as at length perceiving the truth, to which they had before been blind, and reviewing the period of their incredulity. First, in spite of the prophetic "report," or message, pointing to him, few or none, they say, amongst his nation recognized him : he had no outward grace or beauty of form, attracting attention : he grew up in their midst like some mean or lowly shrub, struggling to maintain itself in an arid soil : men despised him, and even held aloof from him in aversion (*v.* 1–3). In truth, however, as the people, still looking back upon the period of their incredulity, proceed to confess, they themselves were the occasion of his distressed appearance : "he was bearing the consequences of *our* sins, although we, in our blindness, imagined him to be 'stricken, smitten of *God*, and afflicted'"—*i.e.*, smitten, as by a judgment, for some specially heinous offence committed by him, —"whereas, in fact, it was *we* who had gone astray and the

---

[1] Both ideas are included. The word means to act with wisdom such as to ensure success (1 Sam. xviii. 14).

[2] In *v.* 15 the rendering "sprinkle," independently of the fact that it forms no suitable antithesis to "were astonished" in *v.* 14, is indefensible upon grammatical grounds. If the word here used were derived from the Hebrew verb signifying *to spirt* (2 Kings ix. 33, "And some of her blood *spirted* upon the wall"), the phrase could only signify *cause the nations to spirt*, as though they were themselves the liquid spirting ! This sense being obviously out of the question, most moderns (including Delitzsch) derive the word from another root, signifying *to leap*, and so obtain the rendering *cause to leap, i.e.*, metaphorically, cause to rise up suddenly in wonder, or (R.V. *marg.*) *startle.* "Shall shut their mouths"—a gesture denoting the involuntary silence of amazement ; see Job xxix. 9 ; Micah vii. 16.

penalty, instead of recoiling upon us, lighted in its entirety[1] upon him, leaving us free." So far, in a word, from being guilty himself, he bore the guilt of others, and relieved them of its penal consequences (v. 4-6). Though he let himself be humbled (*i.e.*, suffered willingly), and made no answer to his accusers, he was still oppressed : first imprisoned by an unjust sentence, he was afterwards led away to execution, not one among his contemporaries considering that he was thus cut off, not for his own sins, but for those of his people[2] : in spite of the innocence of his life, his death was that of a malefactor and his end inglorious (v. 7-9). The fourth and last paragraph introduces a promise for the future. It was Jehovah's pleasure thus to "bruise" him : but out of death will spring a new life : after his soul has been made a guilt-offering,[3] he will live again, enjoy long life, and be rewarded with the satisfaction of seeing God's work, or "pleasure," prospering in his hand.[4] Possessed of an intimate "knowledge" of the dealings and purposes of Jehovah,

---

[1] *V.* 6, "laid," *lit.* made to light, as on the mark of an arrow (Job vii. 20).

[2] So *v.* 8, R.V., *text.* R.V. *marg.* has "and his life who shall recount ? for he was cut off," &c., *i.e.*, who, at the time of his death, would think of dwelling upon his memory ? he had, as it appeared, achieved nothing worthy of remembrance. But the rendering "life" is questionable.

[3] So R.V.—here on marg., elsewhere in text (A.V. *trespass*-offering) : Heb. *āshām* (Lev. v. 14–vi. 7), to be carefully distinguished from the "*sin*-offering," Heb. *chattāth* (Lev. iv. 1–v. 13). In the *sin*-offering, the sin is viewed in its effects upon the sinner, and the idea of expiation is prominent : in the *guilt*-offering, it is viewed *in its effects upon other persons*, as involving an infringement of their rights. The guilt-offering always implies some right or due withheld : if this could be estimated at a money-value, a material compensation was made, the guilt in the eyes of God being met by the sacrifice, or *āshām*, offered at the same time. A *moral* due cannot be estimated in money : where such has been withheld, the sacrifice alone can be offered. The Philistines rendered an *āshām* for the desecration done to the ark (1 Sam. vi. 3, 4). What has been said explains the use of the term here. Sin is viewed as a *sacrilege*, an invasion of God's honour : the *āshām* is the satisfaction paid for it, viz., the innocent life of the Righteous Servant.

[4] In "shall see seed and have long life," the figure of a *patriarch* blessed with longevity and numerous descendants (Gen. l. 22 f.) is in the prophet's thoughts. The "pleasure of Jehovah" is the Servant's *religious* mission (xlii. 1, 4, 6 ; xlix. 6, 8). *V.* 9*a* means that after the travail which he had experienced, he would enjoy a satisfying view of the progress of the Divine work of salvation effected through his instrumentality.

he will "justify the many" (viz., by a method or principle based upon this knowledge) ; whilst his final reward for having submitted to the death of a transgressor will be that he will be ranked as a conqueror, and honoured amongst the great ones of the earth.[1] Thus the ideal Servant's humiliation and death are succeeded by a glorified life ; and the ground of the amazement of the nations (lii. 15) is made fully evident. It will be observed that the idea of *vicarious suffering* is here distinctly enunciated : the subject of the prophecy suffers not *with* the guilty (involved with them in a common catastrophe), but *for* them. The significance of the section, as a whole, will however be considered more fully in Chap. IV. Only one question may be touched upon here. The context, on both sides of lii. 13–liii. 12, deals with the approaching restoration from exile : and in what connection, it may be asked, does the figure of Jehovah's ideal Servant stand to that ? The answer to this question is to be found in the fact that as xlii. 1–7 ; xlix. 1–13 (especially *v.* 5–6, 8–9) show, the future of Israel as a nation is intimately connected, in the prophet's view, with the figure in which Israel's history and character culminate, the ideal Servant. The conception thus reacts upon the prophet's apprehension of the present. His assurance that the impersonation of Israel's character and destiny which he has here pourtrayed is not a *mere* creation of the imagination and will not remain permanently an unrealized ideal, is a pledge to him of the approaching temporal deliverance from Babylon, and a potent confirmation of the promises connected therewith.

Accordingly, in chap. liv., the prophet proceeds to develope the consequences thus implicitly involved in chap. liii. Again, as in xlix. 20 f., Zion is addressed as a woman, who, after years of barrenness, is at length a mother, and may now watch her children "spreading abroad" (see Gen. xxviii. 14) far and wide, *v.* 1–3 : no longer need she fear the reproach of widowhood, for her "Husband" is now about to resume His rights over her : in an "outburst" of wrath, He had indeed for a while hidden His face from her, but with everlasting lovingkindness He will now have compassion upon her, and establish with her an indissoluble "covenant of peace" (see Ezek. xxxiv. 25 ; xxxvii. 26), *v.* 4–10. Tossed to and fro now, Zion will then be at rest

---

[1] *V.* 12*a*, the figure is that of a victor, receiving from Jehovah, and dividing with his peers, the spoils of a successful war.

upon a secure and splendid foundation, her children the "disciples of Jehovah" (comp. Jer. xxxi. 34); and those who think to assail her will but perish in the attempt, *v.* 11-17.

"Ho, every one that thirsteth, come ye to the waters ; and he that hath no money! come ye, buy and eat, yea, come, buy wine and milk without money, and without price." Such is the offer which the prophet next holds out to the exiles ; for that this, though the invitation is evangelical in its comprehensiveness, is the primary import of his words, appears plainly from the sequel.[1] He would have his people prepare themselves to receive the coming blessings worthily : a rich spiritual satisfaction is within their grasp, if they will but come forward and claim it ; the only condition is *obedience*, lv. 3. If this condition be cheerfully and generously rendered, the promise given to David[2] will be confirmed to the nation in a fuller and larger sense : distant nations in voluntary homage will hasten to own the supremacy of Israel's religion (cf. xlv. 14). Exert yourselves, then, before it is too late, that ye may be worthy to partake in the deliverance. Or are you still (xl. 27 ; xlix. 24) incredulous? and do you deem it an idle exhortation to prepare yourselves for a future that may never come? I tell you, My thoughts are not as your thoughts : My purposes are higher than you are able to comprehend :[3] My word is unalterable (cf. xl. 8); it cannot be recalled ; nor will it return unto Me till the object for which it is sent has been accomplished—"For with joy shall ye go forth, and with peace shall ye be led : the mountains and hills shall break forth before you into singing ; and all the trees of the field shall clap their hands." Nature shall sympathize and exult ; and the earth shall burst forth with trees

---

[1] See *v.* 12, "Ye shall *gn forth* with joy," &c.

[2] 2 Sam. vii. 12-16 (Nathan) ; also xxiii. 5 (an "everlasting covenant") ; and Ps. lxxxix. 49. *V.* 4 refers to David. As David became ruler of subject nations (2 Sam. viii.), a knowledge of his religion, however imperfect, spread amongst them : thus he was a "witness" to them. This position of David is idealized in Ps. xviii. 43 ("Thou makest me a *head of nations;* a people *whom I have not known shall serve me*") ; and the position, as thus idealized, is here enlarged, and extended in a *spiritual* sense to Israel (*v.* 5, "Behold a nation that thou knowest not thou shalt call, and a nation that have not known thee shall run unto thee").

[3] The "thoughts of Jehovah," Micah iv. 12 ; and especially Jer. xxix. 10-13 (likewise with reference to Israel's return from Babylon).

of noble foliage (*v.* 13), at the redemption of Jehovah's people (comp. xli. 19 ; xlii. 11).

Once more, however, and from a fresh point of view, the prophet emphasizes the conditions which must be satisfied by those who would enjoy these blessings :—" *Observe judgment, and do righteousness:* for My salvation is near to come, and My righteousness to be revealed" (comp. li. 5). The duties of the first Table are typified by the observance of the Sabbath ; those of the second Table are signified in the comprehensive expression, "That keepeth his hand that it do no evil" (lvi. 2). But no other restrictions are imposed ; and all, the prophet hastens to add, who observe the conditions stated, in spite of any technical disqualification which may attach to them, will be admitted freely to the promised privileges. The alien (or foreigner) who (comp. Deut. xxiii. 3–8) might fear that full religious communion with Israel would be refused to him, the eunuch who (*ib. v.* 1) was permanently excluded from it, are both assured that provided they fulfil the required conditions of a life in conformity with Jehovah's will, no legal impediment will be permitted to bar their admission : the sacrifices of foreigners will be accepted : "For Mine house shall be called a house of prayer *for all peoples.* Saith the Lord Jehovah, who gathereth the outcasts of Israel : Yet more will I gather unto him (viz., from other nations), besides his own gathered ones." With this lofty conception of the future of the Gentile world, and of Jehovah's purpose in relation to it, the prophet closes the present section of his prophecy. In the quotation in Matt. xxi. 13 and Luke xix. 46 (though not in Mark xi. 17), the end of the sentence, *for all peoples,* is omitted. These words, however, it is evident, are of crucial significance in the original context. The passage is, in fact, the counterpart to xlii. 4; li. 5. What is described as the *desire* of the nations there, is shown to be in accordance with Jehovah's *purpose* here.

Very different is the tone of the section which now follows— lvi. 9–lvii. 21. With chap. lix., it forms the most sombre part of the entire prophecy. The prophet turns aside from the glorious future which elsewhere is always uppermost in his thoughts, to the prosaic reality of the present and the past. He dwells upon the faults and shortcomings, which Israel has been only too reluctant to abandon, and which necessitated in the end a Divine interposition for their removal. First, he denounces the unworthy rulers of the nation. "All ye wild beasts of the field, come to devour, yea, all ye beasts in the forest!" Israel is like a neglected flock; and thus he bids ironically the beasts (symbolizing heathen nations) come and devour as they will. The "watchmen"[1] are blind; instead of being on the alert, they are asleep and useless; the shepherds (as in Jeremiah,[2] a figure of the rulers of the people), instead of caring for the flock, are simply intent on their own advantage or pleasure (v. 11 f.). The rulers being thus indifferent, the righteous are neglected, and perish (lvii. 1 f.), no one all the while observing that they are in fact gathered in, that they may be rescued from a judgment to come.[3]

Next (lvii. 3–11a), the prophet reproaches Israel with its idolatry, drawing a vivid description of the nation's devotion to strange heathen rites, such as had been practised (probably) in the evil days of Manasseh, and the tendency to which was still, no doubt, far from extirpated in the mass of the people (comp. lxv. 3–5, 11). Further, under the figure of a woman attiring herself to attract admirers, he shows effectively how ready Israel had been to court the favour of foreign kings, deterred neither by the distance to be traversed by her emissaries, nor by the humiliation involved—"Thou didst get renewal of thy strength, therefore thou feltest not weak." Of whom, the prophet retorts, wast thou in fear that thou wast thus faithless, and forgattest *Me?* But thy works shall not profit thee: let thy rabble of idols, when thou criest to them, deliver thee, if they can! But he that taketh refuge in Me, shall "inherit the land, and take My holy mountain in possession." And again (cf. xl. 3), the voice is heard, bidding the way be prepared for the returning people:

"Cast ye up, cast ye up, clear the way;
Take up the stumbling-block out of the way of My people."

For Israel has a sure ground of salvation. Lofty though Jehovah is, He can yet condescend in His mercy to those of a lowly and contrite spirit; His wrath is now past; and He offers peace to far and near alike of Israel's banished ones. Only the wicked, *i.e.* (in this connection), "those Israelites who persist in the

---

[1] *I.e.*, the prophets: see Jer. vi. 17; Ezek. iii. 17.
[2] Chap. ii. 8; iii. 15; and esp. xxiii. 1, 2. See also Ezek. xxxiv. 2, 5, 8.
[3] Illustrate from 2 Kings xxii. 20.

alienation.from God which they have inherited from their fore-fathers" (Delitzsch), have no part in the promised blessing.

As the second division of the prophecy exhibits an advance upon the first, so the third shows an advance upon the second. At first, indeed, the prophet's strain alters but slightly : as in lvii. 3-21, he continues to upbraid his nation for its moral shortcomings. But after chap. lix. his thought not only leaves behind it the fall of Babylon, but ceases to revert with the same frequency as before to the release and return of the Jews : the vision of Zion restored absorbs more constantly his attention ; he paints its glories in colours of surpassing brilliancy ; and contrasts emphatically the happiness of the true Israelites ("my servants") admitted to be its citizens, with the far different fate reserved for those who indulge in wilful-ness and sin (chap. lxv.–lxvi.). First of all, however, the moral impediments, which disqualify Israel for the enjoyment of these blessings, must be removed. "Cry aloud, spare not, lift up thy voice like a trumpet, and declare unto My people their transgression, and to the house of Jacob their sins" (lviii. 1). Content with the observances of a formal religion, the people nevertheless resort to God boldly, and claim His interposition in their favour. They plead the strictness of their fasts : and affect surprise that they are disregarded. Fasts were a common feature of the old Israelitish religion (*e.g.*, 1 Kings xxi. 9, 12 ; Jer. xxxvi. 9) : in Zech. viii. 19, we learn expressly that during the exile four days were observed annually as fasts, in commemoration of dates connected with the fall of Jerusalem. The prophet replies, Your fasts are no expression of true humility of soul : you exact to the full, on such days, the labour of your dependents ; you become even the more irritable and violent towards them. Has Jehovah pleasure in a fast that is nothing more than an external form? In contrast to fasting such as this, the prophet draws a picture of the true fast, in which Jehovah delights, viz., deeds of philanthropy, unselfishness, liberality, and mercy, and of the blessings which the observance of it will secure, ending, as usual, with that which is foremost in his thoughts, the particular blessing of being able to restore and rebuild Jerusalem (*v.* 6-12). But if the true fast typifies the Israelite's duties towards his neighbour, the Sabbath represents his duties towards God.

The cheerful and ready observance of the Sabbath (cf. lvi. 2, 4, 6) is thus the second condition of Israel's restoration. And, if this condition be complied with, then may Israel, instead of being enthralled in bondage in Babylon, again (see Deut. xxxii. 13) "ride" in triumph over the mountains of Palestine, and resume the possession of its ancient home.

In chap. lix. the prophet enumerates with greater particularity the faults of which Israel is guilty, for the purpose of showing that the cause of the withdrawal from Israel of the Divine favour lies in the people, and not in Jehovah. The picture drawn by him is a dark one: bloodshed, dishonesty, schemes of violence and deceit are prevalent ; in the long catalogue of sins with which Ezekiel in 593 (see chap. xxii.) reproached their fathers, there were many, it is plain, which the exiles as a body had not yet learnt to disown, *v.* 3–8. The prophet, however, proceeds to represent them as confessing their responsibility in the social disorder described, as owning it to be the ground of the helpless condition in which they find themselves, and acknowledging that they have no claim upon Jehovah for assistance (*v.* 9–15*a*). The people's confession is heard : no human champion was at hand to save them : the Divine warrior, therefore, arms himself, and prepares to interpose : his vengeance breaks upon all the authors of disorder and injustice in Israel, and not upon these only, but upon the ungodly world in general at the same time. It is an ideal scene which the prophet here depicts : the restoration of the exiles is described under the concrete image of a manifestation of Jehovah, removing forcibly the obstacles which impede its realization. As a redeemer, then, He will show himself in Zion,—not indeed to all without distinction, but to those who satisfy the needful moral conditions, and have "turned from rebellion in Jacob." And the section concludes with a renewal of the gracious promise made already (xliv. 3) to the true Israel, that it is to continue the permanent recipient of the Divine spirit, the permanent organ of the Divine word.

At length (chap. lx.), the longed-for "light" (lix. 9) bursts upon the prophet's eye ; the dark cloud of night that shrouds the rest of the world has been lifted over Zion ; and a brilliant day there shines. The bright prospect eclipses all besides : and in this most beautiful chapter the prophet gathers together the features belonging to Zion restored into one unsurpassed picture.

He addresses the fallen and ruined city under his favourite figure of a woman, a mother : let her rise from her prostrate condition, and respond to the touch of the Divine glow that is streaming upon her ! And as the rays of this bright light pierce the darkness around, he sees distant nations stirred and attracted by it : they press forward, eager to enter and enjoy it themselves. Amongst them are Zion's own banished sons :—" Lift up thine eyes round about, and see : they are all gathered together, and come to thee : thy sons shall come from afar, and thy daughters shall be borne upon the side " (cf. xlix. 22). Lingering for a moment on the mother's delight (v. 5a) in thus receiving back her offspring, he next imagines the wealthiest and most illustrious nations of antiquity coming in one long train to cast their treasures at her feet, to minister to her wants, to beautify her temple. Violence and destruction will cease, and assured peace and tranquillity will reign throughout the land. No longer will Zion be dependent for light upon the natural luminaries of heaven : for " Jehovah shall be thy everlasting light, and the days of thy mourning are ended." Henceforth the inhabitants will be all righteous, possessing the land for ever, and thriving upon it, like a branch planted and tended by God, whose growth redounds to His honour.

The next two chapters are substantially a continuation of the same theme, the felicity of the ideal Zion of the future. Only, at the beginning, Jehovah's ideal Servant is once more introduced, describing the gracious mission which has been entrusted to him, " to bring good tidings to the afflicted, to bind up the brokenhearted, to proclaim liberty to the captives, and opening of eyes to the prisoners " (cf. xlii. 3, 7 ; xlix. 9). His monologue is immediately followed, as before (xlix. 9–12), by the promise of Jerusalem's restoration (" and they shall renew the ruined cities, the desolations of past generations "), and of Jehovah's blessing, resting visibly upon it, and attracting the notice of the world (v. 4–9). And using figures of supreme beauty (v. 10 f.) the prophet, speaking in the name of the people, expresses its grateful appreciation of the blessedness thus bestowed upon it. Jehovah Himself

conferred upon her by Him. No longer forsaken, she will be taken back into favour by her Husband (cf. l. 1 ; liv. 5), and again become His delight. Upon the walls of this ideal city are set watchers,[1] to remind Jehovah perpetually of His promise, and to "give Him no rest" until He establish Jerusalem in safety, and secure her renown in the earth. And now, for the last time (cf. xl. 3 ; xlviii. 20; lii. 11 ; lvii. 14) the call is heard, bidding the exiles quit Babylon—

> "Pass ye, pass ye through the gates ; clear ye the way of My people :
> Cast ye up, cast ye up the highway ; take ye out the stones :
> Lift ye up a banner over the peoples" (see xlix. 22).

The words of xl. 10 are repeated ; Jehovah is about to return to Zion, leading before Him, as a prize of war, His newly-won people. The ideal character of the nation (Exod. xix. 6) will henceforth be realized; and the sentence passed in Jer. xxv. 38 ("Jehovah *hath forsaken* His covert"), and xxx. 17 ("No man *seeketh* her *out*") is finally reversed.

There follows a passage, lxiii. 1–6, of unique and sublime dramatic power. The impotence of Israel's enemies to retard or interfere with their deliverance has been insisted on before (xli. 15 f. ; xlix. 25, 26 ; li. 23 ; liv. 17) ; and it is here developed under a novel and striking figure. The historical fact upon which the representation rests is the long-standing and impla‑ cable enmity (p. 130) subsisting between Israel and Edom. The scene depicted is of course no event of actual history : it is symbolical : an ideal humiliation of nations, marshalled upon the territory of Israel's inveterate foe, is the form under which the thought of Israel's triumph is here expressed. The prophet sees in imagination a figure, as of a conqueror, his garments crimson with blood, advancing proudly in the distance from the direction of Edom ; and asks—

> "Who is this that cometh from Edom, with dyed garments from Bozrah ?
> This, that is glorious in his apparel, travelling in the greatness of his
> strength ?"

In reply he hears from afar the words—

> "I that speak in righteousness, mighty to save,"

---

[1] Not watchmen (lit. *lookers out*), as hi. 8, lvi. 10, but as in xxi. 11, Cant. v. 7, lit., *keepers*, those who guard the city, especially during the night.

i.e., I who have announced (xlv. 19) a just and righteous purpose of deliverance, and am able to give it effect. The answer is not yet sufficiently explicit ; so he repeats the question in a more direct form—

"Wherefore art Thou red in Thine apparel?
And Thy garments hke his that treadeth the wine-press ? "
"The wine-trough I have trodden alone, and of the peoples there was no man with Me:
So I trode them In Mine anger, and trampled them in My fury ;
And their life-stream besprinkled My garments, and all My raiment have I defiled."

Not Edom only, then, but other nations also have been trodden down and subdued—

" For a day of vengeance was in Mine heart ;
And My year of release had come.
And I looked, but there was no helper,
And I wondered, but there was no supporter ;
Therefore Mine arm wrought salvation for Me,
And My fury—it supported Me ;
And I stamped upon the peoples in Mine anger,
And brake them to pieces in My fury :
And I spilled their life-stream on the earth."

In the hour when the contest *Israel contra mundum* was to be decided, no human agent, willingly or consciously, came forward to assist ; nevertheless, God's purposes were not frustrated : Israel's opponents were humbled and defeated; but human means, in so far as use was made of them, were the unconscious instruments of Providence. And thus the blood-stained colour of the Victor's garments is explained : it is a token of Jehovah's triumph over His people's foes, primarily indeed over those foes who would impede the release of the Jews from Babylon, or molest them when settled again in Palestine, but by implication also, over other foes who might

strain of surpassing pathos and beauty the prophet, as it were,
"leads the devotions" (Cheyne) of his nation, and lends words
by his eloquence to their repentance.

Beginning with the commemoration of the mercies signalizing
the past ("I will make mention of the lovingkindnesses of
Jehovah, and the praises of Jehovah, according to all that Jehovah hath bestowed upon us"), and of the affection with which
Israel was regarded by Jehovah (*v.* 9), he passes quickly to tell
of the people's ingratitude and rebellion (*v.* 10), which obliged
Jehovah to "fight against them," until calamity directed their
thoughts afresh to the glorious past, and caused them to long
again for the Divine help. ⸱ In accents of mingled entreaty and
expostulation they pray : " Look from heaven and behold, from
the habitation of Thy holiness and of Thy glory : where is Thy
jealousy (xlii. 13), and Thy mighty acts? the yearning of Thy
bowels and Thy compassions are restrained towards me.
Why dost Thou make us to stray, O Jehovah, from Thy ways,
and hardenest our heart from Thy fear? Return for Thy servants' sake, the tribes of Thine inheritance." The prayer soon
grows bolder, " O that Thou didst rend the heavens, that Thou
didst come down, that the mountains shook at Thy presence
. to make Thy name known to Thine adversaries, that the
nations might tremble before Thee !" Confession follows, in
tones that remind us of lix. 10–12 : " We are all become as
one that is unclean, and all our righteousnesses are as a polluted
garment. . . . And there is none that calleth upon Thy name,
that stirreth up himself to take hold of Thee ; for Thou hast
hid Thy face from us, and delivered us [1] into the power of our
iniquities." He closes with the beseeching appeal : " Thy holy
cities are become a desert ; Zion is become a desert, Jerusalem a
desolation. Our holy and our beautiful house, where our fathers
praised Thee, is burned up with fire ; and all our delectable
things are laid waste. Wilt Thou, in spite of these things
refrain Thyself, O Jehovah? wilt Thou hold Thy peace, and
afflict us very sore ?"

The supplication is ended ; and chap. lxv. appears to be intended as the answer—an answer, however, in which a distinction
is drawn between worthy and unworthy members of Israel, and
a different prospect is held out to each. God has ever, He says,

---

[1] So Sept., Pesh., Targ., R.V. *marg.* For the thought, cf. Job v.ii. 4.

been accessible to His people, He has ever been ready to renew intercourse with them :[1] it was they who would not respond, but provoked Him with their idolatries. Such as these are "a smoke in My nose, a fire that burneth all the day." Their guilt must first be requited. Israel, however, is not to be rejected on account of the presence within it of unworthy members : a seed of "chosen ones" will be brought out of Jacob, who shall again inherit the mountains of Palestine (*v.* 8–10). Far different, on the other hand, will be the lot of those devoted to heathen gods, whom the prophet next addresses (*v.* 11–16), contrasting their future with the future of Jehovah's true servants. A new order of things ("new heavens and a new earth :" cf. li. 16) is about to be created, in which Jerusalem and her people will be to Jehovah a source of unalloyed delight, and in which care and disappointment, such as are the lot of humanity in the present, will cease to vex (*v.* 17–25). It is a transformation of nature and society, which the prophet here imagines, on the same lines as iv. 2–6 ; xxx. 23–26, &c., but conceived upon a grander and more comprehensive scale.[2]

"Thus saith Jehovah, The heavens are My throne, and the earth is My footstool : what manner of house would ye build for Me? what manner of place for My rest?" Such are the great words with which the last chapter of the prophecy opens. They are a declaration, spoken probably in view of the approaching

---

[1] *V.* 1 as well as *v.* 2 refers to *Israel.* The application in Rom. x. 20 to the heathen is inferential, and has no bearing on the sense of the passage in its original context. The prophet's words are extended by the apostle to other persons exhibiting the same characteristic of not asking or seeking after God. There is a similar extension in the passages cited, Rom. ix. 25 f. and x. 18 : in their original context these relate, the one to the material heavens, the other to the kingdom of Ephraim. Render *v.* 1 "have let myself be inquired of," "let myself be found" (or, "have been at hand ") ; the words used may be illustrated from Ezek. xx. 3, 31 and chap. lv. 6. *V.* 4, "which sit among the graves," &c., viz., for the purpose of obtaining dreams there, which might reveal to them the future. Comp. the ἐγκοίμησις or "incubatio " practised at oracles (*Aen.* vii. 86–88). *V.* 5 alludes to those who claimed superior sanctity, in virtue of certain rites into which they had been initiated ; comp. lxvi. 5, 17. (In *v. ib.* we should read, probably, with all the Ancient Versions, as on R.V. *marg.*)

[2] *V.* 20, observe, the power of death is *limited,* but not abolished (as in xxv. 8) : death at the age of 100 years will be reckoned as early or prema-

restoration of the temple (which, in itself, the prophet entirely approves, xliv. 28, and expects lvi. 7 ; lx. 7 ; lxii. 9), reminding the Jews of the truth which a visible temple might readily lead them to forget, that no earthly habitation could be really adequate to Jehovah's majesty, and that Jehovah's regard was not to be won by the magnificence of a material temple, but by humility, and the devotion of the heart. How needful the warning was history shows. Jeremiah (vii. 1–15) argues at length against those who pointed, with a proud sense of assurance, to the massive pile of buildings that crowned the height of Zion, heedless of the moral duties which loyalty to the King, whose residence it was, implied. And at a yet more critical moment in their history, attachment to the temple, as such, was one of the causes which incapacitated the Jews from appropriating the more spiritual teaching of Christ : the charge brought against Stephen (Acts vi. 13, 14) is that he ceased not " to speak words against *this holy place* and the law"; and the argument of Stephen's defence (chap. vii.) is just to show that in the past God's favour had not been limited to the period during which the Temple of Zion existed. Here, then, the prophet seizes the occasion to insist upon the necessity of a spiritual service, passing on (*v.* 3–5) to denounce in particular certain superstitious usages which had apparently at the time infected the worship of Jehovah. In his concluding paragraph (*v.* 6–24), he contrasts the glorious blessedness in store for Jerusalem, with the terrible judgment impending over her enemies. First, he hears in spirit the sound as of one stirring in the temple (which he views in imagination as now restored) : it is the sound of Jehovah preparing Himself for vengeance—

" A sound of uproar from the city, a sound from the temple !
The sound of Jehovah who rendereth their deserts to His enemies !"

The time of Zion's birth is at hand, and will no longer be delayed. " Was a nation ever born in a day?" Yes, he replies, in the case of Zion, the paradox is the reality. Henceforth peace and joy shall reign in Jerusalem (*v.* 10–14) : for Jehovah is about to execute judgment upon her foes—"with fire will He hold judgment, and by His sword with all flesh ; and many shall be the slain of Jehovah " (comp. Jer. xxv. 31, 33). And those Jews also who, by a strange abnegation of their rights, abandon themselves (cf. lxv. 3 f.) to heathen mysteries, will share the same fate. Distant nations, when they hear of the "sign" thus wrought upon Israel's enemies, will hasten to escort back with reverence the exiles still in their midst (*v.* 18–21). An unending future will then commence for the restored nation,[1] in which the rites of Israel's religion will be honoured by the entire world. Month by month, and sabbath by sabbath, "all flesh" will come to worship at Jerusalem. The thought of lvi. 7 is here expressed by a figure, which, understood literally, involves a physical impossibility : but the prophet cannot altogether emancipate himself from the forms of the Jewish economy (comp. pp. 94, 114), and clothes a spiritual truth in a garb which in strictness is too narrow for it (comp. Zech. xiv. 16–19). And the memory of the signal act of judgment (*v.* 18 f.) will not be forgotten : the carcases of those who fall in it will remain, a never-ending and loathsome spectacle, in one or other of the valleys outside Jerusalem : and both pilgrims, and residents in the city, will go out from time to time to gaze in horror upon the scene (*v.* 24). Such is the picture with which the great prophecy of Israel's restoration closes.

[1] Comp. Jer. xxxi. 35 f. ; xxxiii. 20–26 (similarly of the returned exiles).

NOTE.—The most recent account of Cyrus and his conquests will be found in Maspero's "Histoire ancienne des peuples de l'Orient" (ed. 4, 1886), chaps. xii., xiii., where references to the original authorities are also given. The Rev. J. M. Fuller, in "The Expositor," Dec., 1885, p. 437 ff., seeks to evade the conclusion that Cyrus was a polytheist, by the supposition that the Inscription probably does not represent his true belief, and was drawn up, not by Cyrus himself, but by the priests of Merodach and Bel (whose worship Nabo-nahid had neglected), with the view of reconciling the Babylonians to the change of master. At least, however, the Inscription leaves no doubt that Cyrus was so far a polytheist that he *restored the worship* of the Babylonian gods.

CHAPTER IV.

THEOLOGY AND LITERARY STYLE OF. CHAPTERS XL.–LXVI.

The author's distinctive teaching determined in part by his historical
situation—Characteristic features of his theology—The figure of "Jehovah's Servant"—The author's literary style—The character of his
poetry.

THE general argument of chaps. xl.–lxvi. has been expounded,
it is hoped, with sufficient completeness ; it remains to estimate
—so far as space will permit—the author's position and literary
characteristics, and to define the more prominent aspects of his
theology.

As in the case of the prophets generally, the author's attitude
and teaching, viewed in their broader features, are determined
by his historical situation. Like Isaiah in 701, like Jeremiah on
the eve of the exile, he stands at a critical moment in the his- ✓
tory of his nation. Was Judah to lose its individuality in the
land of its exile, to be gradually assimilated, like its brethren of
the Ten Tribes, to the nations among whom it dwelt? There
were many among the exiles upon whom the promise of Jeremiah had produced no impression ; who were content to remain ✓
where they were ; who had no high aspirations for the future :
others, who were ready to quit Babylon if the opportunity
should offer, were despondent, over-awed by the power and
magnificence of the great imperial city (xl. 27 ; xlix. 14, 24).
The prophet saw the future with a truer eye. Though Cyrus,
pursuing his triumphal progress, may throw the nations of
Asia into consternation, and drive them in terror to their idol-
gods (xli. 2–7), Israel has no ground for alarm (*v.* 8 ff.) : the
promise has been given, and cannot be recalled (xl. 8 ; lv. 11) :

Israel must yet return to its ancient home. and complete the destined cycle of its history. The approaching restoration from exile holds in his view a similar position to that occupied in Isaiah by the triumph over the Assyrians. It marks the commencement of a new epoch, in which the powers of the world and of evil, now holding sway over Israel, will be rendered harmless ; it inaugurates the advent of the perfect kingdom of God. Hence the importance assumed by it in the prophet's eyes, and the brilliant colours in which he depicts it. It is a manifestation of the Divine glory (xl. 5 ; xli. 20 ; lii. 10) ; it is an event of world-wide significance, to be told, and acknowledged gratefully, in the remotest regions of the earth (xliv. 23 ; xlviii. 20 ; lxii. 11). But he stands upon a loftier pedestal than Isaiah, and pierces further into the future. He has a more distinct consciousness of the greatness of Israel's mission : he is aware that, in some mysterious way, a "light of the Gentiles" is in the ᵥ future to proceed from it ; he has received, in even larger and fuller measure than Isaiah, a revelation of God's purposes of grace. Hence the extraordinary comprehensiveness of his view, and the wealth and richness of his prophetic teaching. "No thought is too lofty or too wide for the Prophet, in the passion of enthusiasm, which the vision of a restored nature and regenerated world raises within him." [1]

In considering the theology of chaps. xl.-lxvi., we are impressed not merely by the profusion, and (to speak from a human point of view) the originality of the theological ideas which they contain, but also by the novel aspects under which many of these ideas are presented. Not only has revelation materially advanced since Isaiah's day, but the *form* in which theological truths are stated implies a more mature stage of theological thought—a stage in which the truths are not merely *affirmed*, as in Isaiah, but are made the subject of argument and reflection. To a certain point, a relation may be traced between the truths which the prophet chiefly emphasizes and his historical situation. Thus one of his main objects is plainly to kindle the aspirations of his countrymen in exile, to stimulate their faith, to convince them that the future which he promises will assuredly be theirs. Hence he insists, as no other prophet does, on the *evi-*

empty splendour of Babylonian idolatry, he dwells upon the very different character of Israel's God—His transcendence, His illimitable sovereignty, His absolute supremacy over nature, His sole and incommunicable Deity.   These are the attributes of the Divine nature which, with an eloquence rivalled only by the poet of Job (chaps. xxxviii., xxxix.), he sets forth in his opening chapter.   He does not set himself to *prove* Jehovah's existence ; assuming that, he proceeds to establish His character and attributes : " Who hath measured the waters in the hollow of His hand, and regulated the heavens with a span, and comprehended the dust of the earth in a measure, and weighed the mountains in scales and the hills in a balance ? Who hath regulated the Spirit of Jehovah, and, as His counsellor, informed him ?"   Alone He projected and carried out (cf. xliv. 24) the mighty work of creation : none was with Him to counsel or assist.   Not only, however, did He create the universe : He also sustains it ; to His behests it instantly responds (xlviii. 13) ; and night by night He musters His host, the stars, in their majestic parade, the visible token of His Deity—" Lift up your eyes on high and see : Who created these, bringing forth their host by number ?   To all of them He calleth by name ; through the greatness of (His) might, and the strength of (His) power, not one is missing ! "   Exalted and transcendent, He looks down upon the earth, " and the inhabitants thereof are as grasshoppers : " the forests of Lebanon cannot provide Him with a worthy altar-fire, nor the beasts thereof with a worthy offering (xl. 16) ; no temple which man can construct is adequate to His greatness (lxvi. 1).   He is without beginning and without end ; again and again does the prophet declare that He is the First and the Last, the Unchanging One (xli. 4 ; xliv. 6 ; xlviii. 12).   As the Creator of a universe vast as this, He is the Incomparable One ; no human imagination can express Him (xl. 18, 25) ; nought besides can claim the name of God (xliii. 10 ; xliv. 6, 8 ; xlv. 5, 6, 14, 21, 22 ; xlvi. 9).   But exalted though Jehovah thus is, He is in intimate relation with the earth : He did not design it to be an uninhabited waste (xlv. 18) ; He place i man originally upon it, and still, as ever, summons into being the successive generations of mankind (xli. 4).   He has, moreover, His purposes in history, breaking up the most powerful combinations of rulers (xl. 23 f.), and never permitting His plans to be frustrated (xlvi. 10 ; liv. 16 f.)   And, in particular, the prophet has a profound sense of Jehovah's *personality;* under the one limitation of lv. 8, he represents Him as " a living moral Person, possessing all the powers of personality in a degree transcending conception, and showing all the activities of moral being in perfection." [1]   If such be Jehovah's character, if He be thus all-powerful and all-wise, why should the idols of Babylon inspire the exiles with misgivings? Why should it occur to them to fear that the promised release would never come, or that unforeseen obstacles would defeat His declared purpose? (xl. 28*b* ; lv. 8–12).

Further, Jehovah is a God who *knows the future.* This is a truth to which in chaps. xl.–xlviii. the prophet repeatedly reverts, and to establish which he represents dramatically the Jews and their heathen opponents as engaged in forensic dispute.   The test of divinity being taken to be the power to predict the future, the representatives of the heathen gods are invited to adduce instances of predictions proceeding from such gods, and unquestionably fulfilled : they are permitted the option of either offering examples from the past, or producing predictions now, the truth of which may be tested by the immediate future (xli. 22 f. ; xliii. 9 ; xliv. 7).   No examples are forthcoming : the idols and their worshippers can respond only by silence.   To the Israelites, on the other hand, the prophet appeals confidently (xliii. 10 ; xliv. 8) as able to adduce from their own past history well-accredited instances of predictions truly fulfilled.   This is another evidence of Jehovah's godhead, another proof that the Babylonian idols are nonentities (xli. 24, 29), unable either to save their city from Cyrus (xlvi. 1 f.), or to impede the deliverance of the Jews. Throughout the first division of the prophecy (chaps. xl.–xlviii.) it is thus the prophet's aim to establish in its true nature, as against the pretensions of idolatry, Jehovah's true Deity.   Nowhere else in the Old Testament is there such an emphatic assertion of the latter, or such a sustained polemic against the former.   Idolatry in Babylon was practised with an imposing magnificence and completeness, to which in Palestine there had never been any parallel : and hence it was the more necessary for the prophet to refute its claims in detail.

In dealing with God's relation to *man,* the prophet lays unusual stress upon the motives upon which He acts, and the

[1] Prof. A. B. Davidson, in " The Expositor," Oct., 1884, p. 255.

principles exemplified in His actions,—the latter being not
merely described, but referred to the motive or principle from
which they spring.   Thus, as one such principle, *justice*
(ẓedek) is emphasized : the path of Cyrus, xli. 2 (R.V.),
xlv. 13, the commission of Israel, xli. 10, or of the ideal
Servant, xlii. 6, are, by the use of this term, exhibited in the
light of a manifestation or furtherance of God's righteous
purpose.   Similarly, *righteousness* (ẓedākāh) is often specified
as the principle determining the approaching deliverance,
xlvi. 13 ; li. 6, 8 ; lvi. 1*b* ; lix. 16, 17 (in all, parallel with
"salvation ").[1]   Another motive of Jehovah's action is the
Divine Name, xlviii. 9, 11 : being jealous of His honour, He
cannot any longer permit His name to be reproached, or the
glory which is His due to be transferred to idol gods, by the
nation which He has chosen to be His own people remaining
permanently in exile (cf. Ezek. xxxvi. 20-24).

Jehovah's gracious purposes towards Israel are naturally
those which are most fully developed by the prophet.   The lines
along which he moves are, for the most part, very different
from those followed by Isaiah.   The basis upon which God's✓
purposes rest is His *choice* of Israel, a choice made in the
distant past and irrevocable, xli. 8, 9 *end ;* xliii. 10 ; xliv. 1,
2, 21 (" thou shalt not be forgotten of Me ").   Jehovah has
founded the nation, taken it for His own, impressed upon its
history a character and an aim (see more fully below) ; and
this choice determines His attitude towards it in the present,
xli. 8-10 ; xliii. 1-2 ; xliv. 2 ; xlv. 4 (Cyrus called *for Israel's
sake*).   For a while, indeed, He had permitted it to be chas-
tened for its sins (xlii. 24 f. ; xliii. 28 ; lvii. 17 ; lx. 10) ; but this
"outburst " of His wrath was but transient, and was to be
succeeded—if Israel, at least, should not again prove itself
unworthy—by a period of never-ending favour (liv. 8-10).
Accordingly love may now re-assert itself (xliii. 4), forgiveness ✓
is freely offered (xliii. 25 ; xliv. 22 ; lv. 7), God will now
compassionate His people (xlix. 13, cf. 15 ; lx. 10) ; twice does
He receive the title (which occurs nowhere besides) of Israel's
"compassionater " (xlix. 10 ; liv. 10).   Comfort and consolation
is the burden of the prophecy throughout (xl. 1, 2 ; xlix. 13 ;

---

[1] When Isaiah uses this term with reference to the Divine righteousness,
he conceives it always as a principle of *judgment :* i. 27 ; v. 16 ; x. 22 ;
xxviii. 17.

li. 3, 12 ; lii. 9 ; lxvi. 13). The immediate proof of the
nation's restoration to favour is, of course, the release from
Babylon and return to Palestine.   In jubilant and commanding
tones the prophet bids his people leave the land of their exile
(xlviii. 20 ; lii. 11 f. ; lxii. 10) : and the progress homeward is
depicted by him in ideal colours (xli. 18 f. ; xliii. 19 f. ; xlviii. 21).
More particularly the restoration itself is viewed by him as the
renewal of a *covenant:* Jehovah's "covenant of peace" is
unalterably established (liv. 10): the "everlasting covenant"
with David is confirmed to the nation, upon the one condition
of its obedience, with ampler promises and a larger hope
(lv. 3–5 : cf. lxi. 8).[1] The promise of permanency is repeated
elsewhere, as xlv. 17 (idolaters put to confusion : Israel saved
"with an everlasting salvation "), lxvi. 22.   In virtue of the
covenant concluded with it, Israel, thus restored, is to be the
perpetual bearer of prophetic gifts, the perpetual recipient of
prophetic illumination, lix. 21.

The prophet's representation of the ideal, restored Zion is
developed gradually.   First there is the bare notice of the glad
tidings brought to the ruined city, xl. 9 ; xli. 27 : then follow the
passages xlvi. 13 (salvation to be placed there) ; hi. 1 (no more
to be desecrated by insulting foes), 8 f. (joy at Jehovah's
return to Zion) : in liv. 11 f. the prophet catches in imagination
the first glimpse of her glittering walls : in chap. lx. the
full vision of the restored city bursts in all its splendour upon
his raptured eye.   As in his conception of the new covenant
to be established with Israel, the prophet is in harmony with ✓
Jeremiah and Ezekiel, so in this vision of the future Zion he
shows himself to be influenced by Isaiah (comp. *e.g.,* iv. 3–6 ;
xxx. 26 : also xxiv. 23 ; xxv. 6–8), but the imagery is more
brilliant, the picture more magnificent and complete.   The
inhabitants of the ideal Zion, while free from all anxiety on the
ground of material welfare (liv. 14 ; lx. 18 ; lxii. 8 f.), will exhibit faithfully their ideal character : they will be impregnated
with Jehovah's teaching (the "disciples of Jehovah," liv. 13) ;
"all righteous," they will become to Him a source of pride
and delight (lx. 21 ; lxi. 3 *end*; lxii. 5 ; lxv. 19), an example of
righteousness conspicuous in the world, and attracting the

---

[1] Comp. Jer. xxxii. 40, Ezek. xvi. 60, xxxiv. 25, xxxvii. 26, where the
same expressions occur.   Isaiah never uses in this connection the figure of

world's reverential wonder (lxi. 11*b*; lxii. 2, 7*b*). The desolated tracts of Palestine will be repeopled and repastured
(lvii. 13 ; lviii. 12 ; lxv. 9 f.) : no invader, no pestilence or drought,
will stay the sower from reaping the fruits of his toil :
death will not indeed be abolished, but it will attack none
prematurely : ready then, as they are now (l. 2 ; lxv. 12 ;
lxvi. 4) the reverse, to invoke Jehovah's name, their prayers
will receive His immediate response (lxv. 19–24). Only the
unworthy Israelites, especially those addicted to heathen
superstitions, will be excluded from these blessings (lv. 6 f.,
lvi. 1, chap. lviii., by implication : lix. 20, lxv. 3–7, 11–15, lxvi.
3–5, 17, expressly). Extreme reverence and respect will be
rendered to the restored community by the Gentile nations.
Their good-will will be shown first in the readiness with which
they will escort the exiles back (xlix. 22 f. ; lx. 3, 4, 9; lxvi.
12*b*, 20) : afterwards in the eagerness with which they will
come forward to claim the same religious privileges (xliv. 5 ; xlv.
14; lv. 5 ; lx. 9, 14), and in the regard which in other ways
they will exhibit towards them. Thus not only will they
offer generously of their best (lx. 16 ; lxi. 6*b*), and pour their
wealth at their feet (lx. 6 f., 11*b*; lxvi. 12) : they will execute
for them menial offices (lx. 10 ; lxi. 5) ; they will acknowledge
them as the authorized dispensers of spiritual blessings (lxi. 6) ;
they will honour them as a nation upon which Jehovah's blessing
evidently rests (lxi. 9).

As regards the nations of the world, the prophet's conception
of their future is singularly comprehensive and large. Great as
are the thoughts expressed on this subject by Isaiah (ii. 2–4 ;
xi. 10; xix. 23–5 : comp. xxv. 6 f. ; Jer. iii. 17 ; Zeph. iii. 9),
those expressed by the prophet of the exile may be said,
without fear of contradiction, to be greater. The world, in his
view, is *expectant :* no sooner does it hear the message of truth
than it at once recognizes in it the salvation for which it had
more or less consciously yearned (xlii. 4*b*; li. 5*b*). In the
approaching restoration of his nation the prophet sees a great
evidential act enacted in the eyes of the world (xl. 5 ; lii. 10),
and adapted in the end to create a revolution in the religious
feelings of mankind (xlv. 6). God's purposes of salvation
embrace the entire earth. "Unto Me every knee shall
bow, every tongue swear" (xlv. 23) ; "I will make My judgment (*i.e.*, My religion) to rest for a light of the peoples" (li.

4); "Mine house shall be called a house of prayer for all peoples" (lvi. 7): week by week, and month by month, "all flesh" will come to worship before Jehovah at Jerusalem (lxvi. 23; cf. p. 167). The same thought reappears from a different point of view in connection with the work of Jehovah's ideal Servant: xlii. 1*b* (where judgment, as li. 4, signifies "religion"); xlii. 6 ("a light of the Gentiles"); xlix. 6*b*; cf. lii. 15 (the wonder which the spectacle of his exaltation will arouse in nations and their kings).

The last-mentioned feature of the prophecy remains yet to be considered. The figure of the "Servant of Jehovah" is as conspicuous in the prophecy before us as is the figure of the Messianic king in Isaiah, to which indeed it holds in chaps. xl.–lxvi. an analogous position. What, now, does the prophet mean by this term? What does the figure denoted by it represent to him? What attributes or functions does he associate with it? The term itself denotes in general one who is God's agent or representative, and who is loyal and devoted, according to the knowledge possessed by him, in the discharge of the work entrusted to him. It is thus applied to many different persons, as Abraham (Gen. xxvi. 24), Moses (Num. xii. 7), Caleb (*ib.* xiv. 24), Joshua (Jud. ii. 8), David (2 Sam. vii. 8), Isaiah (ch. xx. 3), Eliakim (ch. xxii. 20), Job (Job i. 8), the prophets generally (Amos iii. 7 and frequently), even to a heathen, as Nebuchadnezzar (Jer. xxv. 9; xliii. 10). In the present prophecy, however, the application of the term is peculiar, nor is it easy to form a perfectly consistent picture of the idea expressed by it. Let us be guided in our endeavour by the hints which the author affords us himself.

It is reasonable to seek the origin of the idea in the first passage in which the term occurs, xli. 8 f.: "But thou, Israel *My servant*, Jacob whom I have chosen, the seed of Abraham, who loved Me; thou whom I have taken hold of from the ends of the earth, and called thee from the corners thereof, and said unto thee, *Thou art My servant:* I have chosen thee, and not cast thee away: fear thou not, for I am with thee: be not dismayed, for I am thy God." Here there can be no doubt as to what the term denotes. It denotes the *Israelitish nation*, treated, however, not as the mere aggregate of the members composing it, but as a *unity*, developing historically, and maintaining its con-

The nation is viewed by the prophet as a single individual, called by God in the distant past, honoured by Him with the title implying that it is His organ or representative upon earth, and now exiled in Babylon. Again, in xlv. 4, Cyrus is addressed in these words: " For Jacob *My servant's* sake, and Israel My chosen, I have called thee by thy name ; I have titled thee, when thou hast not known Me." Here, not less plainly, the term denotes equally the *nation*, exiled at present in Babylon, and shortly to be released by Cyrus. The application is the same in xliii. 10 ; xliv. 1-2, 21 ; xlviii. 20. In all these passages, the term is a designation of Israel, the nation being regarded as an individual whose birth (xliv. 2 : Thus saith Jehovah that made thee, and *formed thee from the womb*) coincides with its first appearance amongst other nations, whose ideal charac- ter (" My servant ") corresponds with the design (Gen. xviii. 19 R.V.) stamped upon the nation's history, and whose life repre- sents its subsequent experiences. The nation being thus grasped as an individual, it follows from the continuity of the national life that the term may be applied equally to denote it in every stage of its history. Thus in xlii. 18 f. we read : " Hear, ye deaf, and look, ye blind, that ye may see. Who is blind but *My servant?* or deaf as My messenger that I send ?" Here, as before, the term " My servant " denotes the nation ; but the prophet for the moment thinks only of the masses whom he sees around him, heedless of Israel's mission, and unconscious of its future destiny : these at the time represent the nation in his eyes, and elicit from him accordingly the language of re- proof (comp. xliv. 21, 22). In the other passages that have been quoted he doubtless, in using the term, has in mind those who are more truly its representatives, and are worthy to receive the promises which he has to bestow. Just so, " Israel" is the recipient of promises and encouragement in xli. 14, xliii. 1, xliv. 23, while it is the object of rebuke in xl. 27, xliii. 22.

There exists, however, another group of passages in which the language is often similar, but where this explanation is not adequate. Thus xlii. 1 f. : " Behold, *My servant,* whom I up- hold ; My chosen, in whom My soul delighteth : I have put My spirit upon him ; he shall bring forth judgment (*i.e.,* religion) to the nations. He shall not cry, nor lift up, nor cause his voice to be heard in the streets." And xlix. 1-3 : " Listen, O isles, unto me ; and hearken, ye peoples, from far ; Jehovah hath called me from the womb, from the bowels of my mother hath He made mention of my name ; and He hath made my mouth like a sharp sword, in the shadow of His hand hath He hid me : and He hath made me a polished shaft, in His quiver hath He kept me close ; and He said unto me, *Thou art My servant; Israel, in whom I will glory* . . . (*v.* 5 f.) And now, saith Jehovah, that *formed me from the womb to be His servant*, to bring Jacob again to Him, and that Israel be gathered unto Him : . . . yea, He saith, It is too light a thing that thou shouldest be My servant to raise up the tribes of Jacob, and to restore the preserved of Israel : I will also give thee for a light to the Gentiles, to be My salvation unto the end of the earth." Here, not only does the language describe apparently the acts of an individual person, but the Servant is expressly *distinguished from* the historic nation ; and part of the Servant's office is to consist in the restoration of the historic nation, and (*v.* 8) the re-allotment of its desolated land. The case is similar in liii. 1–6, where (P. 153) the repentant Israelites reflect upon their previous misconception of the Servant's character and work. At the same time, the Servant is still in some sense " Israel " ; for the term is directly applied to him in *v.* 3 : "And He said unto me, Thou art My servant ; *Israel*, in whom I will glory." The other passages belonging to the same group are l. 4–9 ; lii. 13–liii. 12 ; and (probably) lxi. 1–3. It is inconceivable that the prophet should use the *same* phraseology, and apply the *same* predicates to subjects entirely distinct ; the " servant" of the second group of passages must be *Israel*, not less truly than the " servant " of the first group is Israel. The required identity can only be preserved by some such supposition as the following. The prophet always, in using the term " My servant," means Israel ; but sometimes, as he speaks, he has in view the literal historic nation (whether as maintaining its ideal character, or, as in xlii. 19, falling short of it), sometimes he rises from this to the conception of an *ideal personality*, a figure exhibiting the truest and most genuine characteristics of the nation, and realizing them in action with an intensity and clearness of aim which the historic Israel had never even remotely attained. It is a great ideal creation which the prophet constructs, a transfigured reflection of the historic people, a figure conscious of the colossal task allotted to it, but

13

impeded by no moral slackness, or other deficiency, from undertaking it ; a figure (as it appears) which the prophet conceived
would at some time be manifested, as a reality, upon the stage
of history. So vividly, indeed, is this wonderful creation a
figure present to his imagination, that it exhibits all the concrete traits of an individual person, and he expects from it the
performance of works *in which the historic nation has failed.*
But the figure, being delineated on the basis of the historic
Israel, and reflecting its most essential and genuine characteristics, is still designated by the same title.   Thus in the *first*
group of passages the prophet styles the actual nation " Jeho
vah's servant," seeing in it (as has been said) not a mere aggre
gate of individuals, but a society developing historically, and
realizing in its history a purpose and an aim.[1] In the *second*
group of passages he applies the term to an *ideal figure*, which
is the impersonation of Israel's ideal character, and which he
represents as accomplishing what Israel, as he knew it, had
left unachieved.

The chief aspects of the ideal Servant's work may be classed
as follows :

1. He is to be the embodiment of a new covenant between
Jehovah and His people, to restore the actual nation exiled at
the time in Babylon, and to re-establish them in their own land
(xlii. 6 ; xlix. 5, 6*a*, 8*b*).

2. But he has a mission not to Israel merely, but to the
world : he is to teach the world true religion, and to be a
"light of the Gentiles" (xlii. 1*b*, 3*b*, 6*b* ; xlix. 6*b*).

3. He is to be a prophet, patient and faithful in the discharge
of his work, in spite of the contumely and opposition which he
may encounter (l. 4–9).

4. Being innocent himself, he is to suffer and die for the sins
of others (liii. 4–9).

The central idea here is that of the *prophet.* Israel is the
prophetic nation marked out among other nations of the world,
as the organ and channel of revelation.   To maintain and
develop a knowledge of Divine truth is the purpose impressed
upon its history (Gen. xviii. 19).   Upon the basis of the

---

[1] The germ of this conception of the prophet is perhaps to be found in
Jer. xxx. 10 (=xlvi. 27). By Jeremiah the term is applied to the actual
nation, during the period of its exile, and is not yet used in an individual
sense, or idealized.

character thus belonging to it, the prophet constructs his figure of Jehovah's ideal Servant, the ideal impersonation of the theocratic attributes of the nation. Particular traits in the portrait may have been suggested by actual experience. Both the nation generally (Ps. xliv. 22) and individuals (Jer. xv. 15) suffered for the truth : Jeremiah even applies to himself the same figures as are here used of the ideal Servant (Jer. xi. 19 ; cf. i. 19; xvii. 16 ; xviii. 18–20 ; xx. 11). But the portrait as a whole is ✓ a *new* one, and includes elements transcending experience altogether. Especially noticeable is the comprehensiveness of the work assigned to him. The sphere of his operation is coextensive with the world : his innocency imparts to his sufferings a vicarious efficacy ; his death is a "guilt-offering" (p. 154) ✓ rendering satisfaction for the sacrilege of sin; and it is followed by a new and glorious life, in which he carries through successfully Jehovah's "pleasure" or purpose to manifest Himself to the world, and strikes amazement (lii. 15) by his triumph into the hearts of all that witness it. Another noticeable feature is the completeness of the figure drawn by the prophet, and the artistic skill shown by him in its delineation. The character with which he invests it is unfolded gradually, the figure being introduced at different successive stages in the development of the prophet's theme, and some fresh feature, or group of features, being added each time. There is variety also in the manner in which it is introduced. Sometimes, the prophet speaks descriptively in the third person, sometimes he allows the figure, with dramatic effect, to speak in its own person ; sometimes he represents the Israelites themselves uttering their reflections upon it (liii. 1–6). Thus it is no abstract character which the prophet delineates ; his own warmth of feeling and imaginative sympathy are reflected in it ; it is human in its completeness; it speaks in accents of sweetness and pathos ; it is not deficient in strength and decision (l. 7 f.), yet the attributes of resignation (liii. 7), tenderness, and sympathy (lxi. 1–3) predominate; for a moment it is disheartened, but is quickly reassured (xlix. 4) : unobtrusively but surely it accomplishes its ends (xlii. 2 f.) The prophet is master, in a rare degree (p. 183 f.), of the art of personification : and hence the distinctness, and dramatic force, with which his delineation is expressed.

Such is the figure which the prophet projects upon the future, and from which he expects, alike for his own nation and for the world, the highest benefits to accrue. How were his expectations fulfilled? It cannot be doubted that, as Christendom from the beginning has seen, the character thus delineated by the prophet with such genius and power was realized by Jesus of Nazareth. As has been explained, the figure itself is constructed upon the basis of the historic Israel, and exhibits, in their ideal delicacy and completeness, the most characteristic attributes of the nation. But it is just these attributes which were also realized in their fulness and perfection by Jesus Christ. If, for example, it was the function of Israel to be the organ and channel of revelation, to manifest the character and purposes of God to the world, to perpetuate and exemplify the practice of religion and holiness of life, to be a witness to the truth, even (in the persons of its individual members) to the endurance of persecution and death, it is evident how in all these aspects the mission of Israel was far more effectively and completely realized by Christ. In Christ the genius of Israel found its fullest and most intense expression the character imperfectly realized either by the nation as a whole, or by the best of its individual members, was exhibited in its completeness by Him. The work and office of Christ, as Teacher, as Prophet, as Example, as Sacrifice, exhibits the consummation of what was achieved imperfectly and partially by Israel. As, on the one hand, the figure sketched by the prophet reflects, as in a miniature, the best and truest features of the nation ; so, on the other hand, it is a prefigurement of the human personality of Christ. The ideal *King*, or Messiah,[1] so conspicuous in the prophecies of Isaiah, has no place in the visions of the great prophet of the exile. The ideal *Prophet*, realizing in their perfection the attributes of the nation, appears instead, and occupies a strictly analogous position. In the Old Testament, however, these two figures are distinct : they start from a different basis, and are projected in different planes. Only in the fulfilment is it seen how the two characters thus distinct can be combined in one Person. As under one aspect of His work, Christ realizes (p. 114) the attributes which belong to Israel's ideal *king;* so under another aspect, He realizes the attributes belonging ideally to the *prophetic nation.*[2]

[1] See p. 111, *note.*

[2] The greatest difficulty which arises out of the prophet's delineation is to understand how he conceived the ideal Servant as the agent *in restoring the*

The prophet's poetical genius and literary style will appear most distinctly when they are compared with those of Isaiah. The contrast between the two prophets is in many respects very marked. Not indeed that particular figures, or particular verses, found in either prophet, might not have been written by the other, as they might have been written also by Amos or Nahum or even by Jeremiah ; but as a whole, both the poetry and the literary form are different. Isaiah's style is terse and compact : the movement of his periods is stately and measured : his rhetoric is grave and restrained. In the prophecy before us, a subject is often developed in considerable detail : the periods advance more rapidly : the rhetoric is instinct with animation and passion. It is remarkable how it could have occurred to any one to describe this series of discourses as a "chamber-prophecy," as written by their author in the seclusion of a study. If any prophet in the Old Testament gives evidence that he speaks in public, and that his desire is to stir and move those whom he addresses, it is the author of these chapters. What meaning have appeals and protestations, such as those in xl. 21, 26, 28 ; xliii. 10 ; xlviii. 8; l. 10 f. ; li. 6, 12 f. ; lviii. 3 ff., except as spoken in the very presence of those whose assent the prophet seeks to win ? The author's warm and impassioned rhetoric, the *personal* appeals with which his prophecies abound, show conclusively that he is not writing a literary essay in the retirement of his chamber, but, like a true prophet of his nation, is exerting himself in all earnestness to produce an impression by the force of his own personality upon the hearts of those who hear him. The very first words of the prophecy, " *Comfort ye, comfort ye* my people," mark a

---

actual Israel from Babylon (for the expressions in xlix. 6*a*, 8*b*, are certainly not to be understood in a spiritual sense)—at least, if his conception is to be brought into agreement with the fact. Jehovah's ideal Servant being, as we have seen, a figure reflecting Israel's ideal character and destiny, perhaps it may be supposed that, instead of saying simply that Israel's destiny was the guarantee of its restoration, he conceives its destiny as embodied in this personality, which he then sets over against the actual nation, and views as acting independently on its behalf. Obviously, this part of the Servant's office was completed long before the advent of Christ ; so that the figure

rhetorical peculiarity of the author. The emphatic duplication
of a word, significant of the passion and fervour of the speaker,
is a characteristic feature of the entire prophecy [1]; in the
prophets generally, it is rare; in Isaiah the only examples—and
those but partly parallel—are viii. 9*b*; xxi. 9; xxix. 1. The
rhetorical structure of the verses just referred to, as illustrating
the intensity of the prophet's feeling (to which may be added
xl. 24; xli. 10*b* and 26*b*; xliv. 15*b*; xlv. 21; xlvi. 11*b*), is also
characteristic of the prophecy, and unlike anything to be found
in Isaiah. Another striking feature of the prophet's style is
the addition of participial adjuncts [2] to the Divine name,
especially in corroboration of a promise, or other solemn
asseveration: xlii. 5; xliii. 1, 14, 16 f., &c. (see p. 198); notice,
in particular, the fine series in xliv. 24-8 culminating in the commission of Cyrus to permit the building of the Temple, and
introducing the promise of his conquest of Babylon, xlv. 1-8.[3]

If the predominant characteristic of Isaiah's imagination be
grandeur (p. 115 f.), that of the author of chaps. xl.–lxvi. is
pathos. The storms, the inundations, the sudden catastrophes,
which Isaiah loves to depict, will be sought for in vain in this
prophecy: the author, either, if he uses the same figures,
applies them differently, or draws his imagery from a different
region of nature altogether.[4] The "river," for instance, suggests
to him no destructive agency; its placid and smoothly rolling
waters are twice the expressive emblem of serene and heavenly
peace (xlviii. 18; lxvi. 12). Isaiah describes the *majesty* of
Jehovah: the prophet of the exile is filled with a sense of His
loftiness and immeasurable power: hence the profoundly
impressive figures by which he indicates the insignificance in

---

[1] Chaps. xl. 1; xliii. 11, 25; xlviii. 11, 15; li. 9, 12, 17; lii. 1, 11; lvii.
6, 14, 19; lxii. 10*a*, *b*; lxv. 1. The duplication in lvii. 19 (*Peace, peace!*)
is not quite so characteristic as the others, the phrase being probably one
in current use (see Jer. vi. 14, viii. 11; 1 Chron. xii. 18: the words occur
also, though *not* as an exclamation, in chap. xxvi. 3).

[2] In A.V., R.V., often represented by a relative clause, and thus disguised.

[3] There is nothing resembling this in Isaiah. Some peculiarities of a
more technical character will be noticed in Chap. V.

[4] The passing allusions to a tempest or flood, xli. 16, lix. 19*b*, lxvi. 15,
are no real exception to what has been said. It may be observed that while
Isaiah is apt to *develop* his similes at some length (*e.g.*, x. 33 f.; xviii. 4 f.;
xxix. 8; xxx. 27, 28, 30), the prophet is here usually content with the
simple particle of comparison (*e.g.*, li. 3, 6, 8, 20, 23).

His eyes of all things human—the drop of a bucket, the fine dust on the arms of a balance (xl. 15), the fragile grasshopper (xl. 22), nonentity itself (xl. 17, 23 ; xli. 11). Under images hardly less suggestive, he pictures again the futility of man's opposition to the purposes of God—the grass scorched at Jehovah's blast (xl. 6 f. ; li. 12), the moth- or worm-eaten garment (li. 8) ; or the distance which separates human intelligence from the Divine, lv. 9 ("as the heavens are higher than the earth," &c.). If there is a figure from inanimate nature which the prophet uses more frequently than another, it is that of the wind carrying away with it the powers opposed to Israel (xl. 24 ; xli. 16), or false gods (lvii. 13), or the Israelite himself enervated and rendered helpless by sin (lxiv. 6b). Figures drawn from grass or plants are also not infrequent, xl. 6 f. ; xliv. 4 ; liii. 2 ; lv. 10 (the earth fertilized by rain—a striking figure of the effective and fruitful operation of the Divine Word) ; lviii. 11 ; lx. 21 ; lxi. 3b, 11 ; lxv. 22 ; lxvi. 14.

But the region from which the prophet's figures are by preference derived is animate nature, and in particular the sphere of human emotion. How expressive are the figures drawn by him from animal life ! the grasshoppers, already mentioned, in xl. 22 ; the eagles mounting upwards, in xl. 31 ; the antelope entangled in a net, in li. 20 ; the straying sheep, in liii. 6 ; the lamb dumb before its shearers, in liii. 7 ; the basilisk's eggs, the spider's web, and the viper, in lix. 5 f. How picturesque, in lx. 8, the comparison of the ships bearing the exiles, and speeding homeward with outspread sails, to clouds drifting in the breeze, and *doves* returning to their cotes !

More characteristic, however, are the figures derived from human emotion : it is these, especially, which impart to the prophecy its peculiar pathos and warmth. Thus in xlix. 18 ; lxi. 10b ; lxii. 5, the joy of the bride, or of the bridegroom, is made the basis of a singularly beautiful comparison ; in lxvi. 13, the solace administered by a mother to her grown-up son : in xlix. 15, a mother's affection for her offspring. But the prophet's fondness for figures drawn from this source is most abundantly exemplified by the fine and powerful personifications which are a distinguishing feature of his prophecy. Since Amos (v. 2) it became habitual with the prophets to personify a city or community as a *maiden*, especially where it was desired to represent it as vividly conscious of some keen or sharp

emotion.[1] In the adoption of this usage by the prophet there
is, of course, nothing remarkable ; what is remarkable is the
independence and originality which he shows in the application
of it. Zion is represented as a widow, a mother, a bride, *i.e.*,
under just those relations of life in which the deepest feelings
of humanity come into play : and the personification is con-
tinned sometimes through a long series of verses. The principal
examples are xlix. 18–23 (Zion, a mother welcoming back her
children) ; li. 17–23 (Zion, prostrate and dazed by trouble, but
now bidden to lift herself up) ; lii. 1 f. ; liv. 1–6 (Zion, a bride
reclaimed by her husband) ; lx. 1–5; lxii. 5 ; xlvii. 1–15
(Babylon). This, however, is not the only type of personification which the prophet employs. He personifies nature :
he bids earth and heaven shout in exultation at the restoration
of God's people (xliv. 23 ; xlix. 13 ; lii. 9) ; he hears in imagination the voices of invisible beings sounding from the desert
(xl. 3, 6 ; lvii. 14) ; he peoples Jerusalem with ideal watchmen
(lii. 8) and guardians (lxii. 6). Whatever he touches is at once
aglow with life and animation : the nations themselves
become eager and interested spectators in the Divine drama
about to be enacted, or are summoned up by him *en masse*
(xliii. 9) to dispute with Israel. And lastly, as the most original
and impressive, as well as the most complete, of the prophet's
personifications must be reckoned naturally his great dramatic
conception of Jehovah's ideal Servant.

[1] Amos v. 2 (Israel prostrate and helpless) ; Isa. i. 8 (Zion desolate and
abandoned) ; xxiii. 4 (Zidon lamenting her bereavement) ; xxix. 1–6
(where the pronouns in the Hebrew are feminine) ; xxxvii. 22 (Zion disdainfully mocking the retreating invader) ; Mic. iv. 8, 10, 13 ; Zeph. iii. 14
and Zech. ix. 9 (Zion exultant) ; Jer. iv. 31 ; vi. 26 ; xlvi. 11, 19, 24 (Egypt) ;
l. 42, and li. 33 (Babylon). Isaiah, unlike the author of chaps. xl.-lxvi.,
displays no *exceptional* preference for personification.

NOTE.—In the preceding chapter, it has naturally been impossible to
notice more than the most salient features in the theology of II. Isaiah.
Those who desire to study the subject in greater detail may consult with
advantage the well-written monograph of F. H. Krüger, " Essai sur la
Théologie d' Ésaie xl.-lxvi." (Paris, 1881), and a series of papers by Prof.
A. B. Davidson in " The Expositor," 1883, Aug., Sept. ; 1884, Feb., April,
Oct., Nov., Dec.

CHAPTER V.

AUTHORSHIP OF CHAPTERS XL.–LXVI.

IN the two preceding chapters it has been assumed that the great prophecy of Israel's restoration is not the work of Isaiah, the son of Amoz, but has for its author a prophet writing towards the close of the Babylonian captivity. It remains to acquaint the reader with the facts upon which this conclusion rests. Many of these facts will be appreciated without difficulty by the general reader; others, it is true, can only be properly estimated by those who are conversant with the Old Testament in the original Hebrew; but an endeavour will be made to render their bearing, as far as possible, intelligible to all.

I. The primary fact is the *internal evidence* supplied by the prophecy itself respecting the period at which it was written. The historical background of the prophecy is the period of the Babylonian captivity. The reader who has followed the argument of the prophecy, as exhibited in Chap. III., will not need to be reminded how numerous are the allusions to the ruined and deserted condition of Jerusalem (*e.g.*, xliv. 26*b*; lxiii. 18; lxiv. 10 f.), to the sufferings which the Jews have experienced, or are experiencing, at the hands of the Chaldeans (xlii. 25; xlvii. 6; xlii. 22; lii. 5), to the prospect of return which, as the prophet speaks, is imminent (xl. 2; xlvi. 13; xlviii. 20, &c.). The desolation of Jerusalem is even described as of long standing, or "ancient" (lviii. 12; lxi. 4). Those whom the prophet addresses,

Isaiah's age ; the deliverer, Cyrus, rivets his gaze ; the prospect of return to Zion absorbs his thoughts. Judged by the
analogy of prophecy, this constitutes the strongest possible
ground for supposing that the author actually *lived* in the period
which he thus describes, and is not merely (as has been supposed) Isaiah immersed in spirit in the future, and holding
converse, as it were, with the generations yet unborn. Such an
immersion in the future would be not only without parallel in
the Old Testament ; it would be alien in itself to the nature of
prophecy. As has been before observed (p. 86, 126), the prophet
speaks primarily to his contemporaries ; and his predictions rest
upon the basis of the history of his time. This principle of
prophecy has been exemplified repeatedly in Part I.: Isaiah's
greatest prophecies have, one and all, as their human occasions,
the crises and circumstances of his own age. The same principle is observed equally in the case of the other prophets.
Jeremiah, for instance, predicts the restoration of Israel ; but
how ? He predicts first the exile, then the restoration (ch. xxx.–
xxxiii.) ; but he never abandons his own historical position ; he
speaks uniformly from the period in which he lives ; exile and
restoration are alike viewed by him as future. Ezekiel, in
prophecies written *before* the fall of Jerusalem, does the same
(chaps. xvi., xvii.). There is *no* analogy for the case of a prophet,
transported in spirit to a future age, and predicting *from that
standpoint* a future remoter still. In the prophecy before us,
there is no *prediction* of exile ; the exile is not announced as
something yet future, it is *pre-supposed.* Had Isaiah been the
author, he would, according to all analogy, have predicted *both*
the exile *and* the restoration. He would have represented *both*,
as Jeremiah and Ezekiel do, as lying equally in the future.

Nothing but the strongest and clearest evidence could neutralize the force of this argument. As we shall see, the evidence of
language and thought strikingly confirms it. For the purpose of
meeting it, the following considerations have been urged, which
must be briefly noticed.

a. It is said that there are passages in which the prophets
throw themselves forward to an ideal standpoint, and describe
from it events future to themselves, as if they were part : *e.g.,*
v. 13, 25 ; ix. 1–6 ; xxiii. 1, 11–12 ; also xxv. 1–5, xxvi. 1–18 (p.
121, 123). This is true ; but the passages are not really parallel.
The transference to the future which they imply is *momentary* :

in the immediate context, the prophet uses future tenses, and speaks from his own standpoint ; the expressions moreover are general, and the figures ideal. The passages quoted supply no analogy for such a *sustained* transference to the future, as would be implied if these chapters were by Isaiah, or for the *detailea* and *definite* description of the circumstances of a distant age. Nor do passages supplying the required analogy exist in the writings of any of the other prophets.

b. It is said that the standpoint of the exile is not consistently maintained, and that there are passages in which the prophet returns to his own present, and betrays by allusions to it the age in which he really lives. The principal passages quoted are : lvi. 9–lvii. 2 ; lvii. 3–10 ; lix. 1–15. In the notice of the righteous perishing unheeded, there seems to be an allusion to the persecutions under Manasseh ; the description of Israel as neglected by its rulers, the mention of its careless " shepherds," and the idolatries with which it is charged, remind us forcibly of passages in Jeremiah, relating to the period of the later kings of Judah (ii. 20–37 ; x. 21 ; xxiii. 1, 2) ; and the picture of national sin in chap. lix. seems to be too dark for the close of the exile. It appears, however, to be sometimes forgotten that whatever difficulty these passages present, the difficulty is precisely the same, whether the author of chaps. xl.-lxvi. be Isaiah or a prophet writing towards the close of the exile. For even those who hold these chapters to be Isaiah's admit that they are designed for an age other than his own, and are, in fact, implicitly addressed to the generation of the exile. This being so, the *unity of the prophet's work* requires it to be accommodated throughout to this situation ; and, indeed, the passages quoted are brought expressly into connection with the return (lvii. 13*b*, 14 ; lix. 19 f.). If now the author be Isaiah, and he refers exclusively to the practices and social condition of (say) Manasseh's time, such passages would have no connection with the main theme of the prophecy, and would be out of place in the argument. The sins of Manasseh's age might form to Isaiah, as they formed to Jeremiah (Jer. xv. 4), the ground for an announcement of impending exile : they can, *in themselves*, have no bearing on the future of the exiles more than

Whether, therefore, it be Isaiah or an exilic prophet who speaks,
these allusions to the idolatry and other sins of the nation,
whilst in Palestine, must be *accommodated to the situation of
the exiles.* This accommodation is—to say the least—as readily
conceivable on the part of the exilic prophet as on the part of
Isaiah ; in the judgment of many, it will appear to be more so.
There are frequent allusions in these chapters which show that
the exiles, as a whole, were far from being as spiritually minded
as the prophet would have desired to see them[1] ; and sins such
as those which Jeremiah and Ezekiel attest as prevalent in
Judah till the very eve of the exile,[2] imply tendencies which
would not be generally extirpated 40 or 50 years later.   The
prophet, we may suppose, borrows here passages written
originally in the age of Jeremiah, and *applies* them to the
generation of the exiles, in so far as these are the true children
of their fathers, and in so far as they may see in the mirror
which he thus holds up before them, their own image reflected.[3]

c. The prophet, in proof of the divinity of Israel's God, appeals
frequently to *fulfilled predictions* (xli. 26 ; xlii. 9 ; xliii. 8-10 ;
xlviii. 3-8 : cf. xlv. 21[4] ; xlvi. 10[4]).   This appeal, it is said, is of
no value, if the prophecy dates from the period of the exile.   The
argument would be of weight, if there were reason to suppose
that the predictions alluded to were those *constituting the
prophecy itself;* but if the passages are read attentively, it will
be seen that they contain nothing which lends support to such a
supposition.   The prophet's standpoint is indicated in xlii. 9
" Lo, the former things *are come to pass :* and new things do I
declare ; before they spring forth, I cause you to hear them "
(cf. xlviii. 3) ; on the ground of prophecies which, as he speaks,
are already fulfilled, he rests his claim to be heard in the *new*

---

[1] Chap. xlii. 19 ; xlvi. 8, 12 ; xlviii. 1 f. ; l. 11 ; lxv. 3-5, 11 ; lxvi. 5.

[2] Jer. ii. 20, 23, 27 ; iii. 6, 13 ; xix. 4 f. ; xxxii. 35 ; xliv. 8 (of the exiles
in Egypt), 15-19 ; Ezek. v. 11 ; viii. (in the precincts of the Temple itself) ;
xi. 21 ; xiv. 1-11 (idolatry among the exiles) ; xxii.

[3] In lxv. 7, which has been cited similarly as evidence of authorship in
Palestine, it has been overlooked that those who " offered incense upon the
mountains " are described as the *fathers* of the persons addressed. And in xliii.
22-25 the *fact* of no sacrifices having been offered by Israel during the exile,
especially if, as the prophet holds (xlii. 24 f.), the exile was due to the nation's
sin, is a sufficient ground upon which to base God's free offer of pardon.

[4] Where the word rendered " ancient time " is literally *aforetime,* and
need not express more than this : see Job xxix. 2 Heb.

announcements now made by him. The new announcements are, primarily, the capture of Babylon by Cyrus, and the release of the Jews—topics to which the prophet repeatedly reverts in the course of chapters xl.–xlviii. What the " former things " are is not distinctly stated : but it is nowhere implied that they are anything contained in the prophecy itself. As Cyrus is alluded to as already "stirred up" (xli. 2, 25 ; xlv. 13 ; cf. p. 139), at the time when the prophecy opens, it is probable that they were prophecies delivered either by the prophet himself or by others, relating to the early stages of Cyrus's career (p. 140).[1] These had been spoken some time before : they had been fulfilled (cf. xlviii. 3–6a) : and now *fresh* prophecies are delivered by him relating to events very soon to take place (cf. xlviii. 6b–8). The language of the prophet is throughout consistent with the supposition that his prophecy was delivered *c.* 540, ten or twelve years (perhaps more) since Cyrus's first appearance, and two years before his capture of Babylon ; and the allusions to fulfilled predictions are, upon the same supposition, thoroughly intelligible and clear.[2]

d. It is said that there is a marked absence in the prophecy of allusions to Babylon and Babylonia, while, on the other hand, the scenery and natural objects which the prophet notices, or from which he borrows his poetical images, are Palestinian, and not Babylonian. Here, firstly, it is to be observed that the prophets do not write as travellers or topographers : they mention objects not for the purpose of describing them, but only so far as the allusion may form an appropriate element in their argument. There are exceedingly few specific allusions to Babylonia in Ezekiel, though Ezekiel's whole book was written in the land of his exile. Moreover, as a prophet of *Israel*, the writer's

[1] Cf. xli. 22, 26 f., xliii. 9, xliv. 7, xlviii. 14, where the representatives of the idol gods are taunted with not having produced, and not being able to produce, any similar predictions.

[2] It has been objected (Smith's "Dict. of the Bible," ed. i. vol. i. p. 888) that the author of the prophecy claims "*fore*-knowledge of the deliverance by *Cyrus*." This objection cannot be sustained : in fact, it involves a fallacy akin to that known to logicians as the fallacy *plurium interroga·*

interest would be centred, not in Babylon, but in Judah. As
Ezekiel's eye was never averted from the home of his people, as
he was constantly contemplating either the impending fall of
Jerusalem (chaps. i.–xxiv.), or its future restoration (chaps.
xxxiv.–xxxix. ; xl.–xlviii.), so the author of the present prophecy,
though he wrote in Babylonia, would have his eyes ever turned
towards the home to which, as he knew, his people would shortly .
be restored.   With his mind intent upon the vision of the ideal
glories of Zion, it would not be natural for him to draw his illustrations from the land of his nation's exile.   Nor, secondly, must
it be forgotten that it is quite gratuitous to suppose that Palestine
was unknown to him.   Individuals were left behind by Nebuchadnezzar's general (Jer. xl. 7, 10 f.; xli. 16; xlii. 1, 10; xliv. 28) :
individuals also in the large community—comprising at least
100,000 or 120,000 souls—which the exiles formed, may have
found the means of re-visiting Palestine: and the author may have
been one of either of these classes.   Or, again, since we are expressly told (Ezra iii. 12) that, amongst those who returned with
Zerubbabel in 538, there were some who recollected the former
temple, there is nothing unreasonable in the supposition that
he may have been one of these : if in the year 588 he was a
youth of seventeen, he would, at the time at which we have
supposed the prophecy to open, be not more than sixty-five years
of age.   Those who attribute the prophecy to Isaiah generally
regard it as written after 701, when he would be (p. 2) at least
sixty years of age ; and if the force and animation which it displays is not incompatible with the old age of Isaiah, it cannot
plausibly be regarded as incompatible with the old age of
another prophet.   In the face of possibilities such as these,
there is nothing arbitrary or extreme in supposing the author to
have been personally acquainted with Palestine ; and, if this
were the case, such preference as he shows, or appears to show,
for images derived from its scenery, is readily explained.

But the silence as regards Babylon and Babylonia is not
complete.   Especially in chaps. xl.–xlviii., where the prophet
chiefly contemplates the approaching conquest of the city by
Cyrus, allusions occur incidentally as definite as would be expected under the circumstances.   Thus, xliii. 14, he alludes to
the shipping of Babylon ; xliv. 27, xlv. 1 f., to its river and
great gates (Hdt. i. 180) ; xlv. 3, to its treasures (cf. Jer. li. 13) ;
xlvi. 1 f. to Bel and Nebo, and the processions of sacred images ;

xlvii. 8-10, to the character and habits of the inhabitants ; *v.* 11-13 to its astrologers and sorcerers ; *v.* 15, to the foreign traders who resorted thither ; xlix. 10, to the mirage [1]; l. 2*b*, to the fish in the river ; liv. 11 f., (perhaps) to the precious stones, for skill in cutting which the Babylonians were famed.[2] The prophet would have had no motive for describing in detail the great Temple and image of Bel as Herodotus does (i. 181, 183)[3] : but it is difficult not to think that he had Babylonian idolatry in his mind, in his satirical descriptions of the methods by which idols were manufactured (xl. 19, 20 ; xliv. 9-18 ; xlvi. 6, 7), or produced as occasion required (xli. 6 f.).[4] Of the animals (about twenty-five) mentioned by the prophet, the majority are expressly named among those familiarly known in Babylonia.[5] As regards the trees and plants mentioned by him, it is no doubt true that several do not appear to be such as flourish in Babylonia. But it is to be observed that the principal passages in which they are mentioned (xli. 19 ; lv. 13 ; lx. 13) are passages in which the prophet's mind is fixed on the restoration to Palestine ; and hence it is natural that he should name the trees which he knew—whether from repute or otherwise—to be characteristic of that country, or to constitute the "glory of Lebanon."[6] The willow—or, rather, poplar—of xliv. 2, which has been specially urged as an objection to the Babylonian

---

[1] An atmospheric phænomenon occurring in Babylonia (Rawlinson, "Ancient Monarchies," ed. 4, 1879, i. p. 30).

[2] *Ib.* ii. p. 566.

[3] We do not know, indeed, that he ever saw them. The exiles must have formed a body too numerous to be congregated within the city of Babylon itself : most of them, no doubt, were dispersed in small communities in different parts of the country, where they were left to till the soil, and support themselves upon its produce (cf. Jer. xxix. 5, 28). It is at least as probable that the prophet belonged to one of these communities, as that he resided in Babylon itself.

[4] The *argument* of the prophecy excludes the supposition that such pas-

authorship, is expressly attested for Babylon by the ancient and high authority of Ps. cxxxvii. 2 (same word). The non-mention of the palm tree, a common and conspicuous feature of the Babylonian landscape, has been observed as remarkable. But is it more remarkable than its non-mention by Isaiah himself and Jeremiah, in spite of its having " ever been intimately associated with Palestine,"[1] and even by Ezekiel, who was acquainted equally with Palestine and Babylonia? The only districts of Palestine specially named by the prophet are Lebanon (xl. 16 ; lx. 13), the Sharon (lxv. 10), and the vale of Achor (*ib.* ; cf. Hos. ii. 15). Mountains, rocks, forests, when mentioned, are mentioned quite in general terms (xl. 12 ; xlii. 11 ; xliv. 14–23 ; li. 1 ; liv. 10 ; lv. 12, 13, &c.) : surely there is nothing incredible in such objects being within the prophet's cognizance, even though he wrote in the flat and comparatively unwooded plain of Babylonia ![2] So little is definitely known respecting the *precise* situation of the author, and the opportunities for observing nature at his disposal, that from the scenes and objects mentioned or not mentioned by him, no argument can be drawn capable of neutralizing the general evidence which assigns for his prophecy a date during the exile.

II. *The evidence of language and style.* When the Biblical writings are examined carefully, individualities of style appear as one of their most prominent features. Contrast, for instance, Hosea, Jeremiah, Ezekiel : each of these prophets has stamped upon his writings an individual character ; each maintains throughout his own characteristic phraseology, and pursues his own distinctive veins of thought. The same feature is observable in the New Testament. The Acts of the Apostles and the Third Gospel profess to be the work of the same author ; and the more minutely they are examined, the more fully is this confirmed by the discovery of a multitude of minute similarities of expression, which as a rule altogether escape the notice of an ordinary reader. Between St. Matthew and St. Luke a difference declares itself in a phrase which it might have been thought antecedently would not have varied. The one says nearly always (32 times) *the kingdom of Heaven ;* the other uniformly

---

[1] Tristram, " Natural History of the Bible," p. 378 ff.

[2] " Rock " in xliv. 8 is of course rom Ps. xviii. 31 (cf. *v.* 2, Deut. xxxii. 4) ; in xlviii. 21 the figure is evidently borrowed from Exod. xvii. 6 (cf. Ps. lxxviii. 20 ; cv. 41).

(33 times) *the kingdom of God.* Different writers may approximate—as witness Jeremiah and Deuteronomy—in the use of a similar phraseology ; but difference of style is a common, if not a universal distinction, which obtains between different authors. Especially do differences of style sometimes show themselves in types of expression, or, as they may be termed, mannerisms, affected by particular writers, which are employed by them without deliberation, and which betray themselves unconsciously. Thus the word *straightway* is in this way characteristic of St. Mark's Gospel. He employs it nearly forty times. St. Luke, though his Gospel is much longer, uses it but seven times ; St. John only four times. It is St. Mark's habit of mind to view events under the particular relation expressed by this word, which the other evangelists commonly disregard. St. Luke, on the other hand, employs a peculiar form of indirect question, which occurs in no other writer in the New Testament.[1] The example just quoted may be treated as a peculiarity of *expression.* Examples of a more material character may be termed with greater propriety peculiarities of *conception.* Such are the representation of truth, and the reverse, as *light* and *darkness* respectively, or the prominence attached to the idea of *witness,* both of which are of repeated occurrence in St. John's writings. Instances of both kinds might readily be multiplied. Individual Biblical writers exhibit a preference for particular words and turns of expression, and give prominence to particular ideas ; their inspiration, so far from obliterating individualities of style, if possible, intensifying and confirming them.

Now when the prophecies in the Book of Isaiah possessing an evident reference to the events of Isaiah's lifetime are compared with those relating to the restoration of Israel from Babylon, and especially with chaps. xl.–lxvi., many remarkable differences, both of phraseology and conception, disclose themselves. The terms and expressions which, in the former series of prophecies, Isaiah uses, and uses repeatedly, are absent in chaps. xl.–lxvi. ; conversely, new terms and expressions appear in chaps. xl.–lxvi., which are without parallel in the first part of the book. Sometimes the expressions used in one part of the

or twice only in one part of the book, while in the other part
they occur frequently, and often with a peculiar *nuance* or shade
of meaning.   No doubt, if the subject matter of the two parts
varied greatly, it would be natural that to a certain extent different terms should be employed, even though both were by the
same author ; but, as will be seen, the variations between the
two parts of the Book of Isaiah are not to be explained by the
difference of subject matter ; they extend, in many instances, to
points, such as the form and construction of sentences, which
stand in no appreciable relation to the subject treated.

Here is a list of words and phrases *recurring* in Isaiah, and
therefore characteristic of Isaiah's style (those marked † being
used only by him), not one of which occurs in chaps. xl.–lxvi. :

1. *The Lord* [Heb. *Adon*], *Jehovah of Hosts :* i. 24 ; iii. 1 ; x. 16, 33 ;
xix. 4.†

2. *Not-gods :* ii. 8, 18, 20 ; x. 11 (cf. 10) ; xix. 1, 3 ; xxxi. 7 (cf. p. 109).

3. The figure of Jehovah's showing Himself *exalted* (ii. 11, 17 ; xxxiii. 5),
or *lofty* (v. 16), or *arising* (ii. 19, 21 ; xxviii. 21 ; xxxi. 2 ; xxxii. 10), or
lifting Himself up (xxx. 18 ; xxxiii. 3, 10).[1]

4. *Rottenness :* iii. 24 ; v. 24.†

5. *To mourn* (unusual word) : iii. 26 ; xix. 8.†

6. *The escaped* (or *body of fugitives*) : iv. 2 ; x. 20 ; xv. 9 ; xxxvii. 31, 32.

7. A *trampling down* : v. 5 ; vii. 25 ; x. 6 ; xxviii. 18.

8. The *glory* of a nation, esp. with figures signifying its disappearance
or decay : v. 13 (R.V. *marg.*) ; viii. 7 ; x. 16, 18 ; xvi. 14 ; xvii. 3, 4 ;
xxi. 16 : cf. xxii. 18 (of Shebna).

9. *Hay :* v. 24 ; xxxiii. 11.†

10. *Dust* (not the usual word) : v. 24 ; xxix. 5.   Rare besides.

11. The figure of Jehovah's hand *stretched out* against a nation or part
of the earth : v. 25 ; ix. 12, 17, 21 ; x. 4 ; xiv. 26, 27 ; xxiii. 11 ;
xxxi. 3.   A figure used also by other writers (*e.g.*, Exod. vi. 6), but applied
by Isaiah with singular picturesqueness and force.

12. *To hiss* (as a signal) : v. 26 ; vii. 18.

13. *To smear*, of the eyes, *i.e.*, to blind them : vi. 10 ; xxix. 9 ;
xxxii. 3.†[2]

14. *To be ruined* (unusual word) : vi. 11 *bis ;* xxxvii. 26 (=2 Kings
xix. 25).†

15. Figures borrowed from *harvest :* ix. 3 [Heb. 2] ; xvii. 5, 11 ; xviii. 4.

16. *Burden :* ix. 4 [Heb. 3] ; x. 27 ; xiv. 25.†

17. *To spur* or *incite :* ix. 11 [Heb. 10] ; xix. 2.†   A remarkable word.

---

[1] The idea in lvii. 15 is different—not that of *lifting Himself up,* but of
being already lofty.

[2] The word in xliv. 18 is different.

18. *The thickets of the forest :* ix. 18 [Heb. 17] ; x. 34.†

19. The proverbial phrase, *"head and tail, palm-branch and rush" :* ix. 14 [Heb. 13] ; xix. 15.†

20. The figure of *the fat* reduced to leanness : x. 16 ; xvii. 4.†

21. *Garden-land* (R.V. *fruitful field*) : x. 18 ; xvi. 10 ; xxix. 17; xxxii. 15, 16 ; xxxvii. 24. Very rare besides.

22. *Remnant :* x. 19, 20, 21, 22 ; xi. 11, 16 ; xvi. 4 ; xvii. 3 ; xxi. 17 ; xxviii. 5 ; and in the proper name, *Shear-jashub,* vii. 3. The term expressing Isaiah's characteristic teaching (p. 110), used by no other prophet except (in less special applications) chap. xiv. 22 ; Zeph. i. 4 ; Mal. ii. 15 ; and occurring elsewhere in the Old Testament only in Chron., Ezra, Neh., Esther. (The term used generally for *remnant* is different.)

23. *A consummation and that determined :* x. 23 ; xxviii. 22. A peculiar phrase ; only besides, borrowed from Isaiah, in Dan. ix. 27.

24. The figure of the *scourge :* x. 26 ; xxviii. 15, 18.

25. The *swinging* of Jehovah's hand: xi. 15 ; xix. 16 : cf. xxx. 32 ("battles of *swinging*").

26. A *flying fiery serpent:* xiv. 29 ; xxx. 6.†

27. *The devastator :* xvi. 4 ; xxi. 2 ; xxxiii. 1. So *devastated :* xv. 1 *bis* ; xxiii. 1, 14. (Not very common besides, except in Jeremiah.)

28. *Many* (an uncommon word, not the one usually employed in Hebrew) : xvi. 14 ; xvii. 12 ; xxviii. 2. Only seven times in Job besides.

29. A *treading down :* xviii. 2, 7 ; xxii. 5.†

30. *To wither* (not the ordinary word) : xix. 6 ; xxxiii 9.†

31. *To war* (uncommon word) : xxix. 7, 8 ; xxxi. 4.[1]

This list might be readily increased. The expressions which follow are found also in chaps. xxiv.–xxvii., and therefore, so far as they go, tend to support the conjecture (p. 118) that these chapters embody elements derived from Isaiah : but they never occur in chaps. xl.-lxvi. :

32. *Storm* (prop. *streaming rain*) : iv. 6 ; xxviii. 2 *bis* ; xxx. 30 ; xxxii. 2 Also xxv. 4 *bis*. Only twice besides in the Old Testament.

33. *Briers and thorns* (an alliterative phrase) : v. 6 ; vii. 23, 24, 25 ; and figuratively, ix. 18 [Heb. 17] ; x. 17. Also xxvii. 4. (*Briers* also in xxxii. 13; neither word elsewhere in the Old Testament.)

34. *Little* (not the usual word) : x. 25 ; xvi. 14 ; xxix. 17. Only xxiv. 6 besides. A diminutive, derived from the same root : xxviii. 10, 13 ; only besides in Job xxxvi. 2.

35. *To flee* (not one of the words most commonly used to express this idea) : x. 31 ; xvi. 2, 3 ; xxi. 14, 15 ; xxii. 3 ; xxxiii. 3. In an intensive form, xxiv. 20.

---

[1] The following examples of the recurrence of similar figures and expressions are also worth noticing : iii. 12*b* and ix. 16 [Heb. 15]; iv. 2 and

It is plain that Isaiah has a strong preference for particular figures and phrases, in some cases so strong that he chooses words which are used by no other writer in the Old Testament.[1] Yet in spite of this preference not one of the words quoted recurs in chaps. xl.–lxvi., although the similarity of many of the topics would have afforded abundant scope for the recurrence of at least some of them. The contrast is hardly less marked in the case of the two following phrases, though these occur once or twice in chaps. xl.–lxvi. :

1. *In that day:* used by Isaiah more than *thirty* times, especially in the introduction of scenes or traits in his description of the future. Examples from two or three chapters will suffice :—iii. 18; iv. 1, 2 ; vii. 18, 20, 21, 23 ; xix. 16, 18, 19, 21, 23, 24 ; xxxi. 7. This is used also by other prophets ; but by none so frequently as by Isaiah. In chaps. xl.–lxvi., liii. 6 only.

2. *And it shall come to pass :* a frequent introductory formula, *e.g.*, iv. 3 , vii. 18, 21, 23 ; viii. 21 ; x. 12 ; xi. 10, 11, and elsewhere (common also in other prophets). In chaps. xl.–lxvi., lxv. 24 ; lxvi. 23 only.

The reader's attention is directed especially to the first of these phrases. *In that day* is a form of expression into which Isaiah as naturally and readily falls, in his description of the future, as St. Mark falls into the use of *straightway* in his description of the past. It is as difficult to believe that Isaiah, had he been the author of a prophecy as long as chapters xl.–lxvi., and dealing even more with the future than the prophecies in Part I., would have been content to use this expression but once—and that once by no means in his usual manner —as it is to believe that had St. Mark written, as St. Luke wrote, a sequel to his Gospel, the word *straightway* would have been found in it but once only. Of course it will be remembered that this is no *isolated* point of difference between the pro-

xxviii. 13*b* ; ix. 7*b* [Heb. 6*b*] and xxxvii. 32*b* ; x. 27 and xiv. 25*b* ; xiv. 26 and xxiii. 9, 11*a* ; xvi. 14 and xxi 16 ; xxii. 11*b* and xxxvii. 26*a*.

[1] Words occurring *once* only in Isaiah (not being found elsewhere in the Old Testament) are not included in the list. These are numerous ; and a tolerable proportion of them might have been expected to recur in chaps. xl.–lxvi., if these were by the same author. In fact, *four* only so recur (*caprice*, iii. 4, lxvi. 4 ; *thorn-bush*, vii. 19, lv. 13 ; *to swell*, xxx. 13, lxiv. 2 (differently applied) ; *streams* of water, xxx. 25, xliv. 4) ; a smaller number than that of similar words found only in Isaiah and Jeremiah! (Let the reader who is conversant with Hebrew, discover for himself in Isa. iii. 20 ; vii. 19 ; xvi. 9 ; xviii. 5 ; xix. 14 ; xxviii. 7 ; the words which are used besides *only* by Jeremiah.)

phecies of Part I. and chaps. xl.-lxvi. ; it is but the most common and conspicuous of a multitude of expressions which Isaiah uses familiarly, but which are one and all absent from the chapters last mentioned.   And, above and beyond the class of features that have been specified, there is a certain mould or *type*, constituted, it is true, in part by individualities of diction, but consisting largely of elements that refuse to be analyzed or expressed in words, which is impressed by Isaiah upon whatever he writes, and which differs widely from the mould or type of chaps. xl.-lxvi.

But the entire argument has been by no means yet stated. Just as there are a multitude of features characteiistic of Isaiah's style absent from chaps. xl.-lxvi., so, conversely, a number of words and phrases appear in these chapters which are either never found in the first part of the book, or *are found only in those chapters* (Part II. Chap. II.) *which bear independent traces of belonging to a different age.*   Thus—

1. *All flesh :* xl. 5, 6 ; xlix. 26 ; lxvi. 16, 23, 24.

2. *As nothing,* in a comparison : xl. 17 ; xli. 11, 12 ; cf. xl. 23 ; xli. 24.

3. *Lift up thy (your) eyes (on high,* or *round about,* or *to heaven) :* xl. 26 ; xlix. 18 ; li. 6 ; lx. 4.

4. *To choose,* of God's choice of Israel : xli. 8, 9 ; xliii. 10 ; xliv. 1, 2 ; *My chosen :* xliii. 20 ; xlv. 4 ; lxv. 9, 15, 22.[1]   So xiv. 1.

5. *Those incensed against thee* (or *him) :* xli. 11 ; xlv. 24.†

6. *Praise* (substantive and verb): xlii. 8, 10, 12 ; xliii. 21 ; xlviii. 9 ; lx. 6, 18 ; lxi. 3, 11 ; lxii. 7, 9 ; lxiii. 7 ; lxiv. 10.[2]   In the reflexive conjugation, *to boast :* xli. 16 ; xlv. 25.

7. *Things that are coming* (peculiar expression) : xli. 23 ; xliv. 7 ; xlv. 11.†

8. *To be silent* (a rather uncommon word), applied especially to God : xlii. 14 ; lvii. 11 ; lxii. 1, 6 ; lxiv. 12 ; lxv. 6.

9. *To shoot* or *spring forth :* xliv. 4 ; lv. 10 ; lxi. 11*a* ; esp. metaphorically—(*a*) of a moral state, xlv. 8 ; lviii. 8 ; lxi. 11*b* ; (*b*) of an event manifesting itself in history (not so elsewhere), xlii. 9 ; xliii. 19.   (This verb is not used, even in a literal sense, by Isaiah.)

10. *To bow down* (unusual word) : xliv. 15, 17, 19 ; xlvi. 6.†

11. *To break out* (a peculiar word) into singing : xliv. 23 ; xlix. 13 ; lii. 9 ; liv. 1 ; lv. 12.   Also xiv. 7.   Only Ps. xcviii. 4 besides.

12. *Pleasure :* (*a*) of Jehovah's purpose, xliv. 28 ; xlvi. 10 ; xlviii. 14 ; liii. 10 ; (*b*) of human purpose or business, lviii. 3, 13.   More generally, liv. 12 ; lxii. 4.

13. *The Holy City :* xlviii. **2** ; lii. **1**. Only besides in Neh. xi. **1, 18** ; Dan. ix. 24.

14. *Good will* (God's) : xlix. 8 ; lvi. 7 ; lviii. 5; lx. 7, 10 ; lxi. **2**.

15. *The mirage :* xlix. **10** ; xxxv. 7.†

16 The figure of *clothing oneself,* or *being clothed*—often employed with great picturesqueness and beauty : xlix. 18 ; l. 3 ; li. 9 ; lii. 1 ; lix. 17 ; lxi. 10 ; cf. *v.* 3. The same figure xiv. 19, in a different connection. The figure is not one which Isaiah employs. (The use of the word in iv. 1 ; xxii. 21, in a *literal* sense, evidently does not come into consideration.)

17. *Thy sons*—the pronoun being feminine and referring to Zion : xlix. 17, 22, 25 ; li. 20 ; liv. 13 ; lx. 4, 9 ; lxii. 5 ; cf. lxvi. 8. Isaiah, when he uses the same word figuratively, always says *sons* absolutely, the implicit reference being to God (Deut. xiv. 1) : so i. 2, 4 ; xxx. 1, 9.

18. *To rejoice* (a strong word): lxi. 10 ; lxii. 5 ; lxiv. 5 ; lxv. 18, 19 ; lxvi. 10, 14. Also xxxv. 1.[1]

19. The phrases, *I am Jehovah, and there is none else* (or *besides*) : xlv. 5, 6, 18, 21, 22 ; *I am the first, and I am the last :* xliv. 6 ; xlviii. 12 ; cf. xli. 4 ; *I am thy God, thy Saviour,* &c. : xli. 10, 13 ; xliii. 3 ; xlviii. 17*b* ; lxi. 8 ; *I am he,* i.e., *the same* (from Deut. xxxii. 39) : xli. 4*b* ; xliii. 10*b*, 13 ; xlvi. 4 ; xlviii. 12. No such phrases are ever used by Isaiah.

20. The combination of the Divine name with a participial epithet (in the English version often represented by a relative clause) : *e.g., Creator* (or *stretcher out*) *of the heavens* or *the earth :* xl. 28 ; xlii. 5 ; xliv. 24*b* ; xlv. 7, 18 ; li. 13 ; *creator* or *former of Israel :* xliii. 1, 15 ; xliv. 2, 24 ; xlv. 11 ; xlix. 5 ; *thy Saviour :* xlix. 26 ; lx. 16 ; *thy* (*your, Israel's*) *redeemer :* xliii. 14 ; xliv. 24*a* ; xlviii. 17*a* ; xlix. 7 ; liv. 8 ; comp. xl. 22 f. ; xliii. 16 f. ; xliv. 25-28 ; xlvi. 10 f. ; li. 15 ; lvi. 8 ; lxiii. 12 f. Isaiah never casts his thought into this form.[2]

This list also might be increased. It is not, perhaps, such a striking one as the corresponding list on p. 194 f. ; for the power and originality of Isaiah's genius displays itself alike in the rare terms which he alone uses, and in the force with which he invests even those which may be used by other prophets. Nevertheless the list is not less adapted to illustrate the phraseology of chaps. xl.–lxvi., and to show how essentially it differs from that of Isaiah. It may be supplemented by the following list of words or phrases, most of which are used by Isaiah once or twice each, but not with any special force or significance, whereas in chaps. xl.–lxvi. they occur repeatedly, and sometimes possess

[1] *Redeem, redeemer* (xxxv. 9, and twenty-three times in chaps xl.–lxvi.) has been purposely not included in the text, as its occurrence might be justly treated as due specially to the theme of these chapters. In the two passages, i. 27 ; xxix. 22, in which the idea occurs in Isaiah, the Hebrew word used is a different one.

[2] In xxix. 22 the form of sentence in the Hebrew is quite different.

a definite *nuance,* or shade of meaning, which is foreign to the usage of Isaiah.[1]

1. *Isles* or *coasts :* xl. 15 ; xli. 1, 5 ; xlii. 4, 10, 12, 15 ; xlix. 1 ; li. 5 ; lix. 18 ; lx. 9 ; lxvi. 19. In Isaiah, xi. 11 :[2] also xxiv. 15. This word, denoting properly (so chap. xi. 11 ; Gen. x. 5) the isles and coasts of the Mediterranean Sea, is used in chaps. xl.-lxvi. representatively of distant regions of the earth, which are, moreover, in several of the passages quoted, personified by the prophet. This application of the word is a marked extension of the usage in Isaiah.

2. *Nought* (not the ordinary word) : xl. 17 ; xli. 12, 29 ; xlv. 6, 14 ; xlvi. 9 ; xlvii. 8, 10 ; lii. 4 ; liv. 15 ; also xxxiv. 12. In Isaiah, v. 8 only.

3. *From the first* (peculiar use of the Heb. *rosh,* head or top) : xl. 21 ; xli. 4, 26 ; xlviii. 16.

4. *To create :* xl. 26, 28 ; xli. 20 ; xlii. 5 ; xliii. 1, 7, 15 ; xlv. 7, 8, 12, 18 ; liv. 16 ; lvii. 19 ; lxv. 17, 18. In Isaiah, only iv. 5, in a limited application. The prominence given to the idea of creation in chaps. xl.-lxvi. is very noticeable.

5. *Offspring :* xlii. 5 ; xliv. 3 ; xlviii. 19 ; lxi. 9 ; lxv. 23. In Isaiah, xxii. 24. Also xxxiv. 1. Rather a peculiar word. The usage in chaps. xl.-lxvi. is wider and more general than that in xxii. 24, and agrees with the usage of the Book of Job, v. 25 ; xxi. 8 ; xxvii. 14 ; xxxi. 8.

6. *Justice* emphasized as a principle guiding and determining God's action (p. 172) : xli. 2, 10*b* ; xlii. 21 ; xlv. 13, 19 ; li. 5 ; cf. lviii. 2*b.* The peculiar stress laid upon this principle is almost confined to these chapters : comp , however, Hos. ii. 19 [Heb. 21].

7. The *Arm of Jehovah :* li. 5*b*, 9 ; lii. 10 ; liii. 1 ; lix. 16*b* (cf. xl. 10) ; lxii. 8 ; lxiii. 5, 12. Hence Ps. xcviii. 1 (see chaps. lix. 16 ; hi. 10). In Isaiah, xxx. 30. But observe the greater *independence* of the figure as applied in chaps xl.-lxvi.

8. *To deck,* or (in the reflexive conjugation) *to deck oneself, i.e., to glory,* especially of Jehovah, either glorifying Israel, or glorying Himself in Israel : xliv. 23 ; xlix. 3 ; lv. 5 ; lx. 7, 9, 13, 21 ; lxi. 3. A vivid and expressive figure. In Isaiah, only x. 15 of the saw *vaunting itself* against its user.

9. The future gracious relation of Jehovah to Israel represented as a *covenant :* xlii. 6 (=xlix. 8) ; liv. 10 ; lv. 3 ; lix. 21 ; lxi. 8. In xxviii. 15, 18 ; xxxiii. 8, the word is used merely in the sense of a treaty or compact. Isaiah, often as he speaks of a future state of grace to be enjoyed by his people, never represents it under the form of a *covenant.*

---

[1] Of course with words such as these, not the single, but the *repeated* occurrence shows the habit of the author, and constitutes a criterion of

As features of style may be noticed—

1. The *duplication of words*, significant of the impassioned ardour of the speaker. Very characteristic of this prophecy: see p. 182.

2. A habit of repeating the same word or words in adjacent clauses or verses; thus xl. 12 f. (regulated), 13 *end* and 14 *end* (taught him), 14 (instructed him), xl. 31 and xli. 1 (renew strength), 6 f. (courage, encourage), 8 f. (have chosen thee); 13 f. (will help thee), xliv. 1 f., xlv. 4 f (hast not known me), 5 f. (and none else), l. 7 and 9 (will help me); liii. 3 (despised), 3 f. (esteemed him), 7 (opened not his mouth), lviii. 13 (thine own pleasure), lix. 8; lxi. 7 (double). The attentive reader of the Hebrew will notice further instances. Very rare indeed in Isaiah: cf. i. 7 (desolate); xvii. 5 (ears); xxxii. 17 f. (peace).

In addition there are the rhetorical and poetical characteristics referred to in Chap. IV. (pp. 181-4),—the structure of sentences, the movement of the periods, the preference shown by the author for particular figures, especially for those drawn from the sphere of human emotion, and his love of personification —all differentiating him from Isaiah.[1]

Lastly, words and idioms occur in chaps. xl.–lxvi. which point to a later period of the language than Isaiah's age. A remarkable instance of this is afforded by lxv. 25, where in the condensed quotation from xi. 6–9, which that verse contains, the common Hebrew word for " together," used twice in the passage by Isaiah, is replaced by a synonym of Aramaic origin, which occurs besides only in the latest books of the Old Testament. This subject is, however, one which cannot be profitably discussed in a book intended for general readers; and the writer must remain satisfied with a reference to Professor Cheyne's

---

[1] Some other features differentiating the style of chaps. xl.–lxvi. from that of Isaiah could only be apprehended by the Hebrew student, and are therefore here passed by. On this subject generally the writer rejoices to find himself in accord with such a qualified judge of Hebrew style as Prof. A. B. Davidson, of the New College, Edinburgh, who, after remarking on the difference in vocabulary of the two parts of the Book of Isaiah, adds that it is not so much words in themselves as the peculiar uses and combinations of them, and especially "the peculiar articulation of sentences and the movement of the whole discourse, by which an impression is produced so unlike the impression produced by the earlier portions of the book" (*Brit. and For. Evang. Review*, 1879, p. 339).

One such feature may be briefly noted. Isaiah omits the relative particle about six times: in chaps. xl.–lxvi., *it is omitted nearly sixty times*. An analysis of the instances would show that they corresponded to a difference of *habit* in the manner of constructing and co-ordinating sentences.

commentary, vol. ii. p. 257 f.[1] No doubt the language of chaps. xl.–lxvi. is relatively free from the marks of a later style ; but it is not *so* free as the language of Isaiah.

The attempt is sometimes made to meet the force of the argument derived from difference of phraseology and style, by pointing to the examples of similarities, observable between chaps. xl.–lxvi. and the acknowledged prophecies of Isaiah. No doubt a certain number of such similarities exist; but they are very far from being numerous or decisive enough to establish the unity desired. It is the *differences* between authors which are characteristic, and form consequently a test of authorship : similarities, unless they are exceedingly numerous and minute, may be due to other causes than identity of authorship. They may be due, for instance, to a community of subject matter, to the independent adoption by different writers of a current terminology, to an affinity of genius or mental habit prompting an author to borrow the ideas or phraseology of a predecessor, to involuntary reminiscence. To the first of these heads may be referred such topics common to both parts of the book as the denunciation of sin (injustice, idolatry, bloodshed), the threat of judgment, the offer of pardon, the hope of restoration :[2] teaching on these subjects is common to all the prophets, and no specific similarity appears in the manner in which they are treated in the two parts of the book.[3] To the second head may be referred the use of such phrases as " Jehovah of Hosts," [4] " Thus saith Jehovah," &c. Then, thirdly, if there exists

---

[1] Whose list, however, of coincidences with later usage is not complete.

[2] Rawlinson, " Pulpit Commentary " on Isaiah, i. p. xxiii., where the distinctive doctrines of the two parts of the book are painfully confused. Surely the figure in xlii. 1-4 ; xlix. 1-12, is as plainly as possible not that of a *King* who rules, but of a *Prophet* who teaches !

[3] Thus Israel is charged with shedding innocent blood in i. 15 and in lix. 3 : but the same charge is also brought against it in Micah iii. 10, vii. 2 ; Jer. vii. 9 ; Ezek. vii. 23, ix. 9 ; and elsewhere : and in lix. 3 the word for " defiled " is an uncommon one, recurring in lxiii. 3, but used elsewhere almost entirely by exilic or post-exilic writers (Zeph., Mal., Ezra, Neh., Dan., and, in exactly the same form as here, Lam. iv. 14).

[4] Which is used by every prophet except Joel, Obadiah, and (remarkably) Ezekiel. Isaiah uses it with great frequency : in chaps. xl.-lxvi., however, it occurs only six times,—four of these (xlvii. 4 ; xlviii. 2 ; li. 15 ; liv. 5) being in a form of expression which Isaiah never employs.

evidence pointing independently to the conclusion that the author of chaps. xl.-lxvi. wrote during the exile, there is no ground for supposing that the prophecies of Isaiah were a sealed book to him.   There is abundant proof that the later prophets made familiar use of the writings of their predecessors, both quoting from them and availing themselves of their phraseology : and it is arbitrary to hold that the author of these chapters must have been an exception to the general rule.   His debt to Isaiah, after all, would not be a large one. His relation to him is never that of an imitator ; it is that of a genius, always maintaining its independence, but borrowing, as from an equal, one or two expressions suited to his purpose, and finding in the Book of Isaiah's prophecies ideas and thoughts capable of germinating and fructifying in his own mind, and of being ultimately assimilated with what is indefeasibly his own.[1]   The fact that the resemblance with Isaiah is but partial corroborates this view.   Only such elements are appropriated from Isaiah as harmonize with the author's own habit of thought, and are capable of being assimilated to his own conception of spiritual and theological truth.   Sometimes, no doubt, a phrase or expression may have been adopted deliberately : more frequently, it is probable, the process was rather what we should term one of involuntary reminiscence.

By these considerations, the most noteworthy of the similarities alluded to, viz., the use of the phrase "the Holy One of Israel," which occurs twelve times in Isaiah and thirteen times in chaps. xl.-lxvi.,[2] is naturally accounted for.   A preference observable in the two parts for particular figures, as the metaphorical use of the terms *light* and *darkness*, *blind* and *deaf*, may be similarly explained.   Isaiah and the author of this prophecy share one distinguishing feature in common : alone among the prophets of the Old Testament, they live in

---

[1] As other poets of genius have done : witness Virgil and Milton, who are dependent upon their models to a far greater degree than II. Isaiah is. (who, indeed, follows no *model* whatever).

[2] Elsewhere : Jer. l. 29, li. 5 ; Ps. lxxi. 22, lxxviii. 41, lxxxix. 18. That the title is not otiose in the prophet's mouth is well shown by Krüger, "La Théologie d' Ésaie xl.-lxvi.," p. 23 f.   The title contains in it (so to say) the promise of Israel's redemption : the *Holy One* of Israel will vindicate His name (cf. xlviii. 11), and will not permit the nation which He has made peculiarly His own, to continue permanently in banishment, or lose its distinctive unity.

immediate anticipation of Israel's recovery from humiliation
and disaster. Hence, it is not surprising that in his visions of
the restored Zion the prophet should pursue the lines laid
down by his predecessor, and develop ideas originated by him
(p. 110). Generally, however, when the alleged parallels are examined, it will be found that there is a difference of treatment
or application, which more than neutralizes the argument for
identity of authorship, drawn from the coincidence of idea, and
strengthens the opinion that we are really dealing with a
different author, either employing similar figures independently,
or developing in his own manner thoughts suggested by another.
Thus no doubt the "shadow" is a figure of protection in
xxv. 4, xxxii. 2, and in xlix. 2, li. 16; but how differently
applied! The shadow of a *rock* at noon, and the shadow
(*i.e.*, the hollow) of a *hand!* This instance is evidence neither
of identity of author, nor even of reminiscence. The figure, it
is clear, has been chosen in each case independently. The expression "drunken, but not with wine," occurs in xxix. 9 and
li. 21 : but in xxix. 9 it is a figure of moral stupefaction ; in
li. 21 it is applied to a person staggered by some great afflic-
tion. The difference is just what might be expected in the case
of a writer borrowing and applying in a new connection a
phrase used originally by another. The image of the wilderness blossoming occurs in xxxii. 15 ; xxxv. 1-2 ; li. 3 ; lv.
12-13 ; but in xxxii. 15 the phraseology is strongly Isaianic (see
xxix. 17 ; and p. 195, No. 21) ; in the other passages the predominant expressions are of a different type altogether. The
"flax" of xliii. 17 agrees with xlii. 3, but is different from the
"tow" of i. 31. The mention of lifting up an ensign occurs in
v. 26 ; xi. 12 ; xviii. 3 ; it occurs also in xiii. 2 ; but Jeremiah
uses exactly the same expression (iv. 6; l. 2; li. 12, 27) ; so
that nothing distinctive attaches to it. In xlix. 22 ; lxii. 10, the
verb is a different one ; and a change is the less likely to have
been made by Isaiah himself, as the verb used by him gives
rise to an alliteration (*nāsā' nēs*). These are evidently cases of
similar figures employed independently.[1] "And they shall be

---

[1] So the idiom of the bowels "sounding" (p. 90) occurs in xvi. 11 and
lxiii. 15 ; but it occurs also in Jer. xxxi. 20, Cant. v. 4 ; and it is applied
in xvi. 11 to the prophet, while in lxiii. 15 (as in Jer.) it is used with reference to God. The "overflowing torrent" occurs in xxx. 28 and lxvi. 12 ;
but it occurs also in Jer. xlvii. 2 ; and while in xxx. 28 it is an agent bearing

called Oaks of righteousness," in lxi. 3, has been quoted as testifying to the same author as i. 26, "Afterward thou shalt be called City of righteousness;" but it is accompanied by a difference of expression which points strongly in the opposite direction,[1] and confirms the view, that it is (at most) a reminiscence which the author applies in his own way.

Other similarities that have been quoted are merely instances of figures or usages, which are not peculiar to the Book of Isaiah, but are more or less common property of the Biblical writers generally. Thus " Jacob," in parallelism with " Israel " (as ix. 8 ; x. 20 ; xxix. 23 : xl. 27 ; xli. 8, &c.) : so elsewhere, as Mic. i. 5 ; ii. 12 ; iii. 1, 8, 9 ; Jer. ii. 4 ; x. 16 ; xxx. 10 ; the usage is not distinctive, and forms no ground for inferring identity of author. It might be thought that a stronger argument was afforded by the use of the solemn asseverative phrase, "For the mouth of Jehovah hath spoken it," in i. 20 ; xl. 5 ; lviii. 14 (not elsewhere) : but very similar phrases are used by other prophets, as "For Jehovah hath spoken it," in i. 2 ; xxii. 25 ; xxv. 8 ; Jer. xiii. 15 ; Joel iii. 8 ; Obad. 18 ; 1 Kings xiv. 11 (Ahijah); "For Jehovah, the God of Israel, hath spoken it," chap. xxi. 17 ; "For Jehovah hath spoken this word," xxiv. 3 ; "For the mouth of Jehovah of hosts hath spoken this word," Mic. iv. 4 ; and it is clear from these quotations (especially from the first group) that the occurrence of the same type in three particular passages is no real ground for attributing them to the same author. The idiom, *to call* or *name* symbolically (as i. 26 ; ix. 6 ; xix. 18 : xlvii. 1, 5 ; xlviii. 8 ; lx. 14, 18 al.), is also found frequently in both parts of the book but this again is not distinctive; it is an idiom which other prophets constantly employ, *e.g.*, Hos. ii. 1, 23 ; Jer. iii. 17 ;

with it destruction, in lxvi. 12 it is a figure of the abundant riches of the nations flowing in upon Zion. Anything more superficial than the manner in which the ''similarities" between the two parts of the Book of Isaiah have been adduced as evidence of the unity of authorship can scarcely be imagined.

[1] The word rendered *called* is in a peculiar conjugation, which occurs six times in these chapters (xlviii. 8, 12 ; lviii. 12 ; lxi. 3, 6 ; lxii. 2 ; lxv. 1 [see, however, p. 165, *note*]) ; but never in Isaiah, and only once besides (Ezek. x. 13) in the Old Testament. The sequel also, "the planting of Jehovah, that He may glory in it," is in the style of the same chapters (*planting*, as lx. 21, *not* as v. 7 ; *to glory*, p. 199, No. 8).

vi. 30; vii. 32; xix. 6; xx. 3; xxiii. 6; xxx. 17; xxxiii. 16.
"From henceforth even for ever" occurs in ix. 7 and lix. 21;
but it occurs as well in Mic. iv. 7, and in five Psalms; and is in
no respect peculiar. The comparison of vanquished foes, or
other unsubstantial object, to "stubble" is found in v. 24;
xxxiii. 11, and also in xl. 24; xli. 2; xlvii. 14. But this is a
comparison which might occur readily to any author resident in
the East; and, in fact, it is used repeatedly by the poets of the
Old Testament, from Exod. xv. 7 onwards: Jer. xiii. 24; Nah.
i. 10; Job xiii. 25, xli. 28, 29; Ps. lxxxiii. 13, and elsewhere.
The expression, "My mountains," of Palestine, occurs in
xiv. 25 and lxv. 9 (xlix. 11 differently); but it occurs also in
Ezek. xxxviii. 21; Zech. xiv. 5. If three prophets (as all must
allow) agree in the use of this expression, it is difficult to understand upon what principle it can be forbidden to a fourth.

And so we might go on. The fact is, that lists of similarities between the two parts of the Book of Isaiah have been drawn up,
and copied by one writer from another, without the precaution
having been taken to ascertain *how far they are distinctive.*[1]
When examined, the great majority *are found to occur in other
writers:* they are no peculiar possession of the Book of Isaiah,
and are thus no true criterion of the unity of author. If, nevertheless, the similarities of figure or metaphor between the two
parts of the Book (though not *distinctive* similarities) are somewhat in excess of those existing between any other two prophets,
this is sufficiently accounted for by the supposition, in itself a
reasonable and credible one, of the author's familiarity with the
prophecies of Isaiah. Whether, in a particular instance, a
figure has been arrived at independently, or suggested by a reminiscence, it is, of course, impossible to determine: it must
be sufficient to feel satisfied that in one or other of these ways
the similarities can all be explained.[2] What has to be accounted

[1] One writer actually quotes passages, in which the words *dust* and *water*
occur, as proof of the unity of authorship!

[2] Thus the "fading flower" in xl. 6, 7, 8, the impressive emblem of
the transitoriness of a power opposed to God, *may* be a reminiscence from
xxviii. 1, 4 (where it denotes the splendour, soon to be destroyed, of
Samaria); but it *may* also have occurred to the prophet independently; it
is applied similarly, to the life of man in general, in Job xiv. 2; Ps. ciii.
15. The comparison of God to a potter in xlv. 9, lxiv. 8, *may* have been
suggested by xxix. 16: but it may also have been either adopted independently, or suggested (esp. in lxiv. 8) by Jer. xviii. 6.

for, it must be borne in mind, is not the similarities alone, but *both* the similarities *and* the differences.   And the only hypothesis that will account for *both* of these, is that which has been here indicated.[1]

III. *Theology and Thought.* Here it will be sufficient to recall briefly the substance of what was said in Chap. IV., and to compare it with what appeared in Part I. to be the distinctive conceptions and teaching of Isaiah. Of course, the *fundamental* principles of the Israelitish religion are common to both parts of the Book of Isaiah, as they are to the prophets generally : when we look for features that are *distinctive*, we at once find that they are different.   Isaiah depicts the *majesty* of Jehovah ; the author of chaps. xl.–lxvi. His *infinity*.   This is a real difference.   It would be difficult to establish from Isaiah—not the greatness merely, but—the *infinitude* of the Divine attributes : the author of chaps. xl.–lxvi. exhausts the Hebrew language in the endeavour, if possible, to represent it.   Jehovah is the Creator, the Sustainer of the Universe, the Life-giver, the Author of history, the First and the Last, the Incomparable One (pp. 170, 171).   Where does Isaiah teach such truths as these ? Yet it cannot be maintained that opportunities for such assertions of Jehovah's power and godhead would not have naturally presented themselves to Isaiah whilst he was engaged in defying the armies of Assyria.   But the truth is, the prophet of the exile *moves in a different region of thought* from Isaiah. The doctrine of the preservation from judgment of a worthy remnant is characteristic of Isaiah ; it appears alike in his first prophecy (vi. 13), and in his last (xxxvii. 31 f.) ; in chaps. xl.– lxvi., if it appears once or twice by implication (lix. 20 ; lxv. 8 f.), it is not a *distinctive* element in the author's teaching ; it is not expressed in Isaiah's phraseology, and is not more prominent than it is in the writings of many other prophets.[2] Where, in Isaiah, is the destiny of Israel, and the purpose of its call, developed—or even noticed allusively—as it is developed in

---

[1] The fallaciousness of arguing from similarities alone ought to have been apparent from the case of Jeremiah and Deuteronomy, in which the resemblances are far more marked and numerous than those between the two parts of the Book of Isaiah, and yet are not held to establish identity of author.   But it is necessary to *weigh* words, and not merely to count them.

[2] As Amos v. 15, ix. 9 ; Mic. ii. 12, v. 7 f. ; Zeph. iii. 13 ; Jer. iv. 27*b*, xxx. 11, xxxi. 7, &c.

chaps. xl.–lxvi. ? In these chapters, again, the figure of the
Messianic king is absent ; another figure, intimately connected
with the view of Israel's destiny that has been just mentioned
a figure singularly striking and original in its conception—holds
a corresponding position. To say that the figure of Jehovah's
ideal Servant is an *advance* upon that of the Messianic king is
not correct ; it starts from a different origin altogether ; it is
parallel to it, not a continuation of it. The mission of Israel
to the nations is developed in new directions : the Divine purposes in relation to them are exhibited upon a wider and more
comprehensive scale. The prophet moves along lines of
thought different from those followed by Isaiah, he appre-
hends and dwells upon different aspects of truth. The obser-
vation made while dealing with the subject of phraseology
(p. 193 f.) repeats itself—as indeed is but natural ; for what
are words and figures but the exponents of ideas, exhibiting in their combinations and recurrences the palpable impress of the informing mind ? And thus, even where there
is a point of contact between the two parts of the book,
or where the same terms are employed, the ideas attached
to them have, in chaps. xl.–lxvi., a wider and fuller import.
But this is exactly what would be expected from a later writer
expanding and developing, in virtue of the fuller measure of
inspiration vouchsafed to him, elements due, perhaps, originally
to a predecessor.[1]

[1] Thus the phrase, "high and lifted up," is applied in ii. 13 to the
cedars of Lebanon ; in vi. 1, to the throne seen by Isaiah in his vision ; but
in lvii. 15, it is used to express the transcendent loftiness of Jehovah Himself. In iv. 5, *create* appears with a very limited application: contrast the
large ideas associated with it in chaps. xl.–lxvi. (p. 199, No. 4). Contrast,
further, the use of the word "salvation" in xii. 2, 3 ; xxxiii. 2, 6 ; or even
in xxv. 9 ; xxvi. 1, 18 (if these be elements derived from Isaiah) with its use
in xlix. 6, 8 ; li. 6, 8 ; lii. 7, 10 ; lvi. 1 ; lix. 11, 17 ; lx. 18 ; lxii. 1 (cf. also
xlv. 17 ; xlvi. 13 *bis*, where a very similar word, not, however, used by
Isaiah, occurs) : clearly the word expresses much more to the prophet than
it does upon Isaiah's lips. Most of the instances cited, p. 199, exemplify
the same difference. To the same class, also, may be assigned the metaphorical use of *tôhû* (*lit.*, a desolate waste, or chaos), and of the verb signifying *to form* or *frame* (as a potter), which, however, it would occupy too
much space to develop here. Note, lastly, the tendency in chaps. xl.–lxvi.
to treat the Divine Spirit as a *separate personality:* xl. 13 ; xlviii. 16 (where

Our comparative study of the Book of Isaiah has directed us
along *three independent* lines to the same conclusion. The
historical background of chaps. xl.-lxvi., the *phraseology and style*,
the *character of the theology*, each independently points us away
from Isaiah. Were the differences confined to *one* of these
heads, the other two being what we should have a right to expect from Isaiah, we might distrust our conclusion : but "a
threefold cord is not quickly broken."   It is a most remarkable
coincidence that, so soon as we pass from the parts of Isaiah's
book which from internal evidence belong unmistakably to
Isaiah's own age, to those in which the internal evidence
points to the period of the exile, *the accustomed marks of
Isaiah's hand cease, and new conceptions and new phraseology
make their appearance.*   The difference is plainly perceptible in
chaps. xiii. 1–xiv. 23 ; it is yet more evident in chaps. xxxiv.-
xxxv. ; it is naturally seen most fully in chaps. xl.-lxvi. where
the range of topics is not so limited as in either of these shorter
prophecies.   The diversities are not of a nature capable of
being accounted for by the change of subject.   That might account, perhaps, for a fraction of them : it will not account for
those which are most striking and the most fundamental.   The
diversities embrace broader and minuter features equally. They
extend from the character of the theology to the choice of words
and figures, to the rhetoric and poetry, to the structure of
sentences.   They are manifest in the phrases, or turns of expression, such as fall from an author without deliberation, and
are the surest index of his identity.   The more deeply the book
which bears Isaiah's name is studied, the more clearly does it
appear that the resemblances between its two parts do not

which cannot be traced either in xi. 2, or in xxxii. 15 (where the representation does not differ from Joel ii. 28 ; Ezek. xxxvi. 27 ; xxxix. 29).

It may be deemed an omission in the present discussion that no notice
has been taken of the parallelisms of expression between chaps. xl.-lxvi. and
Nahum, Zephaniah, and Jeremiah (esp. chaps. xxx.-xxxi. ; l.-li.), in their
bearing on the question of authorship.   But the writer has examined these
repeatedly side by side ; and is persuaded that, except by assuming the
question in dispute, it is impossible to determine on which side the dependency lies.   Specimens : chap. lii. 7, 1*b*, and Nah. i. 15 ; li. 15, and Jer.
xxxi. 35*b* ; lviii. 11, and Jer. xxxi. 12 ; xlviii. 20 and Jer. l. 2, 8. The resemblances with Jeremiah, where not accidental, appear to be reminiscences
suggested by the general community of topic.

reach beneath the surface ; the differences penetrate to the core.   The differences of style and conception are, in fact, but the external expression of a far more material difference, of a difference of *mental habit*, in other words, of a difference of *personality*.   Isaiah's style and thought, through all the years that we can watch it, is unchanged : it is as visible in his shortest prophecies (*e.g.*, chap. xvii.) as in his longest.   In the prophecies uttered by him forty years after the date of his call, when he was (presumably) not less than sixty years of age, there is not the smallest deviation from the style of his earliest discourses, not the smallest approximation towards the type of chaps xl.–lxvi.   Habits of expression are subject to the same law as habits of action.   It is alien to the constitution of the human mind for an author to cast off the habits of a lifetime, and assume an altered style in his old age.   It is a misconception of the nature of inspiration to suppose that it invests its agents with a new mental constitution, or induces in them new habits of expression ; inspiration does not confer upon a man *new* natural faculties, it quickens and exalts those which he already possesses.[1]   St. Paul and St. John preserve each, in all that they wrote, the same individualities of conception and expression.   The Book of Isaiah exhibits to us in reality two " Men of the Bible," not one ; two " gifted instruments," not one, each endowed with its own special excellence, and each employed by the Spirit of God, in the manifold scope (Heb. i. 1) of its operation, "to pour forth its voice upon the world."[2]

[1] Comp. Westcott, " Introduction to the Study of the Gospels," pp. 8–13.
[2] The phrase is borrowed from Smith's " Dict. of the Bible " (ed. 1), Art. *Isaiah*, towards the end.

Minor, often trivial, objections to the date here assigned to the prophecy, the writer has found it impossible, within the limits of space allotted to him, to consider.   Only one, which from the name by which it is supported claims respectful attention, may be briefly noticed. Dean Plumptre observes that the ideal completeness of the restoration depicted in the prophecy "is more natural in one contemplating the return of the exiles from a distance than to one who as a contemporary watched the somewhat meagre results recorded in Ezra and Nehemiah, in Haggai and Zechariah." The Dean appears here (for once) to have forgotten his history.   How could a prophet, writing *before* the fall of Babylon, *c.* 540, "watch," or be influenced by, occurrences that only took place subsequently, *after* the return which he promised was completed ? (*Nehemiah* relates events occurring a century afterwards, from 446 B.C. : so that in any case the pro-

No doubt this conclusion would have been generally accepted,[1] had it not been imagined that the value of the prophecy was in some manner impaired by it, or that some doubt was cast by it on the prophetic inspiration of the author. Apprehensions of this nature have indeed been expressed by some writers in terms betraying how imperfectly they have understood the view which they were combating, and how seriously they have misconceived the historical situation which it postulated for the prophet. It is hoped that the preceding pages may have been of service in showing such fears to be groundless. In Chap. III. it has been shown in particular how the prophecy, as a whole, is accommodated to the condition and prospect of the exiles in Babylonia some few years before the

phet could not "watch the results recorded" by him!) No doubt, the prophet's representations far transcended the actual event ; but he *idealizes* the age beginning with the restoration, just as Isaiah idealizes the age that is to succeed the downfall of the Assyrian, notwithstanding the fact that what actually then followed were the dark and cruel times of Manasseh.

It is to be observed, that the compiler of the Book of Ezra, in his notice of the edict of Cyrus, permitting the rebuilding of the Temple, specifies not Isaiah, but *Jeremiah*, as the prophet whose word was thereby fulfilled (Ezra i. 1 = 2 Chron. xxxvi. 22). In *v.* 2 there is perhaps a reference to chap. xliv. 28 ; but it is not stated (or implied) that the "charge" was delivered to Cyrus by Isaiah.

[1] The authority of Delitzsch's name cannot be any longer cited against it. It is true, he has not yet re-cast his commentary in accordance with his present views : but it is plain from many allusions in his recent publications that he no longer adheres to the Isaianic authorship of chaps. xl.-lxvi. Thus in his "Old Testament History of Redemption" (1881), he treats (p. 141 ff.) this prophecy *after* Jeremiah, and speaks (p. 137) of passages in it as "echoes" from Jeremiah's mouth ; and in his Commentary on Genesis (1887), p. 8, he quotes chap. lxiii. 10 f. with the remark that it "belongs to the period of the exile."

It is, of course, true that Isaiah, on one occasion (xxxix. 6 f.) held out the prospect of future *exile* to Babylon ; and Sir Ed. Strachey ("Jewish History," &c., pp. 172, 353), seeing in chaps. xiii. 2–xiv. 23, and xl.-lxvi. merely a dramatic development of the idea of restoration from such exile, without any *specific* allusions to the actual circumstances of the captivity, and regarding the passages which mention Cyrus as inserted in the text subsequently, feels himself at liberty to treat both these prophecies as Isaiah's. But, in spite of the considerations advanced on p. 347, it is impossible to think that he has in this respect read the prophecies correctly ; and he has certainly largely under-estimated the differences of conception and style, which characterize chaps. xl.-lxvi., and remarkably confirm the argument based upon the *historical* function of prophecy.

capture of Babylon in 538 by Cyrus, just as Isaiah's prophecies in chaps. xxix.-xxxii., xxxiii., for example, are suited to the needs of the people of Judah on the eve of the invasion of Sennacherib.   It has been shown also that no violence is done to the language used by the prophet by referring it to that date ; and that no claim made by him to prevision of the future is disallowed or weakened (p. 188 f.).   If it is consistent with the inspiration of Isaiah's prophecies to have been uttered at no long interval before the event, it cannot be objected as less con-sistent with the inspiration of this great prophecy of Israel's restoration.[1]

Nor, in conclusion, is it a sound objection to the date here advocated that a prophecy exhibiting unmistakably such brilliancy and power would not have been produced in the period of the nation's decadence.   Genius is not tied to any particular age or period of a nation's life : the secret of its origin is hidden from us : it may be latent in the obscurest of localities, in the most desperate of times : circumstances and opportunities alone are needed, for the purpose of drawing it into activity and developing its powers.   Such circumstances

[1] The suggestion propounded *ib.* p. 352, 359 that chaps. xl.-lxvi. rest upon an Isaianic basis, which was re-edited and enlarged by a prophet living during the exile, has been adopted and developed by the most recent commentator on Isaiah in Germany, C. J. Bredenkamp (1887).   The commentary by this author has independent merits ; but his attempt in this direction cannot be pronounced successful.   If such an Isaianic basis of chaps. xl.-lxvi. ever existed, we do not know what it was, and (so far as appears) it is impossible to discover it.   The criteria which Bredenkamp applies are arbitrary and subjective in the extreme.   There would be no objection in principle to supposing the passages mentioned on p. 187 to have been written originally by Isaiah under Manasseh ; but even thus far the hypothesis is not supported by positive evidence, for they betray no distinctive marks of Isaiah's authorship.   In the rest of chaps. xl.-lxvi., the several parts are so intimately interwoven with one another by links of both conception and phraseology, that it is impossible to point to any particular passage, or group of passages, and attribute it to a different author.   No doubt, the *literary* unity of chaps. xl.-lxvi. is not complete :

and opportunities existed at the close of the Babylonian captivity. No doubt, the eve of the restoration was a time of mingled feelings ; while some were overcome by anxious questionings, others, and especially those who had faith in their nation's future, would be buoyant with hope : it was just the period to warm the heart, to kindle the imagination, to animate the pen, of an exiled patriot. Nor was this all. The age was one exactly suited to the interposition of a prophet. The nation was on the point of reaching a great turning-point in its history. The restoration of the Chosen People to Palestine enabled it to complete its destined work, as the religious teacher of mankind : it brought the nation ultimately into contact with the Greeks, and thereby prepared the way for the diffusion of its religion, so soon as it was transformed into Christianity, among the Gentiles. All the conditions were favourable to the appearance of a prophet able to direct his people, and interpret to it the lessons of the age. And as inspiration ever avails itself of human organs, and adapts to its end the instruments which occasion supplies, so it is reasonable to conclude that one such patriot, whose natural gifts of genius fitted him for the purpose, was empowered to utter this wonderful prophecy, to teach his nation what the age required of it, to hold out to it, in bold, impressive strokes, its future destiny, to conceive in unsurpassed magnificence the vision of Zion's future glory.

THE END.

INDEX OF PROPHECIES.

The Gresham Press,

UNWIN BROTHERS,

CHILWORTH AND LONDON

The Men of the Bible

ABRAHAM: His Life and Times. By Rev. W. J. Deane, M.A.

MOSES: His Life and Times. By Rev. Canon G. Rawlinson, M.A.

SOLOMON: His Life and Times. By Ven. Archdeacon F. W. Farrar, D.D.

ELIJAH: His Life and Times. By Rev. Prof. W. Milligan, D.D.

ISAIAH: His Life and Times. By Rev. Canon Driver, M.A.

SAMUEL and SAUL. By Rev. W. J. Deane, M.A.

JEREMIAH: His Life and Times. By Rev. Canon T. K. Cheyne, D.D.

JESUS THE DIVINE MAN. By Rev. F. J. Vallings, M.A.

DANIEL: His Life and Times. By Rev. H. Deane, B.D.

DAVID: His Life and Times. By Rev. W. J. Deane, M.A.

THE KINGS OF ISRAEL AND JUDAH. By Rev. Canon Rawlinson.

JOSHUA: His Life and Times. By Rev. W. J. Deane, M.A.

THE MINOR PROPHETS. By Ven. Archdeacon Farrar, D.D.

ISAAC AND JACOB. By Rev. Canon Rawlinson.

ST. PAUL. By Rev. Prof. Iverach, M.A.

GIDEON AND THE JUDGES OF ISRAEL. By Rev. J. Marshall Lang, D.D.

PREPARING FOR PUBLICATION.

EZRA AND NEHEMIAH. By Rev. Canon Rawlinson.

London: JAMES NISBET & CO., 21, Berners Street, W.

R760~ 1